1928-1981

This book is dedicated to George Klein whose legacy is his contribution to
East European scholarship

Contents

Maps and Charts

Maps and Charts

Foreword

Stephen Fischer-Galati
Distinguished Professor of History, University of Colorado

The struggle with the communist legacy, the focal point of the George Klein Memorial Symposium of March 1993, is, alas, very much with us nearly ten years since the collapse of communist regimes in Eastern Europe. The guarded optimism regarding the "transition to democracy" of the former communist countries, prevalent at the beginning of this decade, was already tarnished by early 1993. The caveats expressed by the participants at the Symposium reflected the realities of the political, social, economic and, above all, historic experiences of the countries of Eastern Europe. Still, the hope, if not necessarily the belief, that the transition to democracy was inevitable over a period of years -- a period varying between the end of the twentieth century and the first decades of the twenty-first -- prevailed.

At this writing, in late summer 1998, we tend to be more skeptical. The collapse of the Russian economy, the dangerously precarious status of the economies of Romania and Bulgaria, the survival of Slobodan Milosevic, the continuing crisis in Kosovo, the instability of Bosnia, the authoritarianism of Tudjman's regime, the irredentism of the Free Democrats in Hungary, the economic regression of then admired Vaclav Havel's Czechoslovakia, the prevailing political instability throughout the Balkan states, the growth of Islamic fundamentalism, to mention but a few of the current problems cannot, however, be regarded as an exclusive product of the communist legacy.

The convenient assumption that the inherent democratic tendencies, if not necessarily democratic traditions, of the peoples subject to the communist tyranny of the post-World War II era has been proven to be largely fallacious. It is true that the communist totalitarianism was incompatible with traditional authoritarianism and, of course, with the basic aspects of democracy that were evident in most of Eastern Europe during the interwar years. But the communists did insure a modicum, albeit modest, of economic security for the vast majority of the population. When Stalinism became obsolete and when "socialism with a human face" became a possible alternative it seems fair to say that the Hungarian prototype of the 1980s, as augmented by Gorbachev's "glasnost" and presumed "perestroika," could have become a model for reform in Eastern Europe. It could have led, perhaps, to "social democracy."

What is now evident is that "glasnost" should be "perestroika" and that "perestroika" has not been carried out in post-communist Eastern Europe. However, we may well ask whether "perestroika" within the framework of a "social-democratic" system, not based exclusively on privatization and a market economy, might not have been, and still be, a more realistic solution to the problems of Eastern Europe than the western insistence on total privatization as a prerequisite for democracy?

It is difficult to predict the future of the so-called "emerging economies" of emerging democracies. The disarray in the economic orders of the nations of Southeast Asia, Latin America, and most of Eastern Europe cast doubts about the applicability of western economic models to the resolution of the political and social problems of societies subject to communist rule for over half-a-century.

Preface

The papers in this volume focus on the transitions taking place in Eastern Europe as a result of the collapse of communism (symbolized by the fall of the Berlin Wall in 1989). The crises and chaos that resulted from this abrupt change from a stable communist society form the theme of the book. The arrival of the post-communist period in Eastern Europe was not predicted by the political establishment; the few scholars who anticipated it were largely ignored. National policies designed to aid in the recovery and hasten the transition from communism in these societies have violated many established findings of the social sciences and the initial euphoria has turned to despair as corruption, violence, and a lowered quality of life resulted.

This book developed out of the George Klein Memorial Symposium on Central Europe, held at Western Michigan University, March 17, 1993, and is dedicated to this scholar of Eastern Europe. He left behind a rich contribution to East European studies; and, his writings reflect his anticipating many of the changes that took place. The writings of George Klein are reviewed and analyzed in the context of the sudden shift in Eastern Europe and especially in Yugoslavia, which was his special area of interest.

Of course, so much is happening in former Eastern Europe that no symposium or book of reasonable length can provide an exhaustive account and analysis of the developments in that part of the world. Although this collection focuses on the 1989-90 period of the transition from communism, the analysis and contemporary perspective presented form a strong bases for understanding the issues and problems that continue to plague this region as the people take on a different role in the global system. As a result, the editors of this book feel that the dynamics presented here are representative of what is happening in the region. We would like to add that although the impetus for this volume was the symposium, quality and cohesiveness necessitated that some of the symposium papers not be used while the addition of the works of other scholars be included.

This book is divided into three parts: Part One examines Yugoslavia and the underlying forces that led to its disintegration. The introductory paper, "Contributions of George Klein: Prophecy and Reality," by Patricia V. Klein initiates the focus on Yugoslavia. The writings broadly cover the post-World War II period to the death of Tito and are discussed in reference to the break-up of Yugoslavia. The Barbara P. McCrea paper on "The Role of the Titoist System In the Destruction of Yugoslavia" fittingly leads off by exploring the role of the Communist Party and The League of Communists in the decentralization and destabilization of the country, with a special focus on the ethnic and nationalistic repercussions. "The Failure of Institutions in Yugoslavia" by Agneza Bozic follows the development of federalism and its structure in Yugoslavia as outlined within the various Yugoslav constitutions during the post-World War II decades and the final collapse into war between the Croats and Serbs. "Trukese Time" by Pavao Novosel attempts to provide an understanding of the actions of the Serbs in their fight against the Croats and Bosnians. All three of these papers present background information for a better understanding of how and why Yugoslavia moved into internecine warfare during its transition from communism to nationalism.

Part Two presents a broader view of the Balkan countries immediately after the collapse of communism. Robin Remington begins by dealing with security issues for both Eastern and Western Europe resulting from the fall of the Berlin Wall. Remington's paper, "Security in the Post-Communist Balkans," postulates on the effects of war in former Yugoslavia on the security of the entire area. This is followed by two papers, "Romania and the Struggle for New Directions" by Arthur Helweg, and James McCollum's "Romania's First Steps Toward Privatization" which provide a more micro analysis of the single country of Romania.

Part Three focuses on various aspects of post-communist Poland, Czechoslovakia and Hungary. Z. Anthony Kruszewski explores the fate of Polish minorities in three neighboring countries: Belarus, Ukraine and Lithuania and discusses how they have been treated and what the post-communist future may hold for them. Joanna Regulska examines Poland's development of an independent political system in "The Road To Self-Governance." Her analysis offers graphs and charts to assist the reader in understanding the 1990 Polish elections. It also includes background information on efforts to achieve self-governance in a country which was not historically prepared. Carol Skalnik Leff provides an examination of the role played by dissidents and elites before and during the transition period in Czechoslovakia, Poland and Hungary and where these roles eventually led the participants.

The integrating theme of *Struggling With the Communist Legacy: Yugoslavia, Romania, Poland and Czechslovakia* focuses on some of the ramifications and consequences of the shift from communism in the countries studied. Observations range from severe economic dislocations to growing nationalism and fully developed ethnic warfare. The importance of individual participants during this transition is emphasized in several of the papers.

The editors:
Dr. Patricia V. Klein, Associate Professor of Social Sciences, Emerita, Western Michigan University;
Dr. Arthur M. Helweg, Professor of Anthropology, Western Michigan University;
Dr. Barbara P. McCrea, Joan B. Kroc Institute of International Peace Studies, University of Notre Dame.

Contributors

Patricia Vawter Klein, Department of Science Studies, Western Michigan University

Barbara P. McCrea, Joan B. Kroc Institute of International Peace Studies, University of Notre Dame

Agnezia Bozic, Department of Political Science, Western Michigan University

Pavao Novosel, Political Science Faculty, University of Zagreb

Robin A. Remington, Department of Political Science, University of Missouri-Columbia

Arthur W. Helweg, Department of Anthropology, Western Michigan University

James K. McCollum, Department of Management and Marketing, University of Alabama in Huntsville

Z. Anthony Kruszewski, Department of Political Science, University of Texas - ElPaso

Joanna Regulska, Director, Center for Russian, Central and East European Studies, Rutgers University

Carol Skalnik Leff, Department of Political Science, University of Illinois at Urbana-Champaign

Introduction
Contributions of George Klein: Prophecy and Reality
Patricia V. Klein

Writings by George Klein in books, articles, monographs and papers over his more than twenty years of active scholarship covered such topics as nationalism, ethnicity, democratization, politics, workers' self-management, detente, environmental concerns and energy problems in Eastern Europe, with special concentration on Yugoslavia. Although these writings focused on the Soviet Union, Czechoslovakia and Yugoslavia, it was the latter state that received the most attention and the one I will examine. A review of the material contributed by George Klein reveals both perception and insightful interpretation of the scene in Yugoslavia during the post-World War II period. Many of these writings, which ceased with his 1981 publication, *The Politics of Ethnicity in Eastern Europe* (Klein and Reban) in the year of his death, are found to be prophetic of today's recent events and anticipatory of the conflagration in the former Yugoslav republic. Three themes distinquishable in these writings, when taken together, offer meaningful observations on events leading to the fragmented Yugoslavia of today:

First, there is the underlying theme of national conflict and nationalism, which was described as always present.

Second, there is the theme of greater democratization through workers' self-management and workers' councils in Yugoslavia as a hopeful sign for developing a democratic society.

Third, there is the theme that decentralization, although an indicator of greater democracy, also led to increased nationalism in political and economic institutions combined with the emergence of local leaders in Yugoslavia.

National Conflict and Nationalism

The underlying theme of national conflict and nationalism was a reminder to the reader of their constant presence, as though waiting in the wings to emerge on stage with the proper cue. One of the major obstacles to a move toward democratization was the memory of national conflict during World War II. In *The Changing Face of Communism in Eastern Europe,* written in 1970, Klein said:

> There is always genuine potentiality that the country might disintegrate into fratricidal war, and there is always the ever-present threat of neighbors who show hostility on a great range of problems....Yugoslavia, as a state, needs time to grow into true nationhood.[1]

Time, however, was denied to Yugoslavia by ambitious political leaders who were very much a product of local nationalistic institutions. This was described by George Klein in his 1973 paper "Yugoslavia: The Politics of an Institutional Crisis,"[2] which said that deliberately nurtured nationalism drove the country away from nationhood and in the direction of its current fragmented condition. The opening paragraph in the 1973 paper might have been written in 1998:

> Particularistic nationalism is no new phenomenon in Yugoslavia, nor does it result from new nationalistic feelings. It is rather the constant element in Yugoslav politics. The present re-emergence of nationalism is attributable to the profound changes in the Yugoslav institutional framework over the past years. Previously, the League of Communists and the central government were powerful institutions which could keep expressions of nationalism from rising to the surface. In the past few years the institutional arrangement in Yugoslavia was so profoundly altered that there no longer existed an organization which had the power to keep nationalism contained.[3]

The importance of a strong central government and communist party in control of ethnic or national conflict was stressed in several of Klein's 1970s writings. At the Yugoslav Sociological Association in 1972 at Portoroz the example of the United States was used to show that movement toward resolution of ethnic and racial problems could occur as a result of strong federal action in civil rights and a weakening of states' rights at the local level.[4] The same point appeared in "Yugoslavia and the United States: Divergent Approaches to Ethnicity" (1974) which compared ethnic conflict in the Yugoslav and United States models of ethnic relations.[5]

The importance of a strong central government and communist party was stressed by the Partisans and brought with them into the national government when they took control following World War II. In "The Politics of an Institutional Crisis" Klein commented on the post-war influence of the League of Communists (communist party) and the central government on the issue of nationalism:

> The Yugoslav state machinery, as it took shape after the Second World War, was in effect structured to remain subordinate to the League of Communists.... Nationality problems were submerged under the blanket of memories of World War II during which they played such a tragic role (of the mass atrocities committed in the name of local nationalisms). In those years it was not decent to discuss the very extensive atrocities of either the Ustashi, the Moslems or the Chetniks.[6]

Indeed, during the war the Partisans had promised to build a national party and after the war built the only truly national party within Yugoslavia. However, Klein observed that steps were taken at the Sixth Congress of the League of Communists in 1952 to reduce the role of the party and begin implementation of workers' self-management during the mid-1950s and 1960s through the Fundamental Law of 1953 which brought with it a process of decentralization in the economy, the government and the League. This led to his position that "nationalism grew as central authority and party discipline were weakened by reform from above."[7] The Constitution of 1963 formed the legal basis for these reforms in the government by allowing for direct election of five of the six chambers from locally-based organs of self-management, thus increasing the power of local authorities tremendously. During the years of Tito's control, a determined effort to balance power was repeatedly enforced and this included placing limitations on Serbian dominance. Klein emphasized this point by saying:

> The constitutional amendments (1968) had the effect of formally
> equalizing the influence of nationalities and it was obviously hoped that
> these institutional changes would satisfy those republics which felt
> threatened by Serb hegemonism.[8]

This action was aimed at cutting down on Serb influence in federal institutions. In the 1970 book, *The Changing Face of Communism,* he pointed out that the constitutional amendments of 1968 recognized the paramount position of ethnic problems in the Yugoslav polity and ended Serbian dominance in legislative political bodies in executive organs, which were an expression of the legislative branch.[9] Prior to the 1968 reform Serb and Montenegrin over-representation in federal and party bodies was conspicuous.

Action to discourage Serbian chauvinism included the expulsion in 1968 of persons advocating Serbian preeminence who, in recent years, have returned to power. For example, Dobrica Cosic was removed from the Central Committee of Serbian League of Communists and from the Federal Assembly (Parliament) in 1968 for protesting the unfair treatment of Serbs by the League of Communists and for advocating Serbian interests in Yugoslavia and especially in Kosovo.[10] In 1969 the Ninth Congress of the League of Communists revised the party statute to increase the power of local authorities; it also determined that League members in executive posts could not hold high government positions at the same time.[11]

The constitutional amendments of 1971 further reinforced the position against Serbian dominance. These amendments raised particular opposition in Serbia, where they were viewed as an effort to diminish the role of Serbs and Montenegrins in the machinery of the state and the League. The 1971 amendments also partially federalized the armed forces, which diluted the Serb-Montenegrin domination of the officer corps and aided the organization of locally-based forces for territorial warfare. During the debate over the 1971 constitutional amendments a non-communist at Belgrade University Faculty of Law, Mihailo Djuric, promoted Serbian interests at the possible expense of other Republics.

He was sentenced for "hostile propaganda."[12]

A Klein article in 1975, compared "The Role of Ethnic Politics in the Czechoslovak Crisis of 1968 and the Yugoslav Crisis of 1971." He found the crisis in Yugoslavia at least partly the result of increased autonomy to republics in an effort to defuse charges of Serbian dominance. This tended to institutionalize strong regional party machines at the expense of the federal government and party organs.[13] Nationalism emerged in Croatia in the form of the Serbian-Croatian linguistic dispute and other demands for greater economic and political autonomy which spread to other republics as well. The crisis of 1971 was highlighted by the sentencing of Croatian nationalist leaders who demanded increased autonomy for Croatia. Among those punished was Franjo Tudjman, former Partisan and General in the Yugoslav National Army, since 1990 the elected President of independent Croatia.

This rising nationalism, which threatened the stability of the state, was addressed at the Tenth Congress of the League of Communists and by the Constitution of 1974. Both the party and the government attempted to remove some of the power that had been given to local levels by the Ninth League of Communists Congress and the Constitution of 1963. Klein points out in the 1977 article on "Workers' Self-Management and the Politics of Ethnic Nationalism in Yugoslavia" that "civil rights suffered and police powers increased" in the structural changes of the Yugoslav state; both nationalists and centralists were singled out for prosecution.[14] It was argued by the League of Communists' Executive Committee that unchecked nationalism would bring about a harsh dictatorship and so it must be suppressed.

In the paper, "Self-Reliance and Yugoslav Ethnic Politics," presented to the Ecumenical Institute at Chateau de Bossey in 1976 George Klein emphasized that, "The principle of equal ethnic representation from all national segments was a principle enshrined in every document since the mid-1960s."[15] Although he asserted that nationalism could reassert itself in Yugoslavia regardless of the constitutional forms, he insisted that, "The very survival of Yugoslavia depends on a measure of internal cohesion which can guarantee economic, political and military viability".[16]

He specifically disagreed with the thesis of some scholars at that time that an alliance between liberal communists and nationalists would be a key to the liberalization of communist systems. In his article on the role of ethnic politics in Slovakia and Croatia, written in 1975, his comments are applicable today:

> It would be a prime mistake to equate either Croat or Slovak nationalism with liberalism.... In Croatia, the reform leadership did not exhibit a high degree of tolerance for those elements within the Croat League which opposed them. The struggle was ruthless on both sides, and the methods used did not inspire confidence that nationalism would usher in a new period of socialist democracy.[17]

In support of this observation, Robert M. Hayden pointed out that the nationalist governments that gained power in 1990 in the Yugoslav republics "all promised programs that would discriminate against minorities and favor majorities".[18] They all created systems of "constitutional nationalism" in the new constitutions of the former republics, which favored the dominant ethnic nation over the other residents of the republic.

The rule of Franjo Tudjman in Croatia, who was elected in 1990 and re-elected in 1992, has been characterized by the government's efforts to silence the opposition press[19] and to establish a strong, authoritarian, one-party rule.[20]

A final comment on national conflict and nationality can be found in a 1972 paper, "Yugoslav Views of Social Conflict and Development" continues to be current:

> The tragedy of Yugoslavia is that most Yugoslavs cannot conceive of true Yugoslav solutions but are always locked into identification with their nationality.[21]

Democratization Through Workers' Self-Management

Yugoslavia moved away from centralization--both politically and economically--after the 1948 Cominform break. The move was toward an increase of local control in the government, the party, and economic enterprises after the introduction of workers' self-management. This break with the Stalinist model pointed toward growing liberalism and democratization in Yugoslavia based on the Fundamental Law of 1953. In the chapter on "Yugoslavia: The Process of Democratization" in 1970, optimism on resolving the problem of national conflict was evident in Klein's writings:

> During 1950 to 1970, nationality, for the first time in memory, was not a cause for conflict and slaughter.... Pluralism asserts itself at all levels of Yugoslav society, and it is very difficult to fix with precision where the true power centers lie or where key decisions are made because of widespread public participation in the political process.[22]

During this period, George Klein expressed real hope for the successful survival of a democratized and reformed state, but was fearful of a return to less democratic times:

> Decentralization and self-management, as implemented since the 1950s, has formally triumphed in Yugoslavia, but it has only underlined the existing disparities....and those (forces) which would return Yugoslavia to an "etatist" model.[23]

While self-management was bringing greater citizen participation into organs of government, the League of Communists also thoroughly reorganized and drafted the party statutes at the Ninth Congress in 1969. A freedom of conscience statute was introduced by the League at this time and held promise for individual, independent, critical responses by members of the League in official party positions. The new statute permitted freedom of debate in the League consistent with the preservation of an essentially one-party system designed to serve a very heterogeneous community. On this innovation Klein commented as follows:

> Once League members are permitted to retain opposition views it is only a short step to the organization of those who share them....Factions possess the potentiality of becoming political parties.[24]

Other signs of "democratization" emerging throughout were discussed in "The Process of Democratization in Yugoslavia": formerly suppressed publications, such as the Marxist humanist journal *Praxis* resumed publication; a university faculty member in Zadar published a strongly critical article of the Soviet Union prison camps; Croats demanded that their language become official and separate from Serbian by passage of a constitutional amendment; Belgrade University students demonstrated for more reforms; and some Kosovo Albanians demanded a separate republic.[25] In conclusion, Klein wrote:

> Self-management and a substantial measure of local autonomy are perhaps the best methods by which the country can evolve into a modern state.[26]

Democratization through workers' self-management is further explored in the 1981 book, *The Politics of Ethnicity in Eastern Europe,* where the process is explained as follows:

> The introduction of workers' self-management created a Yugoslav ideology which in time led to the down-grading of most of the agencies of the central government, and substituted pluralized patterns of decision-making.[27]

This meant that building socialism would be through direct participation by Yugoslavs at the level of enterprises and communes and was seen at the time as "a pathway to the withering away of the state."[28] The power of the central communist party also continued to "wither away" so that by the mid-sixties "the League became moribund" and lost much of its power to non-League bodies such as the Socialist Alliance, the councils of the communes, the local units of government, and the executive committees of workers' councils.[29] Workers' self-management and the decentralization of power changed the entire political framework in Yugoslavia. During this period of liberalization most institutions were staffed on the basis of one Serb, one Croat, one Slovene and then other nationalities as needed and dictated by the local ethnic composition.

In a book on the Hungarian revolution of 1956 Klein noted the external ramifications of workers' self-management and democratization in Yugoslavia on such divergent states as Hungary and the United

States. He pointed out the great influence exercised over the events of 1956 in Hungary where the Imre Nagy regime legitimized the role of workers' councils and, prior to the intervention by the Soviet Union in Hungary, the Hungarian leadership visited Yugoslavia in the summer of 1956 to study the system of workers' self-management in that country.[30] United States foreign policy toward Yugoslavia was different than that toward any other communist state. Yugoslavia provided the United States government with a new model of a communist state which offered an opportunity for better relations between the two countries. About this relationship Klein said:

> When the United States started actively backing Yugoslavia, albeit at times reluctantly, few would have suspected that this Balkan country would be regarded a cornerstone in safeguarding the stability of the area.[31]

Yugoslavia became a pivotal area to the United States in the context of the cold war. The end of the cold war brought an end to the United States policy of safe-guarding the stability of the area.

An early examination of the development of workers' self-management and the local political base as an important source of emerging leaders appears in "A Perspective View of Self-Management in a Socialist Context" in 1970. Klein recognized very early that the devolution of power in Yugoslavia to the local level meant that the base of power for new political leaders would be rooted at the community, and at the republic level:

> At the present, a new generation of political leaders is coming to the fore best symbolized by the League executive bureau whose best credentials can be a record of administrative and political success in the republic or area in which they originate. In this regard, the self-managerial system is in effect moulding all political institutions above it.[32]

This same observation is found in the 1973 paper "The Politics of an Institutional Crisis":

> Power was diffused and pluralized (in both government and the League) amongst a variety of republican and local institutions and these became the logical base for political leaders who had to find their support in local constituencies. Since most of these organizations were circumscribed by nationality, nationalism became a very logical appeal for a political leader who wished to consolidate his support in a republican constituency. It was also quite congruent with this configuration of power that the same political leaders who tried to draw a wider public into their base of support should appeal to non-communists or even to anti-communists to join their cause.[33]

This pattern of power-seeking enlarged the potential political base of support for political leaderships and weakened the party. Office-holders in the republics would maximize their influence within their constituencies by appealing to ethnic self-interests. No republic political leadership could afford to lag behind.

This analysis anticipates the emergence of a Slobodan Milosevic at some future time. At the time of the writing of this 1973 paper, Tito was still alive but he had erased from power all potential national leaders who might emerge as his replacement. A collective state presidency on which each republic was represented equally, established by constitutional amendment in 1971, was the substitute favored by Tito. It was in this paper that Klein concluded:

> Ultimately the Yugoslav leaders will have to find a balance between the powers of the republics and the federation....Only a revitalized League would be able to impose a measure of discipline on the institutions of government as well.[34]

An effort to strengthen the central power of the League of Communists and restore it to its position of maintaining order among the various ethnic groups occurred at the Tenth Party Congress and the Constitution of 1974. However, from the point of view of civil rights the Tenth Party Congress and the Constitution of 1974 represented a serious regression. This was demonstrated by an increase in arrests and suppression of hostile acts toward the state. This increased repression also protected "nations and nationalities" from hostile acts and forbade ethnic conflict. The democratization process appeared to succumb to the rise of nationalism. As power devolved to the local level and to the republic, it became captured by the national group in control. This formed a barrier to the continuation of democratization.

A regression from civil rights and democratization was noted at the Tenth Party Congress and in the 1974 Constitution:

> The 1974 Constitution abolished the concept of direct contested elections for the National Assembly which were present in the 1963 Constitution and provided for a system of delegation from communal bodies to a hierarchy of republic and federal assemblies.[35] The Tenth Party Congress called for a return to the older comrades and a move toward more authoritarianism. "The Tenth Party Congress brought back Party discipline to full bloom".[36]

There would be no more "liberalism," "pluralism" or federalization of the Party. Trials took place in all parts of the country to bring home the message that no particularistic nationalist movements would be tolerated. Croatia, where secessionist sentiments were strong, was especially targeted. Many of those same people prosecuted in 1972 became active again in Croatian nationalist politics in the early 1990s. President Tudjman is one example.

Self-Management as an Underlying Determinant of Nationalism

The nationalistic crisis that developed and resulted in the crackdown by Tito on republican leaders was seen by Klein as the logical outcome of the system of workers' self-management:

> There no longer existed an organization which had the power to keep nationalism contained.... My position is that the present situation results more from a shift in the direction of power and that the roots of the crisis are closely associated with the concepts of workers' self-management and general decentralization of power in Yugoslavia.[37]

Klein mentioned that this view was at variance with other scholars who saw the crisis largely as an outgrowth of nationalism and the personal ambitions of individuals.[38] He considered the institutional changes to be a major source of the crisis and thus not one easily resolved. He pointed out in his 1973 paper on the institutional crisis:

> It is extremely questionable that the self-managerial organs and
> communes, which have become comfortable with their powers, will
> abdicate these willingly to the League or to any new call for discipline.[39]

Indeed, they did not willingly give up these powers, but bided their time
during Tito's illness and death and through ten years of a post-Tito
collective presidency.

In "Workers' Self-Management and the Politics of Ethnic
Nationalism in Yugoslavia," in 1977 he related nationalism and
decentralization in this way:

> The crucial event which led up to the crisis of 1971 was the reemergence
> of nationalism as an overt organizing principal for various sub-units of
> the federal state. The occurrence marked the end of an era in the
> development of post-World War II Yugoslavia.[40]

The linking of workers' self-management, nationalism and
decentralization also appeared in his 1981 book, *The Politics of Ethnicity
in Eastern Europe*; he described the loss of power by the League to the
organs of self-management and the increased attention on nationality as
"Citizenry defined its participatory role in terms of members of their
national community."[41] The power base shifted to the local level as a
result of the reforms and as local nationalistic, non-communist
organizations competed with the League itself.

The Constitution of 1963 had reinforced the increase in the power
of local authorities through the system of representation from locally
based organs of self-management as did the revised statutes of the
Ninth Congress of the League of Communists in 1969. The statutes
established an Executive Committee composed on the basis of
nationalities; delegates came from republic parties; Presidium members
also came from the republics. Consequently, "under these
circumstances no political leader could develop a national following,
except Tito."[42] This system was perpetuated through the collective
Presidency, which was, again, an effort to maintain an ethnic balance.

Elements of Inequality in Self-Management

In addition to the institutional and structural changes occurring through the forces of self-management and decentralization which fueled nationalism, there was the problem of increasing economic inequalities among the republics. In the article, "Workers' Self-Management and the Politics of Ethnic Nationalism," George Klein noted that all federal sub-units were constituted along ethnic lines and this meant that participants in workers' self-management and self-government were members of a discrete nationality and organized their area of competence along ethnic lines.[43] In the author's words, "Worker's self-management thus became not only a method of management but also a means of favoring one's co-nationals".[44] He concludes in this article that, "workers' self-management...tends to reinforce particularistic nationalism" since it is a locally integrated institution.[45] "Perhaps," he says "Yugoslavia's ethnic complexity... demands this ambiguous solution to achieve the compromise necessary to the maintenance of the system".[46]

It had been hoped that workers' self-management would achieve something other than local integration; that it would go beyond local interests and lead to communities of interest among the broader proletariat. Contrary to this anticipated result, workers' self-management contributed disproportionately to the economic development of some areas of the country, such as Slovenia and Croatia, so the gap was actually increasing between the developed and underdeveloped parts of the country.[47]

In view of this evident disparity between the more developed North and the less developed South the centralists, who supported a strong central government and were led by Alexander Rankovic, opposed the liberalizing reforms that began in the 1950s. The poorer republics, such as Bosnia, Macedonia, Montenegro and parts of Serbia, favored the centralist position, while the more prosperous republics of Croatia and Slovenia favored the liberalizing reforms of self-management and decentralization. The economic gains in these two republics, which were much greater than in other republics, led to their resentment toward sharing their gains with the less developed areas of the South.[48] The centralists lost the struggle after the dismissal of Rankovic from his office as head of the secret police in 1966. Then, fed by decentralization and the devolution of power to the republican and local levels, liberalization flourished. This led to the increasing expression of nationalistic enthusiasm in the late 1960s and 1970s and the eventual rewriting of the Constitution of 1974. The Rankovic case itself had "some earmarks" of a nationality conflict insofar as the greatest support for Rankovic, a Serb, came from the Serbs and Montenegrins. Although Rankovic had demonstrated his desire to seize control of the Party, "the threat of a centralist coup led by Rankovic and a Serbian-Montenegrin coalition faded into the realm of the impossible."[49]

It is interesting to notice that this Serb-Montenegrin coalition finally came to fruition in 1991 as the remnant of the Socialist Federal Republic of Yugoslavia. The most prosperous republics of Slovenia and Croatia led the exit from Yugoslavia in June of 1991, followed by the less prosperous republics of Bosnia-Hercegovina and Macedonia; Serbia and Montenegro remained to form a new Federal Republic of Yugoslavia.

Recent Realities

"All multinational states are balancing acts," wrote George Klein in 1981.[50] Ultimately, however, the Yugoslav leaders failed in their major responsibility to "find a balance between powers of the republics and the federation...." as Klein called for in a 1973 paper.[51]

The efforts in Yugoslavia to maintain an ethnic balance were sustained throughout Tito's lifetime by methods varying from strong authoritarian control and penalties in law for acts of ethnic hatred to greater autonomy and self-management for the various national populations. Although there was little expectation that the system of the State Presidency would survive Tito's death in 1980, in practice it was sufficiently stable to function during ten post-Tito years until deliberately undermined by nationalist leaders in Serbia. A poisonous variant of nationalism soon spread to the other republics.

As a Slovenian magazine noted, Slobodan Milosevic was the first to realize that "Tito is dead".[52] He built his political fortunes on Serbian frustrations over the limitations placed on Serbian dominance by Tito, the Constitution, the League of Communists of Yugoslavia and the legal system. He was aided in these criticisms by the Memorandum of the Serbian Academy of Sciences in 1986, partly credited to Cosic, which listed Serbian grievances and presented Serbs as the most persecuted people of Yugoslavia.[53] At the time of the Memorandum, Milosevic was President of the League of Communists of Serbia. On April 24, 1987 he appealed to the nationalism of the Serbs and Montenegrins in Kosovo by using inflammatory nationalistic rhetoric and presenting himself as a charismatic Serbian leader.[54] He openly favored limiting the autonomy of the provinces of Kosovo and Vojvodina in contradiction to the Constitution of 1974 and finally succeeded in this endeavor after he forced out of office Ivan Stambolic, who had sponsored him for his various posts and who disagreed with the Milosevic position on Kosovo and his strident nationalism. Milosevic was elected to the position of his former mentor and became President of the Socialist Republic of Serbia on November 12, 1989. From that position he continued to agitate national conflict. In Kosovo, violent repression of the Albanians took place in February and March of 1989 and the Kosovo autonomous provincial government was abolished by Serbia in 1990. Rights to govern themselves, retain jobs, use their own language and control their own schools were also abolished. The appeal to Serbian nationalism was not restricted to Serbia, but also reached the Serbs in Croatia, who demanded their own autonomous republic in August of 1990[55] and the Serbs in Bosnia-Hercegovina, who declared their own republic in December of 1991 and boycotted the referendum for an independent state of Bosnia-Hercegovina in February of 1992.

No longer was nationalism contained by central government action, the rewriting of the constitution or revision of League statutes as it was in the past, but it was deliberately provoked by government leaders. In George Klein's words, "there no longer existed an organization which had the power to keep nationalism contained".[56] By 1990, the principle of equal ethnic representation had been violated and replaced by Serbian dominance. Nationalism became more important than communism and it was an ideology that all Serbs could share.

Nationalism should not, as Klein pointed out, be confused with liberalism and Milosevic showed little tolerance for those who did not support his nationalist agenda. Milosevic operated a strong centralist government but used it to increase Serbian power rather than to balance power among nationalities. Political repression and media control are more characteristic of the Milosevic Yugoslavia than the democratization and self-management of the period described by Klein in the 1960s and early 1970s. The balancing act was deliberately toppled.

A Local Power Base

Milosevic is a product of the devolution of power, which occurred largely through the process of self-management, and the consequent emergence of local leaders. A Serb who built his political career in Belgrade, he climbed the ranks of power strictly within the republic. His road to power did not lead through the Federal State Presidency, which was carefully crafted by Tito to avoid a take-over by any one nationality. Milosevic became the strongest leader in the Federal Republic of Yugoslavia without such federal credentials.

His credentials instead were a record of political success in the republic of Serbia and his strong appeal through the use of Serbian nationalism. Again, quoting from Klein, "nationalism became a very logical appeal for a political leader who wished to consolidate his support in a republican constituency".[57] If the self-management system, in effect, did "mould all political institutions above it"[58] then it also moulded the leaders who emerged from it. The importance of a local power base, emphasized by Klein, has also been affirmed by scholars in 1990.[59]

The current emergence of nationalist leaders in Yugoslavia was predictable. The origins can be found in the decentralization of the system of workers' self-management which afforded the opportunity to combine localized power with national interests and decision-making. This heightened national conciousness threatened the stability of the state in the 1970s, then temporarily contained by Tito through institutional changes, but eventually proved to be the destruction of the state. The spread of nationalism was not limited to Serbian leaders, of course. Serbian leaders were simply the most blatant about using the overt expression of nationalism as a unifying force for its nationals. Serbian nationalism was deliberately used to promote the political fortunes of those leaders, an easy means to political support and legitimacy.

Slovenian and Croatian Leaders

In both Slovenia and Croatia nationalist leaders also emerged to win control of their governments in the first democratic elections in those republics, in 1990. Both republics had discussed the possibility of secession and had expressed dissatisfaction with their role of contributions from their higher levels of income to the less prosperous republics.

Slovenia took the unusual step of amending its constitution in 1989 to permit its secession from the federation. Both Croatia and Slovenia called for a loose confederation and multiparty system in 1990, but Serbia was not sympathetic. In January of 1990, both Slovenia and Croatia broke with the Yugoslav League of Communists. Serbia imposed an economic blockade on Slovenia. Both Slovenia and Croatia elected nationalistic leaders to power in multiparty elections during April and May of 1990, respectively. Both Milan Kucan, in Slovenia, and Franjo Tudjman, in Croatia, had been strong communists as was Milosevic. Milosevic increasingly made clear his position that all Serbs had the right to live in one state.[60] The demands by Serbs in Croatia for self-rule were denied by President Tudjman and armed clashes occurred. The Yugoslav National Army soon intervened and Serbian irregulars in Croatia joined with the Army to secure Serbian lands.[61]

Serbian irregulars, spawned by Milosevic nationalism and responsible for many of the atrocities during the conflict in Croatia and Bosnia-Hercegovina, included Vojislav Seselj, former Assistant Professor of political science at the University of Sarejevo, who headed the "chetniks", Dragoslav Bokan, former journalist, and the infamous Arkan (Zeljko Raznjatovic) who headed the White Eagles and carried out "some of the most frightful crimes of the Yugoslav war".[62]   It was a long way from the time that the United States supported a Yugoslavia that became "a cornerstone in safeguarding the stability of the area".[63]

The Use of Nationalism
The prediction by George Klein that the State Presidency would not succeed was eventually realized. However, the fact that it lasted for ten years after Tito's death and only collapsed when it was blocked by Serbia in 1991 was not predicted.

Particularistic nationalism did not erupt spontaneously and throw the country into ethnic conflict, as might have been expected, but it was deliberately fanned into an eruption by ambitious politicians such as Slobodan Milosevic, in Serbia, Milan Babic, in Croatia Krajina, Radovan Karadzic, in Bosnia-Hercegovina, and Franjo Tudjman, in Croatia. The initial conflicts that erupted in Slovenia, Croatia and Bosnia arose over territory in Serbia's drive to consolidate all Serbs into one territorially-based nation. Ethnic hatred was developed to accomplish this goal.

Serbia wanted Yugoslavia to remain as a federation under Serbian control, and wanted to control all lands they considered "Serbian." Both Croatia and Bosnia-Hercegovina witnessed declarations by Serbs living in those republics for establishing autonomous provinces; these were supported by Milosevic's Serbia.

In a 1992 article, Robert M. Hayden maintained that "the results of the first free elections in Yugoslavia since World War II, held in 1990, set the stage for the civil war that broke out in summer and fall of 1991".[64]   A more consistent position with the George Klein analysis would be that the stage for civil war was set by the deliberate efforts of Serb leaders to catalyze ethnic (national) hatred in order to further the Serbian national interests. Prior to that the decentralization of power to the level of national populations prepared the stage for this later development. This was reinforced by locally based politicians anchoring their careers in their national constituencies, unifying them   through nationalism. Milosevic was a member of this new generation and shared no loyalties with the old guard that had worked so hard to avert national conflict and maintain the "balancing act."

Conclusions

George Klein was a person who had experienced Naziism first-hand in Europe. From this background I believe he would indeed see the tragedy of Yugoslavia as a tragedy for Europe; a Europe that sat by stoically, with averted face, as though the deliberate slaughter of people never happened before in this century and could never happen again. At the same time, both the European Community and the United States moved closer to rewarding the aggressors with bounty taken by force in exchange for an end to the war. Klein might well paraphrase his 1972 comment:

> The tragedy of Yugoslavia is that most Yugoslavs cannot conceive of true Yugoslav solutions but are always locked into identification with their nationality.[65]

to read:

> The tragedy of Yugoslavia is that most Europeans (and Americans) cannot conceive of true Yugoslav solutions but are locked into nationality identification as defined by the Serbs.

To accede to Serbian demands for ethnic divisions is not a solution to the problems of national conflict, nationalism and the process of democratization as analyzed by George Klein. He showed that national conflict could be subjected to a higher level of government control and that overt expressions of violent nationalism or acts of ethnic hatred could be successfully subordinated by law. With national conflict and nationalism neutralized, a form of democratization began a slow development in Yugoslavia which was compatible with communism. Eventually the devolution of power to the local level destroyed the federation and nationalism replaced communism. At a time when Yugoslavia needed a democratic leader to respond to a new era, only nationalist leaders emerged. This is the tragedy of Yugoslavia.

Notes

1. George Klein, "Yugoslavia--The Process of Democratization," *in The Changing Face of Communism*, Peter Toma, ed. (Tucson: University of Arizona Press, 1970) 240.

2. George Klein, "Yugoslavia: The Politics of an Institutional Crisis," presented at the Southwestern Association for Slavic Studies, The Statler Hilton Hotel, Dallas, Texas, March 22, 1973.

3. Ibid., 1.

4. George Klein and Patricia V. Klein, "Some Approaches to the Problem of Ethnicity (Nationality) in the United States and Yugoslavia," presented at the Sixth Annual Meeting of the Yugoslav Sociological Association in Portoroz, Yugoslavia, February 10, 1972.

5. George Klein and Patricia V. Klein, "The United States and Yugoslavia: Divergent Approaches Toward Ethnicity" in *Ethnic Dynamics*, Chester L. Hunt and Lewis Walker, eds. (Homewood, Illinois: The Dorsey Press, 1974).

6. Klein, "Yugoslavia: The Politics of an Institutional Crisis," 9.

7. Ibid., 2.

8. Ibid., 17.

9. Klein, "Yugoslavia--The Process of Democratization," 230.

10. Milan Andrejevich, "What Future for Serbia?" *Radio Free Europe* (RFE/RL) Research Report 1, 50 (December 18, 1992) 11. Cosic would later become President of the rump Federal Republic of Yugoslavia set up in 1991 by the Serbs.

11. Klein, "Yugoslavia: The Politics of an Institutional Crisis," 17.

12. Ibid., 18.

13. George Klein, "The Role of Ethnic Politics in the Czechoslovak Crisis of 1968 and the Yugoslav Crisis of 1971," *Studies in Comparative Communism* 8, 4 (1975) 351.

14. George Klein, "Workers' Self-Management and the Politics of Ethnic Nationalism in Yugoslavia," *Nationalities Papers* 5, 1 (1977) 16.

15. George Klein, "Self-Reliance and Yugoslav Ethnic Politics," in *Report: Self-Reliance and Solidarity in the Quest for International Justice* (World Council of Churches, Celigny, Switzerland, April 3-9, 1976) 11.

16. Ibid., 14.

17. Klein, "The Role of Ethnic Politics in the Czechoslovak Crisis of 1968 and the Yugoslav Crisis of 1971," 357.

18. Robert M. Hayden, "Constitutional Nationalism in the Formerly Yugoslav Republics," *Slavic Review* 51, 4 (Winter 1992) 655.

19. Patrick Moore, "Croatia," *Radio Free Europe* RFE/RL Research Report 1, 39 (October 2, 1992) 82.

20. Patrick Moore, "Issues in Croatian Politics," *Radio Free Europe* RFE/RL Research Report 1, 43 (November 6, 1992) 10.

21. George Klein, "Yugoslav Views of Social Conflict and Development," presented at the Fifth National Convention of the American Association for the Advancement of Slavic Studies, The Statler Hotel, Dallas, Texas, March 1972, 4.

22. Klein, "Yugoslavia--The Process of Democratization," 217.

23. Ibid., 220.

24. Ibid., 233.

25. Ibid., 224.

26. Ibid., 241.

27. George Klein and Patricia V. Klein, "Nationalism vs. Ideology: The Pivot of Yugoslav Politics," in *The Politics of Ethnicity in Eastern Europe*, George Klein and Milan J. Reban eds. (Boulder: East European Monographs, 1981) 256.

28. Ibid., 257.

29. Ibid., 261.

30. George Klein, "Yugoslavia," in *The Hungarian Revolution of 1956 in Retrospect*, Bela Kiraly and Paul Jonas, ed. (Boulder: East European Quarterly, 1978) 107.

31. Klein, "Yugoslavia--The Process of Democratization," 218.

32. George Klein and Milos Samardzija, "A Perspective View of Self-Management in a Socialist Context," *Studies in Comparative Communism* 4, 3-4 (1971) 177.

33. Klein, "The Politics of an Institutional Crisis," 1.

34. Ibid., 24.

35. Klein and Klein, "Nationalism vs. Ideology," 267.

36. Ibid., 269.

37. Klein, "The Politics of an Institutional Crisis," 1.

38. These scholars included: Paul Shoup, "The National Question in Yugoslavia," *Problems of Communism* 30 (1972) and Alvin Z. Rubinstein, "The Yugoslav Succession Crisis in Perspective," *World Affairs* 35, 2 (1972) 103.

39. Klein, "The Politics of an Institutional Crisis," 22.

40. Klein, "Workers' Self-Management and the Politics of Ethnic Nationalism in Yugoslavia," 4.

41. Klein and Klein, "Nationalism vs. Ideology," 261.

42. Klein, "The Politics of an Institutional Crisis," 18.

43. Klein, "Workers' Self-Management and the Politics of Ethnic Nationalism," 9.

44. Ibid., 10.

45. Ibid., 18.

46. Ibid., 19.

47. See Mary B. Gregory, "Regional Economic Development in Yugoslavia," *Soviet Studies* 25, 2 (October 1973) 213-28 and Nicholas R. Lang, "The Dialectics of Decentralization," *World Politics* 27, 3 (April 1975) 309-35.

48. Klein and Klein, "Nationalism vs. Ideology," 260.

49. Klein, "Yugoslavia--The Process of Democratization," 221-2.

50. Klein and Klein, "Nationalism vs. Ideology," 249.

51. Klein, "The Politics of an Institutional Crisis," 24.

52. Andrejevich, "What Future for Serbia?" 8.

53. Ibid., 11.

54. Steven Engelberg, "Carving Out a Greater Serbia," *New York Times Magazine*

(September 1, 1991) 18. Cited in Agneza Bozic, *The Rhetoric of Slobodan Milosevic and War on the Territory of Yugoslavia.* A Master's Thesis. Western Michigan University, Kalamazoo, Michigan (June 1992) 32.

55. Misha Glenny. *The Fall of Yugoslavia* (New York: Penguin, 1992) 17.

56. Klein, "The Politics of an Institutional Crisis," 1-2.

57. Ibid.

58. Klein and Samardzija, "A Perspective View of Self-Management in a Socialist Context," 177.

59. Bogdan Denitch. *Limits and Possibilities* (Minneapolis: University of Minnesota Press, 1990) 24.

60. Glenny, 37.

61. Ibid.

62. Ibid., 39.

63. Klein, "Yugoslavia--The Process of Democratization," 218.

64. Hayden, 654.

65. Klein, "Yugoslav Views of Social Conflict and Development," 4.

Part One

The Making of Yugoslavia's Successor States

1.
The Role of the Titoist System in the Destruction of Yugoslavia
Barbara P. McCrea

A dozen years ago, Yugoslavia was a stable member of the international community, respected for its independent foreign policy and domestic political innovations. Much of the Titoist state's favorable reputation was based on its success in creating a system which treated its multinational citizenry more equitably than other communist-party states. Yet, this very success masked the suppressed conflicts, political irresponsibility, economic piracy, and exclusivist nationalisms which helped bring about the violent dissolution of the former Yugoslavia.

Although there are many lenses through which this catastrophe may be examined, this analysis will focus on the institutional structure and internal political dynamics of the ruling Yugoslav communist party, the League of Communists of Yugoslavia (LCY), and the political dynamics that were engendered by this structure. The argument is that much of the origins of the violent conflict can be found in the system created by Tito, one of fragmented, decentralized political power based in ethnically-bounded territories, where there eventually was little rational political reason to pursue the common welfare.

In the 26 years between Yugoslavia's break with the Soviet bloc in 1948 and the 1974 Constitution, Tito engineered a system which, although Leninist in inspiration, breached a fundamental tenet of

Leninism: the unity of the ruling communist party. Instead, under Tito's direction each of the six republican communist parties gradually acquired real political content, operational autonomy, and control over their own territories and political cadres. The agent of this transformation of the Leninist model was the decentralization and devolution of power enacted by Tito. Titoism itself, then, provided a crucial catalyst for the dissolution of Yugoslavia.

The Titoist revolution was carried out from above; it thus was not democratic in thrust nor supportive of pluralist alternatives.[1] In 1950 Tito announced that the concept of workers' self-management would replace central state control and mandatory central planning, the first major step in the long series of innovations that would distinguish Titoist Yugoslavia from its Soviet model.[2] By the late 1960s the Yugoslav economy had lost much of its Leninist nature. Most economic and fiscal responsibilities were devolved to the six constituent units of the Yugoslav federation, the republics, and with the 1974 Constitution, also to the two provinces, Kosovo and Vojvodina, that were attached to Serbia. As economic power flowed to the republics, political power followed. The mechanism which in a sense substituted for democratic pluralism, the devolution of power from the center to the regional authorities, preserved party control by disaggregating it to the party units of the constituent republics.

Tito formally initiated Yugoslavia's federal system in 1943, during the communist-led Partisan War against the Axis. The system was Leninist in design, modeled after the Soviet example. Nonetheless, from the beginning there were real differences among the constituent units, even in the early postwar period of Leninist orthodoxy.[3] Once economic power was devolved from the center under the impetus of self-management, the republican political hierarchies began to acquire separate, individual bases of power which did not depend upon the central political authorities. Republican political hierarchies developed their own cadres, methods of doing business, and for that matter, levels and modes of corruption.

Conflict soon developed between the more economically developed northern republics, Croatia and Slovenia, and the less developed republics, Bosnia-Hercegovina, Macedonia, Montenegro, and Serbia, and between reformist liberals and conservatives. With Tito on their side, the reformers won out and in the mid 1960s embarked on a program of economic modernization based on workers' self-management, market principles, and competition. A key event occurred in 1966 when Tito broke the power of the secret police and removed from office his potential rival, Aleksander Rankovic, a Serb who was Tito's Vice-President and head of the secret police. With Rankovic's ouster, the Serbian hold on the secret police was broken, as well as the power base of the conservatives.

In many of the republican parties liberals came into leadership positions after the Rankovic ouster. However, substantive moves toward political pluralism were blocked by Tito. As the economy came under the control of republican and local interests, Yugoslav politics became particularistic, based on local networks of power, influence, and interests--the famous "VIP" of Yugoslav politics, "connections and protection." Tito himself, by the 1960s a major international figure, intervened only occasionally in domestic politics, usually to break deadlock among the regional bosses.

New elites, their legitimacy grounded in regional power bases, arose. The structure of Yugoslav federalism, which like its Leninist model rested on ethnically-defined administrative units, accelerated this shift; the conflictual history of the Yugoslav state, where no single nationality comprised a majority, almost guaranteed that politics would flow through these ethnically-defined channels. The denouement between ethnic reassertion and retention of central control came in 1971-73, when Tito reined in a burgeoning nationalist movement, especially in Croatia, that had allied with liberal reformers. The ensuing Titoist revisions and the 1974 Constitution created a complex system of self-management institutions in all public and economic institutions which was coupled with a radical decentralization of power. Republics were granted wide-ranging powers and the two provinces attached to Serbia, Vojvodina and Kosovo, were constitutionally elevated to near-republican status.

Although Tito successfully broke the power of the liberals and nationalists, his actions cemented in place a system which based power and legitimacy in the republics. Liberal reformists in the party, especially in Croatia, Slovenia, and Serbia, were bracketed with the nationalists and ousted from power. Any chance for an early Yugoslav version of perestroika was cut short. Liberals and technocrats, generally the least Leninist and hence in favor of decentralization and pluralism, were a primary target. But, the power of the republican parties, now far more conservative as the result of Tito's actions, was preserved.

Fueled by easy access to foreign investment funds and economic assistance, the system worked throughout the 1970s.[4] But, the political economy was fragmented. Power flowed through republican channels to local levels, where complex networks of power, influence, and interests prevailed. Decision-making was accomplished largely through bargaining among regional elites; economic rationality took second place to political ends. Yugoslavia didn't have a de-controlled market, it had a federalized controlled market in which each unit competed against all others for better distributive outcomes.

The Economic Debacle

Yugoslavia exemplifies in many ways the failure of the distributive state. By the 1980s the consequences of republican autarky had emerged fullblown amid a declining economy. Rather than risk unemployment and the consequent loss of political legitimacy, republican leaderships shored up unprofitable enterprises. Competition among the republics and provinces, each of which possessed its own financial system and central bank, was perceived as zero sum. Many decisions were made at opcina (county) levels, where powerful local politicians controlled the enterprise management boards and financial institutions on their territories. The economic differences among the republics and provinces widened. By 1980 the disparities were stark: Slovenia, with an unemployment rate of 1.3%, had a per capita social product more than double that of the Yugoslav average and eight times that of Kosovo, which suffered a 27.3 percent unemployment rate.[5]

The dynamic set in motion by the federalization of the LCY and devolution of economic power impelled a drive for economic self-sufficiency in the republics. By 1988 over 70 percent of all Yugoslav trade was carried out within republican/provincial boundaries.[6] It was almost impossible to counter the interlocking "directorates" of local party, government, management, and banking. This meant that if Yugoslavia was to reform it had to do so from an extremely disadvantageous position. Although still nominally a communist state, Yugoslavia was so decentralized as to be almost confederal. Without Tito, it lacked a political center strong enough to impose reform. The various measures the federal government reluctantly undertook under severe pressures from western financial institutions were at best inadequate. All eventually foundered on obstruction by powerful republican and local politicians. With republican and provincial politicians unwilling to resist workers' wage demands lest they loose popular legitimacy and federal organs lacking the means to impose reform, inflation wrecked the various proposed reform programs. Inflation rose steadily, to over 80 percent by early 1985. By December of 1989 it would be around 2000 percent.

The potential burden of economic reform was particularly onerous in the poorer regions: Macedonia, Montenegro, Bosnia-Hercegovina, Serbia proper, and its autonomous province of Kosovo. It is at this time, in the mid 1980s, that the Serbian nationalist leader, Slobodan Milosevic, became a major political player. But, although the economic situation helped fuel Milosevic's accession to power, his path was largely determined by the peculiar structure of the Yugoslav communist party itself.

The Party in the Eighties

The Yugoslav communist party was an anomaly in the communist-party universe, its political structure a mirror of the decentralized economy. By 1980 and Tito's death it had evolved into a virtual confederation of competing, and frequenting contentious, republican and provincial party hierarchies, each basically responsible only to their own constituencies. Party membership was open to almost all; there was no candidacy period required or uniform requirements. The BOAL (Basic Organization of Associated Labor) reforms of 1976 which disaggregated the factories and social sector institutions into free-standing self-managed work units (BOALs) generated an analogous disaggregation in the party. Between 1969 and 1982 the number of basic party units increased from 14,382 to 66,875.[7] Most primary party units were based in the BOALs and were consequently small in size. Few members actively participated. The way was left open for the powerful regional oligarchies. Tito's party, originally federalized in structure but unified in governance, was gone; scant political gain accrued to those politicians who still tried to build and maintain a federal consensus.

Careers were made and remained in the republics and provinces; there was no unified central cadre system.[8] The federal organs of both party and government were delegated from the eight constituent units, not coopted by the center. Control over cadre policy rested with the party units of the republics and provinces, each of which controlled political appointments on its territory. Unlike the Soviet Union, personnel were not transferred from republic to republic at the will of the central authorities. Almost all federal appointments, party or government, required the prior approval of the relevant republican or provincial party and in fact usually originated there. The only exception was the party unit of the military, the Yugoslav People's Army (YPA), which prevailed over its own cadre system and thus drew on all of Yugoslavia.

LCY Party Statute provided for dual membership, or in the case of the provinces, triple. Members could--and did so in large numbers--resign voluntarily without question. The eight republican and provincial parties exhibited differing patterns in levels of voluntary resignations versus disciplinary expulsions, which probably reflected differing levels of party discipline. Thus, in 1983 only 1 percent of the Kosovo party-leavers voluntarily resigned, as compared to 21 percent in Croatia and Slovenia.[9] According to party Statute, party discipline was the responsibility of each party unit.

There were also significant differences in the percentages of party membership among the different nationalities. The most striking were the disproportionately low levels of Croatian and of Moslem (both Bosnian and Albanian) members and the disproportionately high levels of Serb-Montenegrin membership in all eight republican and provincial parties.[10] Overall, Serbs comprised 47.8 percent of the total LCY membership but only 36.3% of the total Yugoslav population; Montenegrins, 5.5 percent of the membership and 2.6% of the population. In the Croatian party, Serbs, who comprised 11.5 percent of Croatia's population, were 23.5 percent of the Croatian party; in Bosnia-Hercegovina, 43.3 percent of the membership and 32 percent of the republic's population.[11]

The Yugoslav state was internally inconsistent. Tito had bequeathed to it an official ideology based on self-managed socialism and local empowerment, mandatory ethnic equality, and political federalism, under the control of eight monocratic units, all of which had depended on the mediation of a single charismatic leader. The Party was caught in a downward spiral. Without Tito's immense personal authority the political dynamic he set in place spun free of constraints. Whereas Leninism drives everything to the center, the politics of the LCY became centrifugal, spinning faster and faster until there was little at the center.

The Crisis in Kosovo

Yugoslavia's final decade began in the spring of 1981 with demonstrations for equality and full republican status among the Albanians of Kosovo, who comprised almost 90 percent of the population of the province. Kosovo was never completely pacified after 1981; by 1989, there would be thousands of national troops there. Each new demonstration among Kosovo's Albanians generated backlashes among Serbs. Yet, each quelling of unrest reinforced Albanians' perception that they had no place in a post-Tito Yugoslavia. Slavs continued to leave Kosovo. Although Serbs tendentiously attributed all Slavic out-migration from Kosovo to Albanian terrorism, anti-Serbianism certainly existed and was a factor in the Slavic migration.

An important stimulant was the widening gap between education and employment in Kosovo which, coupled with the mandatory use of the nationality key to fill positions, worked against Slavs of Kosovo. Educational levels outstripped economic development; Kosovo remained Yugoslavia's poorest area. This was exacerbated by the Kosovar Albanian birth rate, the highest in Europe.[12] The numbers of skilled workers in the work force of Kosovo was the lowest (24.1 percent) in Yugoslavia, yet proportionately Kosovo had more students completing secondary education than Slovenia.[13] The political effects were extraordinarily divisive: in the final accounting, it may be said that Kosovo was the proximate cause of the League of Communists' bitter disintegration in January of 1990. The man most blamed for the eventual sundering of the Yugoslav state, Slobodan Milosevic, rode to the leadership of Serbia on a platform of Serbian nationalism and protection of the Slavs of Kosovo.

For Serbian politicians there was no good answer. Either they continued to deny republican status to the almost two million Albanians who lived on what many Serbs regard as their traditional homeland, stolen from them by the Turks in 1389, and again by the communists after 1945, or they alienated eight million Serbs. There was no bargain possible once the equation, political legitimacy equals ethnic legitimacy, had been sealed.

The Party Without Tito

In 1982 the LCY assembled for its first congress since Tito's death. The Congress avoided the main political issue: the relationship of the LCY to its constituent units.[14] Party discipline remained vested in the eight republican and provincial Leagues; delegates refused to limit the autonomy of the republican and provincial parties. The Congress produced one inescapable conclusion: there was no central authority that could compel compliance with federal LCY statutes and decisions.

In the poorer regions, home to many of the economically unfeasible investment projects, earning capacities fell and living standards declined. The LCY responded by trying to impose curbs on what it perceived as internal dissent. The political elites were now out of synch, trying to liberalize the economy while squelching dissent. Many Yugoslavs came to a not-illogical conclusion that as an effective national body the LCY--much as with U.S. political parties--existed only during national Congresses. Centrifugalism was accelerated by mounting expressions of nationalist particularism. With censorship power over the media vested in each republic, the potential for damage was severe. If only the dominant political elite in each unit had free rein, minorities inevitably felt threatened. As overt expressions of nationalism arose in the post-Tito period, media nationalism became a ready tool for ambitious regional politicians. The indirect, complex electoral system instituted by the 1974 Constitution satisfied few, and motivated even fewer; neither the carefully selected delegates nor the public took much active part in the electoral system or in the policy process.[15] The federal government and party could be effectively immobilized if consensus among the republics and provinces were impossible; local assemblies were ineffective.[16] The Yugoslav system lacked the organizational capacity for reform. All decried political interference in the economy. Yet, it was the power of regional and local elites to do this that lay at the heart of political legitimacy in post-Tito Yugoslavia.

The Politics of Ethnic Grievance

In the inchoate politics of post-Tito Yugoslavia, each republican and provincial political elite not only acted autonomously, they were forced to do so for political survival. The enduring conflict in Kosovo was fundamental for Serbian politicians, who had to deal with it firsthand and to justify their actions to their Serbian constituents. Damned if they did, and further damned if they didn't, Serbia came under increasing criticism from other republics. So divisive was the Kosovo issue that by 1988, with the republics unable to reach any consensus on the matter and the federal authorities incapable of imposing a decision, Yugoslavia was the only state besides Romania that refused to send an official delegation to a CSCE human rights meeting.[17]

As the open animosities mounted, some Serbs began to argue that the 1974 Constitution unjustly reduced Serbian sovereignty by granting virtual autonomy to the two provinces. The issue was sharpened by the fact that the Serbian party could no longer select the leadership cadres of Kosovo and Vojvodina, leading some Serbian nationalists to charge that the Kosovo provincial leaders used their autonomy to sabotage Serbian interests.[18] More radical Serbs argued that from its inception Titoism consistently acted against the interests of the Serbian nation, deliberately leaving large numbers of Serbs in Bosnia-Hercegovina, Croatia, Kosovo, and Vojvodina.[19] Such arguments had first surfaced publicly in the mid 1970s when some leading Serbian communists sought to reverse the constitutional autonomy of the provinces granted by the 1974 Constitution. Their arguments, contained in a report known as the Blue Book, was repressed at Tito's orders.[20] Nonetheless, despite Tito, the juridic status of Serbia was unique; the two provinces were both part of the Serbian Republic and were at the same time federal units, and this did subject Serbia to unique constraints.

In 1984 the arguments of the Blue Book were revived. It is at this point that Slobodan Milosevic began his rise to power in the Serbian party as the champion of Serbianism. Milosevic argued that Tito believed that a "strong Yugoslavia" was possible only with a "weak Serbia." Eventually, Milosevic would argue that Tito's real agenda was the destruction of Serbia.[21] The accusation that an anti-Serb, anti-Yugoslav conspiracy set out to destroy Serbia, and thus Yugoslavia, became a leitmotif in Serbian nationalist rhetoric.

Mounting Pressures for Change

Some, particularly in Slovenia, lost hope in the system as constituted, convinced that some form of political pluralism was necessary if Yugoslavia were to survive--otherwise, powerful republican politicians could always block reform. The first independent organizations appeared in Slovenia in the early 1980s, the now-reformist Slovenian communist party leadership permitting them to affiliate with the Slovenian Socialist Alliance or the Slovenian Socialist Youth Alliance. One group so affiliated, the Slovenian Democratic Alliance, expressly promoted a multiparty system.[22] The Alliance was thus the first official noncommunist political group permitted in Yugoslavia since 1945.

However, Serbia took a different path. In 1986 the Serbian Academy of Arts and Sciences (SANU) charged in a draft Memorandum that for 40 years Titoism had consistently suppressed Serbian religion and culture, denying Serbia its rightful political position. The Serbian charges included the accusation that Croats and Slovenes supported Albanian separatism in Kosovo.[23] The Memorandum was the lineal descendant of the Blue Book. It became the intellectual centerpiece of particularistic Serbian nationalism, dovetailing with the frustrations aroused by the Kosovo issue which were fanned by the politics of Milosevic.[24]

Milosevic became President of the Serbian League of Communists in May of 1986, by mounting an intra-party coup. He solidified his base of popular support by sponsoring mass "solidarity" rallies of Serbs, which used the nationalist rhetoric of the Memorandum as their theme. Rallies were staged in Serbia, Vojvodina, Macedonia, Montenegro, and among the Serbs of Croatia's Krajina region, home to approximately half of Croatia's Serbian population. The demonstrations were especially threatening to Croats. Croatian apprehensions rose, fueled by Milosevic's demands for special rights for the Serbs of Croatia.

Slovenes and Croats, reacting to what they saw as mounting Serbian threats, refused to support Serbia when international organizations began to criticize Serbia's human rights record in Kosovo. But, the more Milosevic's policies were criticized, the more intransigent the Serbian regime became. In the spring of 1989 the Serbian government arrested over 200 Kosovar Albanian leaders and held them in isolation. The action was condemned by the governments of Slovenia and Croatia, the Helsinki Committee (CSCE), Amnesty International, the European Parliament, and the U.S. Congress, all of whose protests were rejected by the Serbian government and Milosevic.[25]

Milosevic Comes to Power

Ultimately, however skillfully Milosevic played upon Serbian nationalism, it was the political federalization of the Titoist structure that empowered him. Milosevic had astutely evaluated the potential power of populist nationalism and the possibilities inherent in the structural changes which had freed the component units of the party from central authority. Essentially, he prevailed by calling hundreds of thousands of Serbs into the streets with demagogic nationalist appeals, inviting them to blame their grievances and economic woes on the Kosovar Albanians and on an "anti-Serbian conspiracy."[26]

After Milosevic assumed the leadership of the Serbian party, moderates were expelled in secret procedures that violated party Statutes.[27] Among those purged were moderate Serbian journalists who were replaced with Milosevic supporters, giving Milosevic control of Serbia's media. In December 1987 Ivan Stambolic, once Milosevic's mentor, was removed as Serbia's State President and expelled from the party,[28] his expulsion accompanied by the now-usual Milosevite charges that Serbia had been betrayed by the Communist Party.[29] Milosevic now controlled the Serbian government, party, and media. He presented himself as the protector of Serbs everywhere, the crowds who rallied at his command chanting the Serbian slogan, "samo sloga Srbina spasava" ("only unity saves the Serbs"). A steady drumbeat of massive street demonstrations erupted, in September and October of 1988 alone totaling at almost one million people.[30]

Milosevic then tried to dominate other republics. In 1988 *Mladina*, the official organ of the Slovenian Youth Alliance, published an alleged plan by the Federal Defense Council for mass arrests of dissident Slovenes using the federal army. The Milosevic forces demanded the imprisonment of the authors. Slovenian authorities refused; federal authorities lacked any mechanism for breaking the deadlock. Eventually, four young Slovenes involved were tried by a federal military court, the only ready instrument available, in a trial which enraged Slovenes and unified them in their determination to withstand Milosevic.[31]

In October of 1988 Milosevic succeeded in bringing down his opponents in the Vojvodina party and government after mounting mass demonstrations there. Similar demonstrations staged in Montenegro resulted in the overthrow of Montenegro's leadership in January of 1989. Milosevic now controlled three of the eight units of the LCY and three of the eight seats on the federal Presidency. Although the SFRY Presidency did not require unanimity, most action did require a two-thirds, or six votes, which gave Milosevic and Serbia a virtual veto.

Kosovo: The Touchstone of Serbian Politics

All this occurred against a backdrop of mounting Serbian human rights abuses in Kosovo.[32] Croats and Slovenes began to fear that the

Serbian actions called into question whether the European Community would, or under its laws could, ever accept Yugoslavia as a member. At the same time, Serbian politicians warned that Yugoslavia should not abandon its ties with the Soviet bloc.[33] In February of 1989 amendments to the Serbian Constitution which abrogated the autonomy of Kosovo and Vojvodina were unilaterally promulgated by Serbia.[34] In June of 1989, one million supporters answered Milosevic's call for Serbs to meet in Kosovo to commemorate the six hundredth anniversary of the Battle of Kosovo Polje, which marks the defeat of the medieval Serbian Kingdom by the Ottoman Empire in 1389. Milosevic declared that the Serbian people must unite, lest they suffer the fate of Serbs over the past six hundred years, from Kosovo Polje to both world wars and to socialist Yugoslavia "...when the Serbian leadership remained divided and prone to compromises at the expense of the people."[35] His speech concluded ominously: "Today...we are again...facing battles. They are not armed battles, although such things cannot yet be excluded."[36]

Milosevic then shifted his focus to Croatia, populated by over a half million Serbs, half of them in the Krajina, the crescent-shaped region that runs along the Croatian border with Bosnia. The Krajina Serbs demanded separate status for the Krajina within Croatia; that is, what was denied to the Albanians of Kosovo, political autonomy within a republic. The Krajina demonstrations mark the shift in Milosevic's political rhetoric from "protecting" the Serbs of Kosovo to proclaiming that wherever Serbs lived is Serbian territory. Despite censure by the LCY Presidium, the Army party unit, and the Croatian party and government, the demonstrations in Croatia continued.[37]

There were no effective means outside of Serbia to brake Milosevic or to forestall the nationalist movements developing in other republics. Serbian nationalists began to funnel arms to the newly created Serbian militia throughout Croatia, supposedly so they could protect themselves against a repetition of the genocide carried out by the fascist Croatian Ustasa in World War II.[38] Croatian nationalism rose, fueled by Milosevic's rhetoric and Serbian actions. As Milosevic demonstrated, nationalism was the surest route to public support. The powerful nationalist forces aroused coincided with a growing push for pluralism. As alternative political groups formed in Croatia, one, the Hrvatska Demokratsa (HDZ) of Franjo Tudjman, a former Partisan general cashiered by Tito in 1972, seized the nationalist card in Croatia. A sort of Gresham's law began to prevail: with republican parties controlling the media of their territories, reasonable political discourse was driven out by particularistic nationalism. Ultimately, Tudjman's HDZ would win the multiparty Croatian elections in May of 1990, and go on to define Croatia as "the state of Croatians," effectively disenfranchising Croatia's Serbian population.

The reformist Slovenian party, under the leadership of Milan Kucan, began to argue that multiparty democracy was the only salvation from Serbian hegemony and authoritarianism. However, the other republics, with their ethnically mixed populations and large Serbian minorities, had far more immediate fears over Milosevic's claim that Serbian jurisdiction extended over all Serbs, wherever, and his repeated promise that "Serbia will be a state or will not exist at all."[39] It is difficult to convey the depths of the poisoning of the political wells. In a state where internecine civil war and atrocities on all sides were all too recent, it is insufficient to say that Milosevic validated the politics of mass nationalism, or made concrete the political dynamic which had long been developing. His actions were pivotal because by now both government and party were powerless to stop him. The instruments of restraint available to Tito no longer existed. Consequently, all who would ride the nationalist tide into power could act without fear.

Prelude to Disintegration

In October of 1988 a severely divided federal party assembled amid massive pro-Milosevic street demonstrations in Belgrade. When a special LCY commission recommended that up to one-third of the LCY Central Committee step down, this resulted in an unprecedented vote of no confidence in a Serbian member, which the Serbian party leadership refused to accept.[40] Milosevic declared to the LCY Plenum that Serbia would have its "own politics" and did not need to depend on [or obey] party Statute.[41] Milosevic defended his actions as necessary to halt the "last genocide in the 20th century," which he described in these terms: "....children are raped, houses are burned, people beaten up, graves desecrated, two nations [Serbs and Montenegrins] exterminated, and a whole culture eliminated."[42]

Serbian delegates argued that Kosovo represented a grave threat to Yugoslavia's defense, and thus Serbia was protecting Yugoslavia's very existence.[43] The Plenum ended in a deadlock, the Serbian leadership unwilling to compromise. Milosevic pledged that

> The wave of democracy that has overtaken Serbia can only trouble the environments that have not yet been reached... the certainty of its proximity disturbs and angers those whom it will sweep away when it comes.[44]

Milosevic's accession to power through populist nationalism and the politics of the street reflects a fateful defect in Titoism. Although Tito sanctioned autonomy for the constituent republican units of the LCY, he refused to license any non-party groups. Hence, republican leaders had the traditional communist front organizations and the resources of their republics at their command, while the opposition within each republic had no such organizational resources. Furthermore, because the LCY had obeyed Tito's ban on pluralism, political debate among republics was carried out in the language of nationalism: only nationalism was licensed as a legitimate difference in Yugoslavia. All politics had to course through republic-bounded channels. Unlike other communist parties, where conflicts over reform, cadre policy and so forth elicited shifting coalitions whose makeup and geographic origins varied across time, in Yugoslavia coalition partners were almost always defined by republican boundaries.

Into Dissolution

On the eve of Yugoslavia's disintegration, Koca Popovic, Tito's former vice-president and Partisan general, incisively described Yugoslav politics as dominated by

> ...eight monopolies based on geographic division of nationalities... the

republic and provincial parties, as the federal institutional linkage has been... reduced mostly to optional bargaining among the national elites of the republics and provinces, have created eight managerial oligarchies.[45]

Popovic perspicaciously predicted that Yugoslavia might shatter if the democratic movement were blunted, as occurred in 1971, and warned that without a "modern democratic civilization" the country could not "keep pace with Europe."[46]

In the spring of 1989 repeated attempts by Slovenian officials at a rapprochement with Serbia elicited only refusals. Milosevic, countering the Slovenian criticisms of Serbian human rights violations in Kosovo, described Slovenia's protests as "primitive, vengeful aggression incompatible with the culture of present-day Europe, which they would like to join."[47] Milosevic's final response to the Slovenes was ominous:

When you finally understand that you cannot interfere in the affairs of Serbia...we will be pleased to welcome you to Belgrade....our talks will have no chance of success if you continue to deliberately misinform your public about the situation in Serbia...."[48]

In the background to this was the mounting concern of the other republics, who feared for their economic livelihoods as Serbian policies increasingly alienated the West.[49] In September of 1989 the Slovenian Parliament adopted amendments to the Slovenian Constitution which included the right of secession and Slovenia's right to reject a federally-declared state of emergency.[50] Throughout most of 1989 Milosevic refused to meet with the U.S. Ambassador to Yugoslavia, denied international human rights groups access to Kosovo, and pressured the other republics to support Serbia's position on Kosovo.

Milosevic then announced that on December 1, Serbs would rally in Ljubljana "to tell the Slovenes the truth about Kosovo." To the Slovenes, calling a mass rally in their capital city was an unacceptable interjection of the street politics of Milosevic into Slovenia, and illegal as well, as all public meetings required permission from the relevant republican authorities. The Slovenes also feared the rally might presage an attempt by Milosevic to topple the Slovenian leadership, as with the rallies which brought down the leaderships of Vojvodina and Montenegro.[51] The Slovenian government banned the rally. Milosevic retaliated with a Serbian boycott of Slovenian trade, scornfully describing Slovenian actions as "... uncivilized...aggression against basic human rights and freedoms...a crime against truth and justice."[52]

The cascade of events in Eastern Europe in 1989 sharpened the conflict over Serbian politics. A Serbian member of the LCY Presidium warned that the LCY "must not relinquish power as in Poland, nor agree to become a parliamentary opposition, as in Hungary."[53] Such positions ran counter to the changes now sweeping over Eastern Europe, as well as to those in the Yugoslav republics outside of Serbia, especially Slovenia and Croatia. A leading Croatian communist put it bluntly: the choice was between democratic reform or maintaining the "monistic system at any cost."[54]

It was in this context that the republican and provincial parties prepared for the forthcoming Extraordinary LCY Congress in January of 1990. As the news from Hungary and East Germany and then from Prague spread throughout the country, liberals, reformers, and nationalists who were not Milosevic allies became more and more apprehensive, fearful that they would be left behind in a communist political backwater which the rest of Eastern Europe had deserted.

The prologue to the LCY's final act occurred in June of 1989, in the LCY Central Committee. The Slovenes, fearing that they would be steamrollered by the Serbian bloc of votes, sought to change the party rule under which the size of party delegations were based on membership size, a rule which benefitted Serbs, disproportionately strong in the party. When their proposal was rejected, the Slovenian leadership announced they would leave the LCY if outvoted at the upcoming Congress. As was the practice since 1969, the republican and provincial LCY Congresses were held first. It was at these republican party congresses, in December of 1989, that the Slovenian and Croatian parties voted to hold multiparty elections, thus paving the way for contested democratic elections in the spring of 1990 in Croatia and Slovenia. The move, hotly protested by the Serbian party, stood because there was no way to compel Slovenia or Croatia to obey the letter of the

Yugoslav Constitution or the LCY Statute, both of which forbade multiparty elections.

In January of 1990 the LCY disappeared. The locale of its self-inflicted demise was the Fourteenth Extraordinary LCY Congress. The fact that the Congress was held at the request of the Milosevic forces supports the thesis that they intended it as a mechanism to reimpose centralism. Instead, all the other party units preferred to preserve their independence at the expense of the party's very existence, rather than accede to domination by Serbia and Milosevic. Although undoubtedly prodded by events in Eastern Europe, the LCY did renounce its 45-year monopoly of power, a majority of the delegates voted against the Slovenes' proposal for a confederal structure. The Slovenian delegation had arrived under instructions to walk if rejected. They duly walked out on January 24, 1990.

The Leagues of Bosnia-Hercegovina, Croatia, and Macedonia refused to continue the Congress without Slovenia, voting down the Serbian proposal to constitute a new quorum and continue. With this, the League of Communists of Yugoslavia self-destructed, affirming in its very collapse the genuine political autonomy of the six republics.

Conclusion

When the Yugoslav system began to disintegrate, a process exacerbated by Tito's death and the consequent removal of the sole authoritative force of mediation, the most readily available substitute was nationalism. It is a truism that, in the former communist party states, nationalism all too easily functions as a replacement for the former ruling ideology. However, in the case of Yugoslavia, the truism had a special edge because the Titoist system was so designed, inadvertently or not, to encourage this.

Under Tito the powerful republican chiefs exercised their powers on their own territories, with implicit permission from Tito. However, once Tito the ultimate arbitrator was gone, there was no effective restraint on the use of particularistic nationalism for political designs. Milosevic could project himself as the protector of all Serbs, everywhere in Yugoslavia, which essentially meant everywhere but

Slovenia--although the Serbian-controlled Yugoslav Army even invaded Slovenia, briefly and futilely, in June of 1991. The combination of a one-party system which disaggregated control into eight autonomous units, bound into a Leninist-style federation which tied nationality to territory, reinforced the traditional nationalisms of the Yugoslav region: Serbian expansionism,[55] Croatian particularism, and Slovenian exceptionalism.[56] Milosevic stoked these fires assiduously, and a "Greater Serbia" which would include all Serbs came to be seen by Serbs as their legitimate birthright. The Serbian-driven territorial war which erupted in Yugoslavia in June of 1991 was driven by these political dynamics, its design clear to all that would listen to history. The Serbian territorial goals were entirely consistent: Bosnia, while by far the bloodiest theater, was absolutely necessary to the Serbia promoted by Milosevic.

By licensing nationalism as the only permissible difference and then institutionalizing this in a federalized party structure where eventually central power evaporated, the Titoist system guaranteed the political autonomy of the ethnically-defined constituent units. It, however, also guaranteed Yugoslavia's destruction at the hands of nationalism and Slobodan Milosevic.

Notes

1. See, e.g., Denison Rusinow, *The Yugoslav Experiment 1948-1974* (Berkeley: University of California Press, 1977).

2. By the 1960s the League of Communists of Yugoslavia had abandoned many of the practices common to communist systems. Its innovations roughly fall into three categories: (1) those aimed at securing domestic support through encouraging widespread citizen participation; (2) those aimed at securing international support, especially through Yugoslavia's leadership of the non-aligned movement and its independence from Soviet control; and (3) those aimed at rationalizing the economy. A partial list includes: private ownership of agricultural land; dismantling central planning; abandoning centrally-determined investment and production goals, extensive importation of Western goods and technology; granting communal and republican governments the power to levy taxes and budgetary control independent of federal authority; participation of non-party members in social institutions; mandated parity for the major ethnic groups in government and party bodies; private ownership of homes and apartments; and the freedom to travel abroad, including the right to immigrate and hold jobs abroad.

3. Paul Shoup, *Communism and the Yugoslav National Question* (New York: Columbia University Press, 1968).

4. Susan Woodward, "Orthodoxy and Solidarity: Competing Claims and International Adjustment in Yugoslavia," in Ellen Comisso and Laura d'Andrea Tyson, *Power, Purpose and Collective Choice: Economic Strategy in Socialist States* (Ithaca: Cornell University Press, 1986) 333-36.

5. *Statisticki Godisnjak* (Belgrade: Savezni zavod za statisticku, 1981) 405, 431.

6. "Funkioniranje jedinstvenog Jugoslovenskog trzista" (The Functioning of a unified Yugoslav market), *Jugoslavenske Pregled 32*, 4-5 (1988), 194-5.

7. Ivan Cifric, "Savez komunista i seljastvo u socijalno-historijskom" 484; in Vladimir Cvjeticanin et al, *Klasno-socijalna struktura Saveza kommunista Jugoslavije* (Zagreb: Globus, 1984).

8. *Kadrovska Lista*, the equivalent of *Nomenklatura*.

9. Boris Vuskovic, Zeljko Rogosic, and Stojan Obradovic, "Kretanje i struktura clanstva SK," *Nase Teme* 29, 1-3 (1985) 1092-93.

10. Boris Vuskovic, "Nacionalni sastav stanovnistva," *Savezni zavod za Statisicki Bilten,* (May 1982) 126.

11. Ibid., 126-158.

12. "Stanovnistvo Kosova," *Jugoslovenski Pregled* 9 (1989) 321-326.

13. "Education and the Work Force," *Yugoslav Survey* 27, 3 (1986) 132.

14. Dusan Bilandzic, *Historija socijalisticke federarativne republike Jugoslavije* (Zagreb: Skolska knjiga, 1985) 509-511.

15. Ivan Grdesic, "Interesi i moc: sadrzaj rada opcinskih skupstina u SR Hrvatska," *Politicka misao* 23, 1 (1986) 108-120.

16. Zdravko Tomac, "Raskrsca delegatskog sistema" *Politicka misao* 22, 4 (1985) 31-47.

17. *Danas*, Feb. 18, 1988; trans. in Joint Publication Research Service-EER (hereafter, JPRS) 88-033 (Apr. 26, 1988) 43-45.

18. Bilandzic, *Historija*, 501.

19. See, e.g.,Luka Miceta, "The Errors and Injustices of History," *NIN* (Oct. 13, 1988); JPRS-EER 88-096 (Nov. 14, 1988) 26. See Milan Kucan, "Jugoslovenski federalizam od speransa do razmisljana o novom Ustavu," introduction to Ciril Ribicic and Zdravko Tomac, *Federal izam po mjeri i buducnosti* (Zagreb: Globus, 1989), for an analysis of Serbian criticisms of Titoism.

20. Bilandzic, *Historija* , 501.

21. E.g., Batric Jovanovic, "The Albanization of Kosovo Supported by an Anti-Serbian Coalition," *Politika* (March 7, 1990) 15; JPRS-EER 90-039 (June 1, 1990) 23-25.

22. Igor Mekina, "Hope Expressed for New Political Creations,"_*Mladina* (Dec. 16, 1988) 16-17; Foreign Broadcast Information Services, Eastern Europe, 89-001, (hereafter, FBIS-EEU) (Jan. 3, 1989) 25.

23. "Grupa akademika SANU" [Group of the Serbian Academy of Sciences and Arts], *Nase Teme* 33, 1-2 (1988) 128-163. Printed in the journal of the Croatian Central Committee, this was the first official publication of the Memorandum, although the Memorandum was widely circulated unofficially.

24. Dragutin Lalovic, "Upotreba Jugoslavije," *Nase Teme* 33, 1-2 (1988) 119-127.

25. Radio Free Europe, *Yugoslav Situation Report* 10 (Aug. 17, 1989) 25-6.

26. A collection of Milosevic's most important speeches may be found in *Godina raspleta* (Belgrade: Beogradski Izdavacko Graficki Zavod, 1989).

27. For details, see the suppressed speech by a *Politika* journalist, Radmilo Kljajic, *Mladost* (Nov. 2, 1987) 18-20; JPRS-EER, 88-009, (Feb. 5, 1988) 36-41. Most of the proceedings of the Serbian League of Communists were kept secret from this time on.

28. It was Stambolic who referred to the Memorandum of the Serbian Academy as "Yugoslavia's epitaph". In Jelena Lovric, "Josip Broz's Second Death," *Danas*, June 6, 1989; JPRS-EER, 89-086 (August 1, 1989) 13-14.

29. For a sample of this line, see the interview of Ljubomir Tadic, in "Political Scientist Defends Serbia's Leadership," *Duga* (Sept. 16, 1988) 14-18; JPRS-EER88-092 (Oct. 28, 1988) 11-16.

30. FBIS-EEU, various dates September-November, 1988.

31. The trial, although held in Slovenia, was conducted in Serbian. The four were sentenced to terms of imprisonment and were later released. One defendant, Janez Jansa, became the Minister of Defense in independent Slovenia in 1991.

32. See Steven J. Woehrel, "Yugoslavia's Kosovo Crisis," Congressional Research Service 89-603F, Nov. 2, 1989. Various reports by Amnesty International, which began reporting on human rights abuses in Yugoslavia after 1982, are also useful.

33. Radio Free Europe, *Yugoslavia: Situation Report* 12 (Dec. 23, 1988) 9.

34. Although the provinces were treated as constituent federal units since 1974, they nonetheless were still part of Serbia under the Serbian constitution, an ambiguous situation. The amendments stated that Serbia possessed "equal status" with the other five republics, and would no longer accept the perceived limitations upon her sovereignty by the existence of the provinces within Serbian territory.

35. "Milosevic Speech on Kosovo Anniversary," Tanjug News Service (June 28, 1989) 9-11; FBIS-EEU 89-124, 62.

36. Ibid.

37. Milosevic used the supposed repression of the Serbs of Croatia as an excuse to arm them; in 1991 their "protection" became the rationale for the Serbian-led invasion of Croatia. In turn, in the summer of 1995 the government of independent Croatia used Serbia machinations as their rationale for expelling Serbs from their homes in the

Croatian Krajina.

38. These arms were augmented by arms seized from the magazines of the territorial defense forces (somewhat similar to a National Guard) of Croatia. The Yugoslav federal Army eventually disarmed all of the territorial militias except Serbia's, but the Slovenes managed to keep some 40-50 percent of their territorial armaments. In James Gow, "Deconstructing Yugoslavia," *Survival* 33, 4 (1991) 291-311. The Serbian government denied any responsibility for the arming of the Serbs in Croatia and Bosnia-Hercegovina until February 27, 1992, when Milosevic admitted this in speech to the Serbian parliament.

39. This statement was repeated in many Serbian nationalist speeches. It became shorthand for what many perceived as Milosevic's real goal: a Greater Serbia which would include all Serbs, first in Croatia and Bosnia and then, the historic medieval Serbian lands of Macedonia, Montenegro, and Kosovo.

40. Radio Free Europe, *Yugoslavia: Situation Report* 2 (Feb. 3, 1989) 3-4.

41. Interview with LCY Central Committee member, Zagreb, May 28, 1990.

42. "Milosevic Addresses Plenum," Belgrade Domestic Service, Oct. 17, 1988; trans in FBIS-EEU 88-201, 84. The accusation that the Albanians of Kosovo were guilty of genocide was a constant theme of Milosevic's speeches, as was the charge that Albanian terrorism included planned mass rapes of Serbian women and children.

43. E.g., Gaja Petkovic, "Kosovo--Weak Link in Defense," *Borba* (Nov. 4, 1988) 12; JPSR-EEU 88-108 (Dec. 16, 1988) 41-42.

44. "The 17th Plenum," *Vjesnik* (Nov. 20, 1988) 3; FBIS-EEU 88-227 (Nov. 25, 1988).

45. Interview with Koca Popovic, *Danas_* (Jan. 31, 1989) 25-7; JPRS-EER 89-039 (Apr. 10, 1989) 14-15.

46. Ibid., 15.

47. Radio Free Europe, *Yugoslavia: Situation Report* 6 (June 27, 1989) 19-20; citing *Politika*, (May 23, 1989).

48. Ibid..

49. Interviews, Ljubljana and Zagreb, November-December 1989.

50. In 1990 the federal Constitutional Court ruled that the amendments to the constitutions of Serbia and Slovenia were in conflict with the federal SFRY Constitution,

but the Court lacked the means to compel conformity. "The Opinion of the Constitutional Court of Yugoslavia," *Yugoslav Survey* 31, 2 (1990) 5970.

51. *Demokracija.* Ljubljana, independent newspaper. (Dec. 5, 1989) 1-2.

52. Radio Free Europe 1, 3 (January 19, 1990) 22.

53. Radio Free Europe, *Yugoslav Situation Report,* 11 (Sept. 18, 1989).

54. Interview with Vladimir Goati, *NIN* (Oct. 8, 1989) 30-38; JPRS-EER 89-126 (Dec. 27, 1989). 19.

55. See David MacKenzie. *Ilija Garasanin: Balkan Bismarck* (New York: Columbia University Press, 1985) 42-45, *passim*; "Serbian Territorial aspirations in 1885, Translation of resolutions from a meeting of Serbians of Old Serbia and Macedonia, Belgrade, c. March 8, 1885," in Anita L.P. Burdett, ed., *The Historical Boundaries Between Croatia, Bosnia, Serbia: Documents and Maps, 1815-1945* (London: Archive Editions, 1995) 411-426.

56. See Ivo Banac, *The National Question in Yugoslavia: Origins, History, Politics* (Ithaca NY: Cornell University Press, 1984) for an examination of nationalism in the former Yugoslavia.

2.

The Failure of Institutions in Yugoslavia

Agneza Bozic

Then there is difference of race or nation, which remains a source of dissension until such time as the two groups learn to live together. This may be a long process; for just as a state cannot be made out of any and every collection of people, so neither can it be made at any time at will. (Aristotle, *Politics*, book V).

Introduction

Until the late 1980s multinational Yugoslavia attracted the attention of many scholars, for its reputation and status as an "outstanding anomaly" among the East European Communist states. Not only did Yugoslavia refuse to be a satellite of the Soviet Union in 1948, it insisted on and really worked on its own version of what would later be termed "national communism." Yugoslavia was home to workers' self-management, an original principle of industrial democracy, and the inaugurator of what others came to label as "Marxism with a human face." Yugoslavia was also a leader and co-founder of the international non-aligned movement. It was a socialist country with extensive political decentralization and economic liberalization; an exceptional communist country where people were allowed to travel freely and work abroad in non-communist countries.

In June of 1991 Yugoslavia became the scene of the bloodiest

war in the Balkans, and since then, a conundrum in search of an
answer: what were the reasons that led it from relative political stability
to tragic dissolution? Yugoslavia was a country with a complex
nationality make-up and intricate history; therefore, any examination of
its demise will inevitably be incomplete. With that in mind, it is
necessary to state that this analysis will not claim more than it intends to
investigate. The purpose here is to look at the institutions of communist
Yugoslavia and to assess their impact on the dismemberment of the
multiethnic state. Two institutions appear particularly pertinent: the
Communist Party of Yugoslavia (CPY), which was the ruling party of
the country and federalism as the underlying structure and organizing
principle of government. Of necessity, any analysis of federalism in
communist regimes must also consider Communist rule itself as a major
variable.

The Communist Party of Yugoslavia was the only authorized
political grouping in the country.[1] It perpetuated its control over the
government even though rhetorically it separated itself from the
government. The developments and dynamics between these two
institutions, as illustrated through historical institutional analysis of the
four Yugoslav constitutions[2] and their impact on the breakup of the
state are the focus of this analysis.

Political Institutions and Cleavage Management[3]

The quest for stability in severely divided societies provides a
challenge for many social scientists. Plural societies have been defined
as those societies in which "...political divisions follow very closely, and
especially concern lines of objective social differentiation, especially
those particularly salient in a society."[4] The lines of cleavages may be
religious, ethnic, linguistic, ideological or racial. The effective
management of these divisions, which translate into political cleavages,
is essential to the functioning of political regimes and their long-term
stability.

The task of cleavage management is complex and demanding
enough in democratic political systems which already provide
institutions designed specifically to accommodate competition among

organized groups. Most democratic regimes recognize the necessity of maintaining a careful and often difficult balance between conflict and consensus. Of the ten specific capabilities of government listed in one analysis, the most important is the ability to "manage political cleavages to ensure that the society does not degenerate into civil war."[5] Institutions designed for the purpose of conflict management in plural society include presidential or parliamentary structures of government, electoral laws, party systems and federalism. In differing democratic countries these institutions have contributed to differing patterns of democratic stability.

However, the task of analyzing the role of institutions in a non-democratic society, in this case the former Yugoslavia, is made difficult not only because of the all-pervasive role of communist ideology but also because of the lack of a history of liberal-democratic norms. These norms are often translated into the way in which institutions perform their functions or tasks. Many observers have noted that the institutions by which the Communist Party of Yugoslavia attempted to maintain stability were inadequate.[6] Ramet describes the effort as a marriage of decentralization and democratization in a one-party context: "The Yugoslav experiment was based on the premise that conflict could be regulated if there was pluralism within the party, even if genuine pluralism was proscribed outside the party."[7]

Others claim that Yugoslavia as a state never developed institutions that were particularly designed for conflict management.[8] The ruling party believed that the autonomy granted to the constituent nations through the federal administrative structure and the devolution of power would be sufficient to maintain peace among different nations and ethnic groups. But, because no autonomous intervening institutions were permitted to exist outside of party channels, ethnic dissent became magnified. The lack of legitimate, competing organizations and institutions meant that all political activity was confined to party channels--which, given the territorial administrative structure, were ethnically bounded.[9] Leninism, the original organizing principle of Titoism, forced all such actions into the party-government administrative structures.[10] To this might be added the judgment that the

LCY resolved to keep Yugoslavia together by whatever means necessary, which, as one analyst put it, meant that "Ultimately, Yugoslav stability has rested on force and the threat of force."[11] Such an assessment leads to an examination of the extent to which federalism of the political system and of the party played a role in weakening the communist monolith, which then gave in to the forces of disintegration.

Although some democracies, such as the United States, Belgium, the United Kingdom and Spain have mixed results in their record of conflict management, the conflicts they suffered and still suffer from did not result in violent conflict or in dissolution. In the case of Yugoslavia, that is precisely what happened. Hence, we turn to the analysis of the institutions that for 45 years seemingly contributed to the stability, even if superficially at times, of the multinational Yugoslav state. Did these institutions eventually facilitate a counter function, helping to lead Yugoslavia to its violent demise? Or were there factors, other than institutional mechanisms, that contributed? Above all, federalism has been cited as a major factor contributing to political stability. Was this the case in former Yugoslavia as well?

Federalism in Theory
Federalism has been described as:

> ...a form of political organization which unites separate polities which still maintain their fundamental political integrity. Federalism distributes power among general and constituent governments to protect the existence and authority of all which all share in the system's decision-making and executive processes.[12]

The very ambiguity of the term "federal" demonstrates that federalism is concerned both with the diffusion of political power in the name of liberty and its concentration on behalf of unity or providing a viable government. The right to some autonomy by the constituent units of a federation distinguishes the federal principle from mere decentralization or devolution of power, where powers so devolved or decentralized can be repossessed by unilateral decision of the central government. In the narrowest sense then, federalism is about the juridic division of power within a state, the constitutionally guaranteed division of power between the central government and the governments of the component units of the federation.[13]

According to Elazar, successful federations are characterized not only by their constitutional arrangements but by the "spirit of federalism," that is a commitment to partnership and active cooperation. This federal commitment is crucial to the system as a whole.[14]

However, the concept of decentralization within the framework of a one-party state directed by a party which tried to implement the Leninist policy of democratic centralism led to the tensions and crises that ultimately relegated Yugoslavia to the grave of lost communist utopias and failed multiethnic states. It appears that such a conception on the part of the regime obscured the process of conflict prevention and regulation by ignoring the foremost source of grievances: the nationality problem.

Yugoslav Federalism

The failure of federalism in Yugoslavia refutes the optimistic statement that once established, federal systems are the most durable political systems: "No authentic federal system that has lasted for even 15 years has ever been abandoned except through revolutionary disruption or foreign conquest, and in most cases, including the aforementioned two, federalism---showing remarkable resilience--has ultimately been restored."[15]

However, there are true federalisms--those that function as vehicles of political integration while at the same time accommodating diverse groups by giving them territorial or other power bases of their own--and federalism in name only, where there is federal structure but not the substance of federal commitment. The question is, was federalism in Yugoslavia true federalism or not and, was federalism a main contributor to the Yugoslav disintegration?

Whether or not the differences in the Yugoslav institutions of government were in name only or were truly substantive, at the very beginning of its post-World War II existence, its rulers distinguished Yugoslavia from other communist-party states in Eastern Europe by declaring it a federal state. The Constitutions of 1946, 1953, 1963, and 1974 established and reaffirmed the federal structure. Yugoslavia remained the only federal state in Eastern Europe until 1969 when Czechoslovakia also became federal.

It is important to note why federalism was chosen as the administrative structure for the state. At the end of World War II the victorious Partisans, led by the Communist Party of Yugoslavia (CPY) and Marshal Tito, possessed the laurels of victory and complete control over the Yugoslav lands. The Communist Party emerged as the winner of an anti-fascist liberation movement and a civil war against various nationalist extremists. Since CPY legitimacy rested on its claim to represent all the Yugoslav peoples, federalism appeared the logical option to solve the "national question." However, since the communists were preoccupied with consolidating power, their decisions about the internal borders of the constituent republics and the treatment of individual ethnic groups were arbitrary, without full consideration of the potential consequences.[16] Such a tactical approach to the national question and territoriality issues would eventually become the source of sharp controversy and violent conflict.[17] Some of the controversy can be demonstrated by looking at the first Constitution of the Federal People's Republic of Yugoslavia (FPRY) and the subsequent three federal constitutions, whose contents reveal the paradox that developed: a federal structure with real political content in the context of the Leninist communist monolith.

The constitution that was promulgated in 1946 established the country's new structure as a multinational federation of eight units: the six republics, Croatia, Serbia, Montenegro, Bosnia and Hercegovina, Slovenia and Macedonia, and two provinces of Kosovo and Vojvodina, which were attached to Serbia. Contrary to the communists' own principle, "to each nation its own territorial unit," one republic, Serbia, was divided into three elements: Serbia proper, Kosovo and Vojvodina. However, similar proposals for other units, namely for an autonomous region for the Serb-inhabited areas of Croatia, were treated as "reactionary" and rejected on the grounds that it would lead to the division of other Yugoslav nations.[18] Forty years later, this division of

Serbia would provide the major rationale for the Serbian leadership to demand a unified state and thus create a constitutional crisis.

The standard monolithic regime featured the nationalization of industry, centralized economic planning, a single communist-front mass organization, and the elimination of all opposition. Thus, in the period 1945-1952, the FPRY was modeled after the USSR in both structure and operation, and was administratively centralized.[19] Its federal structure was hierarchical, modeled after the Bolshevik federalism of Lenin. The federal principle remained to a great extent theoretical, except that both houses of the *Skupstina*, the federal parliament, had equal powers. The *Skupstina* initially was the only bi-cameral legislature among the postwar East European parliaments. It consisted of two houses, the Federal Assembly, *Savezno Vijece*, which was elected by universal suffrage, and the Council of Nationalities, *Vijece Naroda*, which was made up of equal numbers of representatives from the six republics and two provinces.

Despite the federal structure, the system was monolithic. At the top was the Politburo of the Central Committee of the CPY with ten members, each of them in charge of specific parts of the system.[20] The tight interlocking of party and state functions was also symbolized by Tito's position as head of government, party and the army.[21] This system of "administrative socialism" resulted in poor economic performance and general disillusionment among the population, who were waiting for the proclaimed equality to occur. The level of economic development of the regions which were the constituent units of federal Yugoslavia was so disparate that the regions were commonly divided into the "developed" north and the "underdeveloped" south.[22] The ruling CPY distanced people from power and weakened the cooperation that had developed during the Partisan War of Liberation.

The first signs of intranational conflicts, especially over the arbitrary redistribution of "central income" and investment funds, emerged to the surprise of the CPY which firmly believed that the "national question" had been resolved through the federal structure and the supposed formation of a "socialist community" (ignorant of particular differences among its constituent peoples).[23] The CPY recognized the need for change and, as was common to communist-party states, in 1953 a new constitution was written to bridge the gap between the constitutional myth and the regime reality. The Yugoslav constitutional myth was best expressed by Jovan Djordjevic, main author of the third, 1963 Yugoslav Constitution:

> The Yugoslav federation was formed during the Liberation War...on the basis of the right of every people to self-determination...as a voluntary community of equal and sovereign Yugoslav peoples which constituted a common federal state.[24]

This myth was in contrast to reality since the Yugoslav communists were not elected to power but seized it, and thus did not allow free elections to challenge their hegemony.

In 1953 the Constitution was drastically modified, becoming in effect a new constitution. The Constitutional Law of 1953 (sometimes referred to as the Fundamental Law) reflected the cautious steps toward decentralization that had been taken after Yugoslavia broke with the Soviet bloc in 1948. It took into account the development of self-management under the 1950 manifesto, "Factories to the Workers," and the reforms in local government which occurred in 1952. At the Sixth Congress in 1952 the CPY officially changed its name to the League of Communists of Yugoslavia (LCY), supposedly to reflect its avant garde role and rejection of administrative centralism. This was done with the intent of winning the confidence of the population. Local government reforms gave a degree of autonomy to the basic units of local government, the communes (*opstine*), which were to oversee the economic, social and cultural life of the territories under their administration.

The 1953 Law also changed the structure of the Federal and republican assemblies, which now acquired Producers' Councils, *Vijece proizvodjaca*. The Federal Assembly itself was made up of a Federal Council, *Savezno Vijece*, which "incorporated" the former Council of Nationalities (elected by the representatives of the republics and autonomous provinces) and the Council of Producers. The question remains, why did the communists eliminate/change the Council of

Nationalities if the principle of election remained the same? One answer is that suspension of the Council of Nationalities was consistent with the ideological expectation that the republics, before the state itself, would "wither away" and disappear.[25]

The position of President of the Republic was created and its first (and only) incumbent was Josip Broz Tito. As a supreme executive body and the effective government of the country, a Federal Executive Council, *Savezno Izvrsno Vijece*, was created. The members were elected by the Federal Assembly. The first Federal Executive Council (FEC) consisted of 38 members, 36 of whom were members of the Central Committee of the CPY.[26]

During the period between 1953-62, the grip of the communists loosened somewhat, although they still represented the only organized political force in the society and, despite both proclaimed and real liberalization of society, the party still had the option of exercising total control if necessary. This period was characterized by a moderate, one-party centralization, a condition sometimes described as "quasi-federalism."[27] The gap between theory and practice is illustrated by the case of one of the closest wartime allies of Tito, Milovan Djilas, who was removed from office because he strayed too far from the party line by arguing for a second socialist party that would compete with the LCY. Djilas's removal demonstrated that rhetorical changes would not lead to the LCY's abandonment of its political monopoly.

Liberalization occurred in the economic sector with the establishment of another unique feature of Yugoslavia, "market socialism." The powers of taxation were gradually transferred to the republics and local units of government, providing enough basis for them to plan their own policies of economic development. But, this transfer of power contributed to greater inequality in the economic development among the constituent units of Yugoslavia, and would become a major issue in inter-republican affairs.[28]

More than ideology, the need for a more efficient economy ruled the changes, which occurred in the midst of a great debate between economists and politicians, especially those fearful of market reforms which could undermine the socialist basis of the economy. Those who opposed economic reform came largely from the southern, underdeveloped regions, and were generally afraid that the market would benefit the already more prosperous areas of Yugoslavia disproportionately. But, there also was opposition from influential institutions such as the federal army and the police, both dominated by Serbs and Montenegrins who feared that decentralization would erode the Serbian dominance in government and in the LCY.[29]

The third Yugoslav Constitution, adopted in April of 1963, set down a number of principles upon which the socialist system in Yugoslavia had changed; at the same time it provided a framework in which the movement for reform could expand. It also departed from its predecessor in several fundamental respects. The former People's Republic was now renamed the Socialist Federated Republic of Yugoslavia (SFRY). Decentralization was seen as best elaborated in the concept of self-management, which was now extended to all forms and sectors of society. The office of the Premier (whose official title was President of the Federal Executive Council), abolished just the previous year, was restored and a Vice-Presidency of the Republic introduced. The Federal Assembly now was composed of five chambers instead of two. The Federal Chamber consisted of 190 delegates, directly elected by universal suffrage, and 70 delegates who were nominated by the Assemblies of their Republics and Provinces. These 70 delegates could sit separately as a Chamber of Nationalities when certain constitutional matters affecting the relations among the republics were under discussion. The remaining four chambers, the Social Welfare and Health, Education and Culture, Sociopolitical and Economic chambers, represented the interests of the workers in different occupational sectors and were indirectly elected.

The government, the FEC, elected by the Federal Assembly, was responsible for the coordination and supervision of the federal administration. The FEC, as the source of legislative proposals, was the most important government body insofar as the character of day-to-day government operations was concerned. Its 33 members constituted what in fact was a cabinet. Tito, as President of the Republic, proposed one member of the Federal Assembly as FEC President (Premier); the

Federal Assembly then voted to accept. The other members of the FEC were elected by the Federal Assembly on the recommendation of the Premier. The most important consideration regarding the composition of the FEC was that it reflect the various nationalities of the country. The new institution, a Council of the Federation, *Savjet Federacije*, was established. Its role was that of advisory body to the President. Its members, usually distinguished former Ministers, ambassadors, party officials, soldiers, and cultural figures, were nominated by the President. The 1963 Constitution introduced two concepts. First, a system of rotation in office, whereby members of public bodies could not be reelected after a second consecutive term. Secondly, it forbade simultaneous occupancy of the leading political offices in both state and party, except in the case of Tito, who was President of the Republic for life and head of the party. Another significant feature of the 1963 Constitution was the formal acknowledgement of the LCY and its front organization, the Social Alliance, as the only political groups with legal status.

The 1963 Constitution led to developments of disparate nature. The control of the federal government was firmly in the hands of the party, through the President, who now enjoyed enlarged powers, while at the same time introducing a real measure of decentralization. This decentralization, which occurred both at the state and in the LCY, fostered a closer association between nationality and territory since each republic was constituted as the "home" of a titular nationality. But the emerging "national question" was still second to the economic concerns of the leadership.

The period between 1963 and the last 1974 Constitution, can best be described as the period of "cooperative federalism" among central, republican and local authorities. The dynamics between state and party were somewhat paradoxical but reflective of the tendencies that were plaguing the country: separatist tendencies were counteracted by unitarism and hegemonism, which were equally dangerous for the unity of Yugoslavia. The processes of further decentralization and regionalization of the country and of the LCY were mixed with attempts toward recentralization of the party. The party, separated from the state machine, was beginning to lose its role as the sole unifying "Yugoslav" force. After decentralization occurred, the balance of power between communal, republican and federal institutions was constantly in dispute, never fully resolved. This was usually manifested in a power struggle between centralist or conservative forces that argued for unity at any cost, and a liberal stream that leaned toward democratization through decentralization.

The nationalism which crept in openly surfaced in several republics, but in Kosovo in 1968 and in Croatia in 1971 it resulted in the intervention of the Yugoslav Army and in Tito's purge of republican and provincial leaders who were "nationalistically minded." Nationalism was the product of several factors: the growing regional inequalities and differences which did not correspond with the ideal of socialism as a society of equals; the growing powers of the republican/provincial party elites and consequently, the increasing emancipation of the society from the party and from the state.

The growing discontent from the republics mounted by the end of the 1960s. Less developed republics, led by Bosnia and Hercegovina, called for an unprecedented meeting of the Chamber of Nationalities in 1967 to discuss what they termed was the unfair distribution of federal funds for economic development. The more developed republics, Slovenia and Croatia, on the other hand complained about the abuse of the same and about other federal funds (social security in particular) and sought to abolish them. In an attempt to diffuse these threatening developments, a series of constitutional amendments giving wider powers to the republics were hastily prepared and rushed through the Federal Assembly in April of 1967. But, the constitutional changes did not achieve the desired effect of dampening the fervor of the nationalists. Yugoslavism was forced to retreat under growing pressures from local, but this time, Party leadership. It became obvious that sectarianism had not disappeared. Some relate the growing sectarianism to a sense of the impossibility of fostering anything common to all Yugoslavs other than Communism.[30] Others see these national-based movements as new social actors that filled the social space vacated by the party in the 1960s.[31]

The 1971 Croatian national crisis, along with upheavals in Slovenia, Serbia, Montenegro and Kosovo, raised the fear within the LCY leadership that any radical change in the federal framework would threaten the unity of Yugoslavia. The republican leaderships were elected by their republican constituencies and therefore did not directly depend on the LCY for their positions. Consequently, the party focused on how to return Yugoslav politics to more direct party control. As the only factor of unity, Tito decided to firmly hold onto the army and police. Was this a sign that the country could have been kept together only by force? The resurrection of the wartime "triumvirate" of party-army-state was only one safeguard. Self-management and the delegate system were another safeguard, proclaimed as mechanisms of direct election/participation and basically re-intertwined with the party and government. Perhaps the mechanism which most reflected Tito's awareness of the nationality problem was the one created at his suggestion of a Collective Presidium at the LCY level and a Collective Presidency which was formally instituted at the federal government level in the Constitution of 1974 as Tito's successors.[32]

The reaction of the core party leadership to the crisis that ended the 1960s period of liberalism was two-fold. They severely reduced democratization at the price of decentralization, which was acceptable to most ambitious republican party leaderships because this preserved their power. Political democracy was decreased while at the same time greater power was delegated to the republican and provincial party elites. Both tendencies were visible in the Resolutions of the Ninth and Tenth Congresses of the LCY, held in 1969 and 1974 respectively. The Congresses served the function of gathering top party officials for endless discussion about the problems of the country and its future, which usually served as blueprints for change. Thus, the counter-reform had aspects that were anti-democratic and aspects that were confederalist, although the confederate character of Yugoslavia was not admitted. The interesting question about the latter is what were the reasons behind this "hidden process," and if the leadership was even aware of it. Alternatively, the party elite may have thought it had protected itself with the ideology of self-management in allowing greater powers to the federal units.[33] Self-management was intended to hold the country together by sheer strength of belief, serving as the main integrating factor that was supposed to withstand both political decentralization and national unity.

Developments in the 1970s proved this to be a vain hope. Regional party elites, paying lip service to "brotherhood and unity," used the ideology of self-management to promote their own particular political interests and thus to create political legitimacy in their home republics, which in post-1974 Yugoslavia became the most meaningful source of legitimacy.

The Croatian movement of 1971-72, however, was seen as a threat and the leadership of Yugoslavia, under Tito's firm hand, decided to do whatever was necessary to preserve the unity of the state. The Constitution that was introduced in 1974 replaced the 1963 Constitution as amended in 1967 and 1971. The 1974 Constitution delineated a new set of executive and legislative institutions and a new way of decision-making. To Kostunica, the 1974 Constitution marks the beginning of "peripheral federalism."[34] In Yugoslavia, however, most politicians and scholars referred to this development as "polycentric federalism"[35] or "contractual federation."[36]

Tito introduced the 1974 Constitution by stating, "A determined break has been made with all the remnants of so-called representative democracy which suits the bourgeois class."[37] This was a response to the sectarian behavior of the representatives in the Federal Assembly who increasingly argued for the interests of their constituencies rather than for the federation as a whole. The most important institutions promulgated by the 1974 Constitution were the indirect system of elections, the *delegatski sistem*, and the structure and decision-making of the Federal Assembly. The systems of indirect elections was promoted as Tito's way of ensuring the unity of the country. Suffice to say that the elaborate and complicated system of the workers' participation was difficult to achieve. The *delegatski sistem* never fulfilled its function of direct democracy.[38] The failures of the system demonstrate that it, as with every other political innovation, suffered from the party's inability to give up its monopoly of power. In one analyst's evaluation, "In reality, the Yugoslav system is a quest for totalitarian democracy," despite the window-dressing of workers' self-management.[39]

The Federal Assembly was in theory the only body competent to amend the Constitution, pass national laws, adopt federal plans and budgets, call a referendum, ratify international agreements, decide on questions of war and peace, alter the boundaries of Yugoslavia, and supervise the work of the federal executive and administrative bodies. It consisted of two chambers, a Federal Chamber, *Savezno Vijece*, and a Chamber of Republics and Provinces, *Vijece republika i pokrajina*. The Federal Chamber, which decided on the questions of interest to the federation, consisted of 220 delegates (30 from each republic and 20 from each autonomous province), all elected from the communes. The Chamber of Republics and Provinces, in charge of republican and provincial issues that did not require consent of all republics and provinces, consisted of twelve delegates forwarded from the assemblies of each of the six republics and eight from the assemblies of the two provinces.

With equal representation of the constituent units in both chambers, the two chambers differed from one another only in the mode of voting--the Federal Chamber decided by majority vote; the second chamber, by unanimous consent. The claim was that the Yugoslav system was unique because of the emphasis on consensus of all the federal units for all amendments: all constitutional amendments had to be passed, in the same text, by the legislative assemblies of all the units.[40] This provision granted an effective regional veto over federal policy to each of the republics and provinces.

With the adoption of the 1974 Constitution, the Yugoslav decision-making process was marked by a constant tension between federal authority, with responsibility for all-Yugoslav policy, and the regional powers that could obstruct its preparation, adoption, or implementation. But the system appeared to function reasonably effectively as long as Tito was alive. Through his ability to transcend conflicts and to enforce compromises in which all the parties assented, whether they liked them or not, Tito acted as the ultimate aggregator.[41]

After his death in May of 1980 there was neither the instrumentality nor agreement on the criteria for resolution of conflicts. As economic conditions worsened in the 1980s, federal decision-making became extremely difficult as the result of the growing reluctance of the republics and provinces to compromise their short-term economic interests in exchange for uncertain long-time gains.

The three federal institutions, the Chamber of Republics and Provinces, the SFRY Collective Presidency, and the federal cabinet, the FEC, were not able to restore to the federation the formal powers it had lost as the result of the constitutional reforms that shifted power to the republics and provinces. The Chamber of Republics and Provinces, with its provision that decisions be made by consensus, reflected this power shift and this severely affected any attempt to arrive at common solutions. Because the delegates to the Chambers represented a bloc, and each delegate from the federal unit was required to adhere to policies agreed upon by his home base in republic or province, there were often cases of alliance formation and logrolling and the delay of negotiations in controversial areas, such as assistance to less developed areas.[42]

The Collective Presidency, which served as the collective executive head, brought together one delegate from each of the federal units. After Tito's death in 1980, his permanent position as President of the Presidency lapsed and the position rotated annually according to the set Constitutional rota. Even though Tito envisioned this body as the mechanism of party control over the federation, the members of the Presidency were responsible to the respective units which elected them, and thus lacked a common vision and loyalty to the federal union. The decision-making mechanisms of the Presidency were severely endangered by the exercise of regional loyalties. Eventually, this gave Slobodan Milosevic, the Serbian leader after 1987, the ability to produce deadlocks in the Presidency, and served as the catalyst for Slovenia and Croatia to announce their intention to separate.[43]

In the late 1960s and 1970s, the FEC served as the broker in negotiations among the representatives of the federal units and the federal center. By the late 1970s, the FEC became the most important decision-making body outside of the party and a significant actor in inter-regional negotiation. But even this could not bring back the powers that the federation enjoyed before the process of decentralization began. Because of the wide powers granted to the republics and provinces, most federal policies reflected, in effect, a compromise between nine conflicting positions, the eight units and one "all-Yugoslav" position, the FEC. Similar to the processes in the Chamber of Republics and Provinces, the agreements on policy were regularly inhibited by objections from various federal units until the last moment. Even when the policies eventually were passed, they were often reduced to general policy statements and thus subject to differing interpretations in each of the individual federal units.

In general, the developments since Tito's death strengthened the assertiveness of the regional structures, as the policy of the central leadership continued to balance ethnic groups against each other. Political tensions realized themselves in Croat bitterness against Belgrade; they stimulated emotional reactions among Serbs and brought into the open the issue of Serbia as an equal republic, because it was divided by the two autonomous provinces, Vojvodina and Kosovo; they surfaced in an Islamic assertiveness in Bosnia and Hercegovina. The eighties were characterized by the overwhelming decline of confidence of the Yugoslav society, the result of the growing popular disenchantment with the party, socialism and self-management, none of which had lived up to their promises.[44] The decade between 1980 and 1990 was marked by serious economic crisis and the failure of all proposals to deal with it. The LCY failed to apply any mechanism that would enable it to exert an integrating influence at a nation-wide level. The party refused to give up its monopoly of power because that was an essential part of its definition of socialism, but the monopoly was now plural, the political monopolies defined by republican or provincial boundaries. In their drive to become the people's party, the leadership of the LCY turned it into eight national parties. The only institution that could hold the country together, the party, had fragmented into eight autonomous, largely independent parties. The fragmentation of Yugoslavia into eight national units assumed a variety of forms. In addition to a decrease in economic exchange among republics, it was also apparent in culture, communications, science and other fields. This peaceful fragmentation, because of the different political developments within each of the republics, turned violent in 1991.

Conclusion

Federations that consist of constituent units identified with particular ethnic groups, or ethnic federations, have exhibited strong tendencies toward comprehensive decentralization. Pressures from ethnic groups identified with constituency politics have been accommodated by federal governments through the decrease of federal control and the encouragement of additional activity, regulation, and control by the constituent units themselves--all in an effort to limit secessionist tendencies and increase satisfaction within the federation so as to preserve its political integrity.[45]

Yugoslavia was a striking example of ethnic federation with a level of decentralization that brought it closer to confederation than to federation. All three requisites of "true federalism" identified by Elazer, a written constitution, noncentralization, and an areal division of power,[46] existed in Yugoslavia. Although endangered by secessionist trends, the LCY functioned as a "single ruling party to hold together its diverse ethnic groups."[47] It is ironic that Yugoslavia was considered to possess all three requisites of federalism: the constitutions were changed frequently, to reflect the regime changes and the subsequent changes in the division of power between the center and the regions. Noncentralization was obvious in the growing regionalization and individuation of the republics and provinces. The division of Yugoslavia into six republics and two provinces reflected an areal division of power based on ethnic criteria. But, even though Yugoslavia possessed the three elements of federalism, it still lacked the federal principle, the principle by which a federal structure becomes meaningful.

The factor essential to the maintenance of the federation is a commitment "...to partnership and to active cooperation... sharing... mutual forbearance and self-restraint in pursuit of goals and con-sideration of the system as a whole."[48] The history of Yugoslavia shows that such a commitment never existed. The federalism that did function for the thirty years between 1945 and 1974 was imposed from above and maintained by the sheer force of the authoritarian regime dominated by the personality of Marshal Tito and the ruling Communist Party. As soon as liberalization and decentralization occurred, it was obvious that regional loyalties outweighed loyalty to the larger state and a "single ruling party" turned into eight different parties that were not interested in the preservation of a unified Yugoslavia.

Looking at the classic description of federalism as that of a continuing legal contract in which each contracting partner surrenders some autonomy to the federal authority for some anticipated compensatory advantages, it seems that from the beginning Yugoslav federalism did not serve its original purpose. Instead, it became a smokescreen for the Communist Party to assure its monopoly of power, while it seriously compromised federal authority. The high level of compromise at the federal level by Marshal Tito, allowed the republican party elites to use federalism simply as a rhetorical principle while promoting confederal arrangements and deeper cleavages.

The analysis above shows that the dynamics between regional and federal actors were facilitated, or controlled, by the Communist Party, and resulted in the subsequent belief of the regional elites that the federal unit did not provide any advantages worthy of their sustained commitment to the federal principle. If the leaders of the different ethnic groups found such advantages perhaps they would have been willing to cooperate and transcend rather than create cleavages at the mass level, and federalism could have existed as a workable framework.

Notes

1. Officially, the Socialist Alliance of the Working People (*Savez Socijalistickog Radnog Naroda*) was an authorized "interest group," but it really served as a mass transition belt for the Communist Party.

2. This analysis was inspired by the work of George and Patricia V. Klein, "Nationalism vs. Ideology," in George Klein and Milan Reban, eds., *The Politics of Ethnicity in Eastern Europe* (Boulder, CO: East European Monographs, 1981), where they assert, contrary to many analysts of the former Yugoslavia, that the constitutional changes were designed to institutionalize new channels for conflict resolution by directing nationality conflicts along acceptable paths.

3. This section draws mainly on the following works: Lenard J. Cohen, "Conflict Management and Political Institutionalization in Socialist Yugoslavia," in Albert Eldridge, ed., *Legislatures in Plural Societies* (Durham, NC: Duke University Press, 1977); Arend Lijphart, *Democracies, patterns of majoritarian and consensus government in twenty-one countries* (New Haven: Yale University Press, 1984); Arend Lijphart, "Majority rule in theory and practice: The tenacity of a flawed paradigm," *International Social Science Journal* 43, 3 (1991) 483-493; Arend Lijphart, Ronald Rogowski & R. Kent Weaver, "Separation of powers and cleavage management," In R. Kent Weaver & Bert R. Rockman, eds. *Do institutions matter?* (Washington, D. C.: The Brookings Institution, 1993) 302-344.

4. Harry Eckstein. *Divisions and Cohesion in Democracy: A Study of Norway* (Princeton: Princeton University Press, 1966) 34.

5. Richard Gunther and Anthony Mughan, "Political Institutions and Cleavage Management," in R. Kent Weaver and Bert R. Rockman, eds. *Do Institutions Matter?* (Washington D.C.: The Brookings Institution, 1993) 272-301.

6. E.g., Patricia Klein and George Klein, "The United States and Yugoslavia: Divergent Approaches Toward Diversity," in C.L. Hunt and Lewis Walker, eds. *Ethnic dynamics: Patterns of Intergroup Relations im Various Societies* (Holmes Beach, FL: Learning Publications, 1979); Sabrina Petra Ramet. *Nationalism and Federalism in Yugoslavia*, 2nd ed. (Bloomington IN: Indiana University Press, 1991); Stephen L. Burg, "Elite Conflict in Post-Tito Yugoslavia," *Soviet Studies* 38, 1 (1988) 55-68.

7. Ramet, *Nationalism and Federalism*, 35.

8. Mitja Zagar. Concluding Remarks to the International Conference on Constitutional and Legal Regulation of Ethnic Relations, Ljubljana, March 28-30, 1996. George and Patricia V. Klein, maintain that it was not the lack of institutions but rather the hasty changes in the status of institutions. Since political leaders had yielded to the political pressures of the time, each constitutional reform disturbed the institutions set up by the

previous constitution so much so that they never had a chance to regularize their work and prove their efficiency. "Flux in institutions in Yugoslavia has become an institution in itself" best expresses these processes. See Klein & Klein, *Nationalism vs. Ideology*, 252-3.

9. Barbara P. McCrea, *The Political Dynamics of Federalism in a Marxist-Leninist Setting: The League of Communists of Yugoslavia* (Ph.D. dissertation, the University of Notre Dame, Notre Dame, IN: 1992) 186-235.

10. McCrea, ibid., maintains that the CPY, despite Lenin's ideological strictures, permitted meaningful federalism of the party to develop, with the result that party politics might be fairly described as federalized.

11. Ramet, *Nationalism and Federalism*, 38.

12. Daniel J. Elazar, "The Themes of a Journal of Federalism," *Publius* 1, 1 (1971) 3.

13. McCrea, *The Political Dynamics of Federalism*, 55-71.

14. Daniel J. Elazar. *Exploring Federalism* (Tuscaloosa, AL: University of Alabama Press, 1987).

15. Elazar, *Exploring Federalism*, 156.

16. See, e.g., Milovan Djilas. *Wartime* (New York: Harcourt Brace Jovanovich, 1977).

17. Lenard J. Cohen. *Broken Bonds: The Disintegration of Yugoslavia* (Boulder CO: Westview Press, 1993) 24.

18. Vojislav Kostunica, "The constitution and the federal state," in Denison Rusinow, ed. *Yugoslavia: a Fractured Federalism* (Washington DC: the Woodrow Wilson Center, 1988) 78-92.

19. Dusan Bilandzic. *Historija Socijalisticke Federativne Republike Yugoslavije* (Zagreb: Skolska Knjiga, 1985).

20. Bilandzic, *Historija*, 118.

21. Fred Singleton. *A Short History of the Yugoslav Peoples* (Cambridge: Cambridge University Press, 1985) 211.

22. For an analysis of the differences in labor efficiency and per capita social product of the republics from 1947 to 1978, see Ramet, *Nationalism and Federalism*, 142-43.

23. Bilandzic, *Historija*, 135-6; 143.

24. Carl J. Friedrich. *Trends of Federalism in Theory and Practice* (New York: Frederick A. Praeger, 1968) 162.

25. Bilandzic, *Historija*. For a different elaboration on the role of the Council of the Nationalities see Klein and Klein, *Nationalism vs. Ideology*, 252-3.

26. Ibid., 177.

27. Cohen, *Broken Bonds*, 27.

28. Klein and Klein, "The United States and Yugoslavia."

29. Ibid.

30. Stephen Pavlowitz. *The Improbable Survivor* (Columbus: Ohio State University Press, 1988).

31. Gregor Tomc, "Classes, Party Elites and Ethnic Density," in Rusinow, *Fractured Federalism*, 112-130.

32. Bilandzic, *Historija*, 373.

33. Tomc, "Classes, Party Elites, and Ethnic Identity."

34. Kostunica, "The Constitution."

35. Cyril Ribicic and Zdravko Tomac. *Federalizam po mjeri buducnosti* (Zagreb: Globus, 1989).

36. Tomc, ibid.

37. Cited in Singleton, *Short History of Yugoslavia*, 261.

38. Ivan Grdesic, "Interesi i moc: Sadrzaj rada opciniskih skupstina u SR Hrvatskoj," *Politicka Misao* 23, 1 (1986) 108-120.

39. Oscar Gruenwald. *Yugoslav Search for Man: Marxist Humanism in Contemporary Yugoslavia* (South Hadley: J. F. Begin Publishers, Inc.) 173.

40. Kostunica, "The Constitution," 81.

41. George Schopflin, "Nationality in the Fabric of Yugoslav Politics," *Survey* 25, 3 (1985) 1-19.

42. Burg, "Elite Conflict."

43. Gruenwald, *Yugoslav Search for Man*, 200-01; Ramet, *Nationalism and Federalism*, 69.

44. Pedro Ramet, "Apocalypse Culture and Social Change in Yugoslavia," in Pedro Ramet, ed. *Yugoslavia in the 1980s* (Boulder, CO: Westview Press, 1985) 3-26.

45. Elazar, *Exploring Federalism*.

46. Elazar, *Exploring Federalism*, 157.

47. Ibid., 177.

48. Elazar, *Exploring Federalism*, 154.

3.

A Note on Trukese Time

Pavao Novosel

Serbia took to arms and invaded Croatia and Bosnia in response to what would have been the peaceful exit of four out of the six former Yugoslav Republics from the Federation. The explanation for the Serbs' action remains unanswered. The answer would be important, even imperative, not only for scientific but also for practical reasons. The events following the dissolution of socialist Yugoslavia might offer valuable historical lessons as similar crises might occur in other parts of the world.

This author offers an explanation for what happened in former Yugoslavia that, to the best of his knowledge, has not been taken into account so far. This explanation offers the interested student a better understanding of the origins of this region's tragedy than has so far been available. But, first, an examination of various explanations allows us to place our hypothesis--the role of Trukese time--into its context in the sources of the current conflict.

The first, and most plausible explanation has focused on the national interest, which for some were helped and for others were endangered by the disintegration of the Yugoslav Federation. For example, for the Croats, the disintegration of Yugoslavia meant liberation and freedom from a long-endured subordination, and for the Serbs the disintegration meant an end to age-old aspirations for "Greater Serbia." The latter would be a state encompassing most of Croatia,

Bosnia-Hercegovina, Vojvodina and Kosovo, even though Serbs were an
absolute minority in these territories.[1]

The concept of "Greater Serbia" was not merely the chimera of
some irrational Serbian intellectuals and politicians but a national
ideology with specific plans to achieve its ends by whatever means
were available. The phrase--"by whatever means"--should be taken
literally. No means to such ends, however odious, were excluded. So
the plan went into practice by use of force, legalized injustice and
similar means. Such was the approach to the case of the Albanian
population of Kosovo. In other cases, less drastic, but equally efficient
methods were used. For Croatia, the gradualist way seemed best. It
consisted of a slow but long-term demographic infiltration of the
Croatian territory, including the settling of Serbian and Montenegrin
Partisans immediately after World War II and a corresponding takeover
of leading positions in the Croatian society. The way it was planned, a
demographic and cultural change would gradually do away with a Croat
nation.

For example, many retired army officers from the Yugoslav
People's Army (JNA) settled in Croatia. The officer corps was
preponderantly Serbian and reached as high as 90%. After retirement,
such officers enjoyed the legally guaranteed right to settle wherever in
the Federation they wished and, at the same time, had entitlements to
housing in whatever city or town they chose. And, they chose,
overwhelmingly, places in Croatia, especially in the capitol, Zagreb, or
on the Croatian Adriatic coast in Pula, Rijeka, Zadar, Sibenik, Split,
Dubrovnik and others. Thus, whole new settlements, called
appropriately enough "officers' strongholds", mushroomed in the most
attractive parts of Croatia. These were frequently viewed as the seeds
for further Serbian penetration. Inevitably, the newcomers brought in
their families and relatives, and after that their friends and
acquaintances. All of them could expect better than average jobs and
other privileges which was more than enough, without any special
inducements, to persuade them to re-locate.

In addition, there also existed the influence of the traditional
informal social mutual assistance network among Serbs. The network

distributed the better jobs and privileges, thus increasing the percentage of Serbs in the leading positions of industry, the police, and other sectors. As a consequence, some 24% of the managerial positions in Croatia were occupied by Serbs, and almost 70% of the police officers were of Serbian origin[2] although the Serbian population of the Republic of Croatia was only 12%.

Thus, the fear was that the combination of demographics with the operation of the Serbian network could have resulted in the complete Serbian takeover of Croatia within another twenty-five to thirty years. No wonder then that the Serbs reacted with rage when Croatia voted for independence in October 1991 and effectively put a halt to the Serbian plan.

As for the Serbs, there is no mention of the dreams of a Greater Serbia in their explanations for having taken to arms and the ensuing atrocities in Vukovar, Dubrovnik and countless other cities, towns and villages. All that lay buried under slogans of brotherhood and unity and justified by the ideology of Socialist Yugoslavia. Instead, the propaganda spewed out all sorts of excuses. The chief excuses invariably came in defense of the allegedly endangered Serbian minority by the "fascist" Croats.

But, such an explanation stood in obvious contradiction to the history of both Yugoslavias as well as in the period before the first Yugoslav state. In the first Yugoslav experiment after 1918, it was not Croatia, but Serbs, or at least their political leadership, that first tilted toward aggressive and even fascist politics. In 1928, the Yugoslav Parliament witnessed the assassination by Serbs of Croatian political leaders Stjepan Radic, Pavle Radic and Duro Basaricek. It was Belgrade that concocted laws that discriminated against Croats in 1919 and after, not Zagreb that discriminated against Serbs. For example, the former Austrian currency, the krona, which was in use in Croatia, was exchanged for Yugoslav dinars at the rate of 1 dinar for 4 kronas even though the exchange rate on the open market was 1 to 1. That way the Croatian population was plundered of three quarters of their cash possessions just by this one "operation".[3] As another example, the land tax in Croatia was twice as high as in Serbia.[4] There are numerous other examples.

Interestingly enough, Serbs historically have perceived of the Croats as a non-aggressive, peaceful people. For example, in 1902 a Serbian politician, Nikola Stojanovic, *wrote in Serbian Defense (Srbobran)*, published in Zagreb, of his complete agreement with a quote from a Croatian author. Stojanovic endorsed wholeheartedly the Croat's statement that,

> We (Croats) have two great defects which, very probably, originate from our exceptional position throughout the centuries: a mentality that wants to please everybody and is imprudent.

By contrast, the same author noted that the very concept of a Serb included the idea of the hero.[5] The whole body of Serbian folk epics from medieval times to the present conveys this. Take, for instance, the tale of the great deeds of Prince Marko of Prilep, a celebrated medieval Serbian hero who plowed under roads as his revenge for some perceived injustices.

The regrettable World War II "independent" fascist state of Croatia stands out as an exception to the rule of the generally peaceful character of the Croats. This is not to justify or exonerate the acts that Croatian fascists committed under the guise of Croatian nationalism, but to place this episode in the context of the war. Many other European states succumbed to fascist governments and, whether in Slovakia, Baltic states, Greece, Hungary or Serbia, similar atrocities befell Jews. Dawidowicz[6] gives comparative data on the Jews killed in the whole of Europe: in Poland 3 million of 3.3 million were killed (90%), in Baltic states 228,000 of 253,000 (90%), in Greece 54,000 of 70,000 (77%), in Hungary 450,000 of 650,000 (70%). The author's comparative number for Yugoslavia is 26,000 of 43,000 (60%). This is surely underestimated in an effort to keep the number lower.

In Serbia itself, Philip J. Cohen writes:

> In August 1942, following the virtual liquidation of Serbia's Jews, Nedic's government attempted to claim all Jewish property for the Serbian state. In the same month, Dr. Harold Turner, the Chief Nazi Civil

Administrator for Serbia, proudly announced that Serbia was the only country in which the "Jewish Question" had been solved. Serbia became the first *Judenfrei* country in Europe, an "achievement" which reflected the extent of Serbian cooperation. Thus, about 90% of Serbia's 12,500 Jews were exterminated, with collaborators drawn from the Serbian government, the Serbian Orthodox Church, the Serbian State Guard, the Serbian Volunteer Corps, the Serbian Police, and the Serbian public.[7]

Before this happened, Yugoslavia, absolutely dominated by the Serbs, opted for Fascist politics. According to one version:

The one Jew in the Yugoslav Senate was expelled in 1938, and the Prime Minister asked the Regent to appoint a non-Jew in his stead. In October 1940 two anti-Jewish laws were adopted. One limiting the access of Jews to secondary and higher education, the other halting the issuance of licenses for Jewish business and restricting the renewal of others. Though not widely enforced by local authorities, no serious opposition was offered to their enactment.[8]

In 1941 the greater majority of Croats condemned their own state's actions even though that state contained within it for the first time in ten centuries the promise of at least some independence. As an example let us recall an event at Zagreb's stadium in 1941. The "independent" Croat state had only recently been declared. The fascist rulers, the Ustase, ordered Zagreb's high school students to the stadium to denounce publicly their Jewish and Serbian colleagues. They ordered the Jewish and Serbian students to step forward and identify themselves as Jews or Serbs. But the Jews and the Serbs did not stand alone. The Croat youth also stepped forward with them and thereby undermined the intention of the Ustase. In fact, the opposite occurred. The Croat youth demonstrated that they did not share the Ustasa's antisemitism or antiserbianism.[9] The majority of Tito's Partisan troops who fought on the side of the Allies against Germany were Croats who rejected the Ustase, while the Serbian Chetniks slipped into collaboration with the Germans. In fact, Serbs came over to the Partisans in substantial numbers only in late 1944.[10]

Looking at the Croatian vote for independence in October 1991, history supports the thesis that the Serbs in Croatia faced neither physical harm nor the infringement of their rights as equal citizens when Croatia voted for separate statehood and that Serb claims to the contrary served only as a skillful rationalization in behalf of other goals. It was not human rights but the special privileges for Serbs and the dream of a Greater Serbia that was threatened by Croatian independence. But the defense of privilege and visions of a Greater Serbia do not in themselves explain the inconceivable barbarism that occurred. Let us take a close look at this question.

How could a Serb who for decades had lived beside Croatian and Muslim neighbors suddenly see them as a real and personal threat? After all, for a long period of history, they had helped each other and had exchanged goods and services as neighbors. Not only that, many intermarried so that in many instances they had shaped an integrated social life with a common future for their children and themselves. Or, at least, that's how it looked from outside.

Then came the day, no different from other days, much to the surprise of an innocent Catholic or Muslim neighbor, when this very same Serb who had married a Croat or even a Muslim, with no apparent reason or warning, took out his gun and ordered his Catholic or Muslim friends to leave or face death. The neighbors naturally appealed to lives they had shared or to their roles as good neighbors. Such appeals either fell on deaf ears or drove the Serb to even greater cruelties.

In my opinion, such behavior requires an explanation that goes beyond calculated interests or abstract dreams of the Greater Serbia. I would suggest that the explanation must include an appreciation of the Serbs' conception of time. What if the Serbs live in a different sense of time than the Croats and Muslims, what if for them the past never died but governs their behavior in the present?

The idea for this explanation came from reading Edward T. Hall's, *The Silent Language*,[11] and, more specifically, from the concept of time in the chapter, "The Voices of Time". Let Hall speak for himself:

> Time does not heal on Truk! Past events stack up, placing an ever-increasing burden on the Trukese and weighing heavily on the present. They are, in fact, treated as though they had just occurred. This was born out by something which happened shortly after the American occupation

of the atoll at the end of World War II. A villager arrived all out of breath at the military government headquarters. He said that a murder had been committed in the village and that the murderer was running around loose. Quite naturally the military government officer became alarmed. He was about to dispatch M.P.'s to arrest the culprit when he remembered that someone had warned him about acting precipitously when dealing with "natives". A little inquiry turned up the fact that the victim had been "fooling around" with the murderer's wife. Still more inquiry of a routine type, designed to establish the place and date of the crime, revealed that the murder had not occurred a few hours or even days ago, as one might have thought, but seventeen years before. The murderer had been running around loose in the village all this time....

Prior to Missionary Moses' arrival on Uman in 1867, life on Truk was characterized by violent and bloody warfare. Villages, instead of being built on the shore where life was a little easier, were placed on the sides of mountains where they could be better protected. Attacks would come without notice and often without apparent provocation. Or a fight might start if a man stole a coconut from a tree that was not his or waylaid a woman and took advantage of her. Years later someone would start thinking about the wrong and decide that it still had not been righted. A village would be attacked again in the middle of the night.

When charges were brought against a chief for things he had done to his people, every little slight, every minor graft would be listed, nothing would be forgotten. Damages would be asked for everything. It seemed preposterous to us Americans, particularly when we looked at the lists of charges. "How could a chief be so corrupt?" "How could people remember so much?"

To the best of this author's knowledge, Professor Hall never christened such a concept of time that lacked a sense of what is past and bygone. Perhaps, he would not object, if we introduced the term he might well have given it--Trukese time.

The Serbs who suddenly took their guns from hiding and started shooting their neighbors showed precisely the same behavior as the natives of Truk at the end of World War II. For both, there was no line that separated past and present. The enemies and traitors of decades and even centuries past were present and due to be punished. The normal process of forgetting what happened centuries ago was conspicuously absent and past humiliations and defeats festered in the present as open, never healing wounds. The older the past injustice, the more strongly it is felt in the present. Emotions, instead of dying out in the course of time, accumulate and take on more monstrous dimensions. The feelings of shame and hatred become personal, demanding revenge and the humiliation of the culprit. And, the culprit is every member of the hated nation whether neighbor or not, friend or not.

Perhaps, an imaginary example might help illustrate this time sense. Let us conjecture a situation in Dallas, Texas where the "Anglo", i.e. white, non-Hispanic, citizens suddenly one day started to kill any Mexican-American they could find. Worse than killing, they submitted the Mexican-Americans to torture and mutilation while they placed Mexican-American women into concentration camps to be systematically raped and held captive until abortion was impossible. All of this the "Anglos" did claiming that the Mexican-Americans posed a mortal threat and screaming "Remember the Alamo!"

Perhaps, an old joke current during the Vietnam War era makes the point more effectively. Protesters have put the American Embassy in Belgrade under siege. As the joke has it, the demonstrators beat without mercy everyone who came out of the Embassy. Then one man comes out and just as the mob is about to strike he shouts, "Not me, not me, I am a Turk!" Hearing that, one of the Serbs yells back, "Ah! A Turk! I've been waiting for you for 500 years since the Battle of Kosovo!" And he hits him even harder. (At the Battle of Kosovo in 1389, the Ottoman Turks defeated the Serbs and delivered the coup de grace to the medieval Serbian state). If we think of the concept of Trukese time, the joke has a hidden message.

If we apply the concept of Trukese time to the present, it explains the more vicious aspects of Serb behavior in the recent war against Croats and Muslims in the former Yugoslavia. How else to explain such cruelties committed upon completely innocent individuals? How else to explain the dismemberment of Muslim peasants piece by piece in Serbian concentration camps? How else to explain the unspeakable horrors committed against Muslim and Croat women who were systematically and repeatedly raped in designated "rape camps"?

Needless to say, the concept of Trukese time requires much more elaboration and research than this paper permits. But, for now, let us emphasize a few of its more prominent characteristics that might enable one to anticipate certain behavior patterns. First of all, Trukese time defies the law of memory optimism which is referred to in psychology. According to this law, the normal process induces people to forget bad elements of the past and remember only the pleasant and gratifying ones. Exactly the opposite process appears to occur among individuals and nations who function according to Trukese time. Theirs is a process of memory pessimism; they remember the bad elements of their own or their ancestors' past and accumulate negative feelings toward the alleged causes of their plight. In explosive situations, such as the disintegration of Socialist Yugoslavia, such emotions take the lead and serve as the governing force for overt behavior.

Secondly, Trukese time has the characteristics of immediate, intimate experience irrespective of the fact that the particular individual never lived through such experiences. So, the past injustices to the nation as a whole are felt by the individual on a personal level. A battle fought and lost over 500 years ago is felt as a personal defeat today which must somehow be rectified on a personal level. Thus, any individual members of the culprit group (e.g., the Muslim or Croat neighbor) must be attacked and must be made to pay. Within the framework of this psychology, the Bosnian Muslims remain as traitors of the Orthodox religion who should be punished for what they did and, indeed, for what they may do every day--namely, go to mosques to pray.

Trukese time, moreover, does not fit the concept of past orientation of the past-present-future paradigm found in David Riesman.[12] One cannot say that the Serbian nationalists under Milosevic disregarded the future. After all, the plan for a Greater Serbia is future-oriented and required meticulous steps for implementation by Serbian intellectuals, politicians and army officers. The point is that the past did not die; all time is compressed into one dimension. It contains the future as well as the past and present. In other words, one could speak of Trukese time as undivided or unarticulated time in comparison to the time common in Western Civilization.

A final question: What is the origin of this experience of time? In the Serbian case, the connection might lie in the perpetuation of national mythologies, embodied in national epics. Serbs are unlike members of other national cultures in the former Yugoslavia in the way they retain and admire national singers who play the gusle, an ancient string instrument, and who still enjoy faithful audiences that listen and believe the singer's tales. They take seriously the folkloric tales of Prince Marko and other bygone heroes and villains from centuries long past. Perhaps, we should search for the roots for Trukese time in the gusle connection? Or, is the causal sequence the opposite? Is the gusle connection the result of Trukese time? We do not know the answer to this dilemma at this time.

After all is said and done, what are we to think of the Serbs? Should we declare them an immature nation acting out medieval ways at the beginning of the twenty-first century? Should the international community be compelled to undertake some educational measures in Serbia just as it did in Germany after World War II? Or, would some form of "cordon sanitaire" work better? It is tempting to try to answer these questions but that task lies beyond the scope of this essay.

Notes

1. Ilija Garasanin, "Nacertanije", (a long-term program for building the Greater Serbia, 1844), reprinted in D. Stranjakovic. *Kako je postalo Garasaninovo "Nacertanije"* (Spomenik SKA, XCI, Beograd, 1939) 76-102.

2. *Oslobodjenje* (August 11, 1990). See "Tko je sto u armiji" by Vlatko Cvtila in *Danas* 568, 5.2 (1991)16, for composition of the army officer corps.

3. Rudolf Bicanic. *Ekonomska podloga, Hrvatskog pitanja* (Zagreb: Isdavac Vladko Macek, 1938) 42-46.

4. Bicanic, 49.

5. Nikola Stojanovic, "Do istrage vase ili nase," *Srbobran*, 168 and 169 (Zagreb, 1902). Reprinted in Boze Covic (ed.). *Izvori velikosrpske agresije* (Zagreb: August Cesarec and Skolska Knjiga, 1991).

6. Lucy S. Dawidowicz. *The War Against the Jews, 1933-1945* (New York: Bantam Books, 1975) 403.

7. Philip J. Cohen. *Serbia's Secret War: propaganda and the deceit of history* (College Station: Texas A & M University Press, 1996) 12. An excerpt of this work first appeared under the title "Holocaust History Misappropriated" in *Midstream, a monthly Jewish review*, published by the Theodor Herzl Foundation, 38, 8 (November, 1992) 18-20.

8. Lucy S. Dawidowicz, 391.

9. Slobodan Zaric. *Revolucionarni omladinski pokret u Hrvatskoj, 1941-1948* (Zagreb: Centar drustvenih djelatnosti Saveza socijalisticke omladine Hrvatske, 1980) 30-31.

10. Jozo Tomasevic. *Cetnici u Drugom svetskom ratu* (Zagreb: Liber, 1979) 398ff.

11. Edward T. Hall. *The Silent Language* (New York: Doubleday, 1959).

12. David Riesman. *The Lonely Crowd* (New Haven and London: Yale University Press, 1962).

Part Two

Other Balkan States

4.
Security in the Post-Communist Balkans[1]

Robin Alison Remington

In the Balkans, as in the New Europe that is in the process of becoming, Mikhail Gorbachev's "new political thinking"[2] about security issues played a crucial role in the political/economic earthquake that destroyed the foundation of communist regimes throughout Eastern Europe.

During 1989, reform from above became revolution from below. In May the Hungarian citizens with wire cutters joined soldiers ordered to take down the barbed wire on the border with Austria. When President George Bush came to Budapest in July, he was given a piece of that barbed wire on a plaque that read:

> This piece of barbed wire was part of the Iron Curtain along the Austrian-Hungarian border. It represented palpably the division of the European continent into two halves. Its dismantling was made possible by the will of the Hungarian people in recognition of peaceful coexistence and mutual interdependence....It is believed that the artificial physical and spiritual walls still existing in the world some day will collapse.[3]

Thus, during 1989-1990 East European communist governments fell apart like so many humpty-dumpties. Soon hegemonic communist parties were reduced to minor or drastically recast roles in the political drama of democratic transition. By December 1991 *Perestroika* had come home. The Soviet Union came unglued; replaced by a shadowy confederal Commonwealth of Independent States as an arena for working out still undefined political, economic, and military relations among Soviet successor states.

With the disintegration of the Soviet Union, the post-World War II international system essentially disappeared. The most solid concrete symbol of Winston Churchill's "iron curtain," the Berlin Wall, fell; reduced to rubble   from which small rocks sold for whatever the market would bear, from the streets of New York to Long's Drug Store in Eureka, California.

The military institutions of the Warsaw Treaty Organization (WTO) were disbanded at the end of March 1991, followed by the alliance's political superstructure.[4] Soviet soldiers marched home from Czechoslovakia, Hungary, Poland and the united Germany. In short, when what Gorbachev envisioned as minor surgery in intra-alliance relations became a major operation. The patient died. The Warsaw Pact along with communist Eastern Europe and the Soviet Union itself was history. The Cold War that defined national security in Moscow, Washington and the capitals of East and West Europe alike was gone. NATO became an alliance in search of a mission.

This analysis explores what the collapse of communism and this radically transformed political/security environment meant for the relationship of post-communist politicians striving to build multiparty democracies in the post-communist Balkans to the armies that were charged with protecting these societies during the trauma of transition. It asks the core questions: what is security, for whom, from what, by what means? These are straightforward questions.

Unfortunately, there are no straightforward answers. Sorting out the complex, conflicting perceptions was rather like painting a moving train. Nonetheless, by focusing on the initial stage of disintegration that necessitated redefining national security beyond cold war ideological divisions it is possible to identify the relevant variables that parties and armies had to consider in restructuring their relationship; to make some assessment about how the changing nature of security altered the civil-military political game and military mission alike. My analysis explores the working hypothesis that given the embryonic nature of post-communist political institutions and the stated intent of those who considered that the West had won the cold war to monitor the speed on the road to democracy and the market, the gap between rhetoric and reality in the ephemeral "New World Order" inevitably had major influence on the outcomes of stage one of a multi-stage systemic transformation. Therefore, before considering country-specific and regional imperatives, this chapter establishes my view of the emerging international security regime within which unready post-communist politicians and military leaders sought to redefine goals of an unfamiliar national security.

The New World Order

With the end of the post World War II international system came the struggle to determine a New World Order. The very concept of such an order was largely the wishful thinking of journalists in need of new labels and politicians who craved predictability. In retrospect, Kuwait was easy. Industrialized nations joined forces with Middle Eastern allies to prevent Iraq from threatening the energy artery of their economies, Middle East oil. President Bush's ability to put together a coalition under United Nations' auspices to force Saddam Hussein's troops out of Kuwait was skillful diplomacy. However, that diplomacy did not put in place the infrastructure of a post-Cold War new world order.

Notwithstanding popular horror and outraged international rhetoric at the tragic civil war in Bosnia and Herzegovina,⁵ there was no general agreement as to when, by whom or under what conditions such united military action should be taken, on the role, if any, of the European Community (now European Union) of NATO in regional conflict resolution, or if UN peacekeeping forces should be deployed to contain massive violence. Squabbling over the implementation of previously agreed upon NATO air strikes or air support to ensure delivery of UN humanitarian aid continued almost until the signing of the 1995 Dayton Agreement.

Today the power configuration of the current international system is one military nuclear superpower torn between becoming the policeman of whatever New World Order emerges and the imperatives of competition with the economic power players of the early 1990s-- Japan, the united Germany, and an increasingly integrated Europe. Britain and France are members of the nuclear club. Russia has inherited the Soviet membership. Assurances aside, the status of nuclear weapons and nuclear materials in other Soviet successor states-- particularly Ukraine and Kazakhstan--remains ambivalent and will until all nuclear weapons are gone or destroyed.

The traveling international UN/EU permanent peace conference to negotiate the conflicts that tore Yugoslavia apart produced more hot air than substance. Meanwhile in terms of conventional weapons, war and the threat of force to accomplish political goals remain very real.

As the East-West ideological/political dividing line disappears, the threat to West European prosperity is not communism but chaos: a flood of refugees from war, political dislocation, unemployment and economic pain on the way to market economies. Now the North-South division between "haves" and "have nots" on the spectrum of industrialization/modernization/development is the fault line dividing not only developing countries from the industrialized world but Europe itself. In the reality of New World Disorder, those successor states of the former "second world" accepted into the common European home will move towards the Northern end of the spectrum. It is likely that for all practical purposes the others will slide backwards into what cold war terminology called "the Third World", i.e. the problem-ridden South.

This dynamic, fluid international environment is the womb of post-communist parties and armies alike. In the East European Balkans, it is strewn with security problems for politicians who must continually juggle tradeoffs between the pressures to create viable democratic institutions, prosperous market economies and as Daniel Nelson has put it, "a new basis for national security"[6] side-by-side with more-or-less restructured military establishments desperately seeking identity, resources, and mission. To understand these security problems and perspectives, it is useful to look at what these countries share and how they differ from Central European post-communist societies and each other.

The Legacy of Communist Rule

First, unlike the peoples' revolutions in Central Europe (Poland, East Germany , Hungary, and Czechoslovakia), East European Balkan communist governments collapsed from the weight of the demonstration effect upon party leaders willing to change political horses and swim with the tide in order to save a bigger piece of the political action for themselves. This phenomena might be called "born again communists". Within days of the November 1989 collapse of the Berlin Wall, the Bulgarian Communist Party had changed its name and platform to reemerge as the Bulgarian Socialist Party (BSP). By December, Romanian dictator Ceausescu's "socialism in one family" came to a sudden, violent end to be replaced by Ion Iliescu's National Salvation Front that many viewed as a front for former communists.

Seeing the handwriting on the wall, the League of Communists of Yugoslavia (LCY) renounced its own "leading role" and accepted opposition parties at the extraordinary 14th Party Congress in January 1990 only to die a lingering death when the Congress proved impossible to reconvene. In the multiparty elections that went forward at the republic level Serbian strongman Slobodan Milosevic won with a restructured Serbian League of Communists in the form of the Socialist Party of Serbia (SPS), while in Montenegro reform communists defiantly remained the Communist Party of Montenegro. By the end of 1990 Albanian president Ramiz Alia yielded to student demands for a multiparty system, but it took until the March 1992 elections for the Albanian Democratic Party (ADP) to make much headway in national politics.[7]

It is fair to say that the nature of the transition to a multiparty system in the East European Balkans left communists and 'born again communist' parties and politicians in positions of power for longer than was the case in Central Europe. Thus, while the East European Balkans share the crisis of leadership that exists throughout post-communist Europe where fallen away communist politicians lacked credibility and democratic opposition leaders lacked political experience, the difference is that in Albania, Bulgaria, Romania and most of former Yugoslavia, the initial transition to multiparty systems and market economies was in the hands of renamed, repackaged communist parties and politicians.

Quite apart from the credibility question, the political socialization and professional experience of these former communist cadre are poor qualifications for the job. The strength of Leninist organizational theory was intra-party coherence in the name of democratic centralism. Acceptance of the inevitability of opposition parties does not necessarily mean willingness or ability to play by democratic rules of the game, tolerance for political pluralism, or skill at compromise and negotiated settlement. Many who benefitted most from the command economy were not necessarily seriously committed to dismantling it. Those who were committed may or may not be capable of navigating these uncharted waters without grounding the ship of state.

Moreover, when it came to politics from below, communist political systems in the East European Balkans, like in Central Europe and in the former Soviet Union, operated according to *de facto* social contract: political acquiescence for economic security. On a country-specific basis this deal was reinforced by varying combinations of propaganda and repression. It was a relationship in which the Marxist myth of future utopian society had considerably less drawing power than a job virtually impossible to lose, subsidized food, an apartment, medicine and education. The rhetoric of democracy aside, communist politicians landed on the rubbish heap of history in 1989-1990 because they had steadily increased expectations and failed to deliver. Their successors are left with massive structural economic problems, few resources, and politicized populations.

Albania set out on the road to democracy and the market as the poorest country in Europe.[8] Bulgaria and post-Tito Yugoslavia were struggling to cope with the consequences of the international credit card economy of the 1970s that had addicted these economies to hard currency debt. Ceausescu had starved his economy and impoverished his people to wipe out that debt. In each case the myth of democracy and the market had become the hope and the promise; a panacea that would somehow miraculously allow political access, create stable political institutions, correct economic deformations and restore the eroded economic security of increasingly impatient workers, peasants, housewives, academics, managers, and bureaucrats.

Armies in Transition

Still more directly related to security in a traditional sense was the problem of communist military establishments that did not collapse along with the communist governments they served. What to do with the soldiers? Again, this problem has different country-specific contexts rooted in quite the differing security environments of communist Albania, Bulgaria, Romania and Yugoslavia.

Of these four East European Balkan countries only Bulgaria was a Warsaw Pact member in good standing. When allied socialist troops marched into Czechoslovakia in 1968, Albania denounced the Warsaw Treaty Organization as a "treaty of slavery" and unilaterally withdrew from the alliance. Romania had long been the maverick within communist coalition politics; refusing to engage in pact military activity or pay what Moscow had pressured the other East European alliance members into accepting as their fair share of defense costs. Yugoslavia was never a member. Stalin's mini-Cold War with Tito had forced Yugoslav communists to rely on their own armed forces.

However, in all four communist regimes civil-military relations were highly politicized. Whether or not this was a consequence of Nordlinger's penetration model[9] as in Albania, Bulgaria and Romania or what amounted to a party-army partnership in Yugoslavia, the end result was that professional socialization and military corporate self-interest combined to put former communist armies high on the list of internal security problems.[10]

Whether or not these military leaders and soldiers would always have preferred to defend a country instead of an ideology, they are suspect. In post-communist Europe, officer corps are seen as potentially dangerous havens for communist hardliners. Any Cold War peace dividend required cutting into their privileges and professional needs. In short, the line between ideological objections and   personal self-interest was significantly blurred. On both grounds military officers had and have reasons to resist political/economic reforms needed in other sectors of society.

In the search for a new military mission, post-communist politicians must depoliticize communist militaries and learn about democratic civil-military relations. This dilemma is all the more acute due to the felt need for reliable armies and security forces to deal with internal and external perils that threaten to overwhelm still fragile post-communist governments. Such threats compound the danger flowing from still another cognitive remnant of communism.

A fundamental aspect of Marxism-Leninism had been the attempt to transform what the prophets of communism saw as parochial national identities into "proletarian internationalism". Ideologically this class-based identity was more suited to struggle with world capitalism. After the Russian revolution its task was to protect Soviet Russia from being strangled in the cradle. Thereby, proletarian internationalism became the rationale for the vertical, dominant-subordinate organization of the world communist movement, for the Stalinist interstate system in Eastern Europe following World War II, and for the Godfather role of Soviet leaders in the family of socialist nations. The cornerstone of proletarian internationalism was love of comrade Stalin, devotion to the Soviet Union. By definition what was good for the Soviet Union was good for the international communist movement.

In this manner proletarian internationalism elevated Russian national communism, thereby depriving East European communists of the right to appropriate their own national traditions. It created a communist subsystem with its own political culture, "embodied in its own prolific literature...(with) its own distinct language and symbols, its own history and its own heroes, villains, and martyrs...its own special ritual behavior."[11]

More importantly, at the heart of the single largest experiment in social engineering in history was the goal of creating the 'new socialist' man and woman. With the discrediting of that vision, class and international identities alike have become suspect. Thus, as in Central Europe, four decades of communism have left East European Balkan politicians and societies in the grip of a mammoth identity crisis. Hence the question: security for whom?

Back to the Future

Although these East Central European revolutions are a response to the scientific, technical and information revolutions that are creating the infrastructure of the world order that will define the 21st century, there is no generic 21st century identity to take off the shelf. The identities that exist in the East European Balkans are historic national identities. These are the closest identities that were cherished in the privacy of the family and church to counter the abstraction of socialist citizens. At its most basic level, the rebirth of East Europe[12] that Michael Roskin writes about is the rehabilitation of the nation.

This is both a political and security problem. In newly independent East European societies there is substantial confusion about basic democratic concepts. In the West, democracy is associated with the rights of individual citizens to political access and governmental accountability. That has never been the most common assumption in the East European Balkans.[13] Here, among the political parties proliferating like mushrooms, the most passionate are those reclaiming national identities who think of democracy as the right to national self-determination.

In these multinational societies how does one build political parties to bridge ethnic cleavages? How can such parties find a common denominator of national security that will satisfy the Bulgarian majority and Turkish minority in Bulgaria; Romanian and the Hungarian minorities in Transylvania; Serbs, Croats, Muslims, and Albanians in the former Yugoslavia?

Communist political systems put an end to inter-ethnic violence and within the commonwealth of socialist nations there were no Balkan wars. Under the Brezhnev Doctrine, the Soviet godfather might use military means to "save socialism". However, national/ethnic feuds were not tolerated within the family of socialist nations.

One does not have to go as far as those who argue that the violence of post-communist ethnic outbursts is directly related to unnatural repression of national identities under communism to accept that what was seen as perhaps the greatest Soviet success story in Eastern Europe, the solving of the national question, has turned out to be an illusion. Conflicts were not solved so much as put into a kind of suspended animation. The removal of the Soviet veto on systemic change and the disbanding of the Warsaw Pact reopened the Pandora's box of national/ethnic hatreds and agendas.

East European Balkan politicians in search of security must transverse ethnic land mines and territorial irredentas that define country-specific and regional security problems and perspectives alike. The interaction of rediscovered national identities and the temptation of politicians to posture as saviors of the nation blurs the line between external and internal security.

No Albanian politician can ignore the shadow of the war waged between former Yugoslav republics or, in Tirana's view, the denial of human rights of two million Albanians captive in Serbia. There is also concern, if less so, for the situation of the 20-40 percent (depending on whose figures you use) Albanian minority in Macedonia. Romania must worry on two fronts: about Hungarian action to protect the Hungarian minority in Transylvania and for fear of spill-over from rising violence in Moldova between the Romanian majority and Russian minority. Bulgaria's assimilationist policy towards its Macedonian minority makes sorting out Sofia's relationship with the self-proclaimed independent Macedonia delicate, to say nothing of the implications of relations with its own politicized Turkish minority. In or outside of Yugoslavia, Serbs feel threatened by what they see as Albanian interference in Kosovo, Hungarian deals with Croatia and meddling in Vojvodina.

From the internal perspective, nationalist passions, economic hardships, and weak political parties are a potentially deadly combination. War between former Yugoslav republics and, especially in Bosnia and Herzegovina stand as tragic reminders of the cost in life and treasure of giving up on pluralism; of abandoning dialogue for sectarian rhetoric; of rejecting negotiated solutions for military means.

As the EC debated whether to give Greece a copyright on the name "Macedonia" and the Bush administration quibbled about the cost of UN peacekeepers, the war clouds broke over Bosnia and Herzegovina and witnessed 200,000 dead and around 2.5 million refugees in a little over a year.[14] This is not Ivo Andric's romanticized combat that advances "in complete accord with the deep sense of our history and racial destiny." From Karageorge's words in the early 1800's: "Let each kill his Turkish chief," the social problem in the Balkans has always been solved by the way of national liberation movements and wars. "It all moves beautifully, logically from the less to the great, from the region and tribal to the national and formation of the State...."[15]

Here there are no winners. This war has shattered the security of Croats, Serbs and Muslims alike. Moreover, there is always a real danger that the vortex of violence in Bosnia and Herzegovina will draw in neighboring countries as well if the Dayton Agreement fails. Notwithstanding Serbian opposition and police harassment, Kosovar Albanians voted overwhelmingly to secede from Yugoslavia.[16] The post-communist Albanian Democratic Party pledged to support "our martyred brothers" in Kosovo. Bulgaria and Turkey recognized Macedonia, and Greece was outraged. Athens fears Skopje's expansionist ambitions and points to Macedonia maps as proof of aggressive intentions. There are unconfirmed rumors that former Romanian Securitate fought along side Serbian paramilitary irregulars. True or not, Romanian sympathies are with the Serbs both for historic reasons and because the Hungarians are on the side of the Croats. Failure between Zagreb and Belgrade for tentative normalizing of relations under the January 20, 1994 joint declaration prolonged the war;[17] ultimately contributing to Croatia's resort to a military campaign that expelled some 150,000 Serbian civilians from Krajina and Western Slavonia[18]–the single largest refugee flow in Europe since the Hungarian Revolution in 1956. The potential for war in Kosovo is becoming the primary security problem for all Yugoslav successor states, their East European Balkan neighbors, and the new Europe alike. Indeed, unless politicians and policymakers in the neighborhood learn from the tragic Yugoslav experience, they may be condemned to repeat it. Therefore let us consider the perspectives on security at the heart of the violence that has detoured what might have been Yugoslavia's road to democracy and Europe into a barren dead-end.[19]

The Yugoslav Road to Civil War[20]

Twice since 1918 the attempt to establish a viable south slav state has collapsed in inter-ethnic violence.[21] The first Yugoslavia (1918-1941) and Communist Yugoslavia (1945 to 1991) both sought and failed to integrate the conflicting political cultures of Serbs and Croats into a stable political union. Journalistic accounts that see the new Europe as an economic revival of the Austro-Hungarian empire[22] assume a superficial cultural determinism. However, the founders of the interwar Kingdom of Serbs, Croats and Slovenes clearly came together on the basis of a major misunderstanding. The Council of Croats and Slovenes wanted a confederal Yugoslavia, a partnership of equals. For Serbs the new Yugoslavia was confused with longings for the historic Serbia empire, a "greater Serbia". The tensions between these two visions were sharpened by Serbian centralizing tendencies and Croatian tactics of political obstructionism to expand their autonomy in face of what many Croats experienced as Serbian colonization.

These widely differing agendas for the relationship did not disappear when Hitler's war machine dismembered the first Yugoslav state in 1941. Rather, when the League of Communists of Yugoslavia deadlocked at the January 1990 14th Extraordinary Congress, these conflicting visions of Yugoslavia as a community of equal nations (the EC model) and Yugoslavia as an integrated federal system in which Serbian numbers would add up to political advantage (a "greater Serbia" model) were central to the choreography of political struggle. These two visions are much more than competing modes of governmental organization. They are directly related to conflicting perceptions of security. Although the impetus for Slovenian and Croatian independence is frequently cast in terms of an ideological clash between these republics and a Serbian "bolshevik" leadership, at the heart of that clash was an agreement of a fundamental principle of Gorbachev's new political thinking about security in Ljubljana and Zagreb.

In short, the more economically developed republics of the

former Yugoslavia saw their future security in economic/political terms, and feared that to continue in a federal Yugoslavia the population numbers would guarantee Serbian political advantages that would prevent them from walking through the door into Europe. In Serbia security remained the physical safety and political/economic position of Serbian minorities that would be outside of Serbia without the umbrella protection of a Yugoslav state in territories where the fate of such minorities at the hands of an indigenous fascist Croatia during World War II was still a matter of family memory.

For Slovenia, the answer was to cut and run. For Croatia the June 1991 timing of the Slovene declaration of independence was a golden bandwagon, not to be missed because if Slovenia succeeded Croatia's position would be less secure within the remaining Yugoslavia. Clearly Slovenia and Croatia saw "self-determination" and independence as the key to their security. As demands for Slovenian and Croatian sovereignty mobilized these republics' populations, Serbian president Slobodan Milosevic made clear that in his mind security meant a reuniting of the Serbs in one homeland, i.e. a redrawing of the borders so that Serbian minorities no longer existed outside Serbia. This strategy in turn fed into non-Serbian fears of "greater Serbia" ambitions harking back to Tsar Dusan's medieval empire. What in Belgrade was and is perceived as security-related expansion was seen by Croatia, then by Bosnia and Hercegovina as unjustified Serbian aggression.

On the road to civil war, the Croatian elimination of the Serbian minority's political rights in the new Croatian constitution threatened the political/economic status of the 600,000 Serbs in Croatia. When that minority responded by declaring its own "sovereignty" and threatened to join Serbia if Croatian separatism won the day, this was a threat to the territorial integrity of Croatia. When the Serbian militants demonstrated their self-proclaimed sovereignty by harassing tourists and blockading the main road from Zagreb to the Adriatic coast, thereby cutting the artery of Croatian tourism, they endangered the economic security of Croatia and Yugoslavia alike. For the Zagreb government, this was an internal security problem. The Serbian minority saw the resulting Croatian paramilitary force as a threat to their physical security. In

Belgrade the safety of Serbs in Croatia became a security concern of Serbia proper. The scandal surrounding an alleged purchase of Hungarian arms by the Croatian defense minister further highlighted the external security dimension of rising Croatian nationalism.

These conflicting conceptions of security were entangled in domestic political agendas in Serbia and Croatia alike. Milosevic's virtually iconic image faded due to his authoritarian style, economic mismanagement, and Serbia's growing isolation at home and abroad.[23] The Serbian president needed to reverse his declining popularity. In Croatia Tudjman's Croatian Democratic Union (CDU) needed to deliver on its promise to make Croatia the republic of Croats. The political needs of a Croatian president struggling to consolidate his power and the Serbian president fighting to hold on to his power clashed disastrously.

Meanwhile, Washington and Brussels alike viewed security as avoiding the downhill slide into civil war. These efforts came too late. Neither President Bush's assurance to Prime Minister Ante Markovic that the United States would not "encourage or reward those striving to disrupt the country"[24] nor European Community promises of a 1.1 billion dollar loan to underwrite Yugoslav unity and the opening of negotiations on associate membership for that united Yugoslavia within the EC itself were enough to stem the tide.

For the army and the federal government what had begun as a show of force to demonstrate federal authority in Slovenia became a fateful misstep on the road to civil war.[25] Once the shooting started, control over the Slovene political spectrum went from the hands of policymakers who saw the declaration of independence as part of the ongoing jockeying for position in the struggle for a confederal Yugoslavia into those for whom independence equated with separation.

Notwithstanding, the European Community brokered a cease-fire and placed EC monitors in Slovenia; the Yugoslav National Army (JNA) was deeply humiliated. As one colleague told me while we watched a defensive JNA press conference on Belgrade television, "This is our most dangerous time. The army is unpredictable; a wounded animal."

The damage to civilian control and the corporate identity of the

JNA interacted with rising militancy in Serbian Krajina and criticism of Tudjman for not following the Slovene example of military resistance. In short, as moderates in the JNA were purged, violence escalated and JNA armed forces more and more openly supported Serbian irregulars battling Croatian militia.

Internationalization of the Yugoslav Civil War

This was not the same army that had backed down in Slovenia. The fragile control of the federal Yugoslav government under Prime Minister Ante Markovic was already damaged beyond repair. In these circumstances, German threats to recognize Croatia if the federal army did not exercise restraint inevitably backfired. One does not have to agree with the Serbian "Fourth Reich" theory[26] in which Tudjman, as the leader of the wartime Croatia before him, was considered as a German pawn to acknowledge that German policy only shifted the violence into high gear.

In turn the resulting decision to recognize Croatia before the Zagreb government had met the human rights conditions of the EC commission establishing criteria for recognition of breakaway Yugoslav republics played a direct role in spreading the war to Bosnia and Herzegovina. Repercussions of the EC corollary demand that any former Yugoslav republic seeking recognition must request it by December 23, 1991[27] continued in the form of hundreds of thousands of refugees created by policies of ethnic cleansing.[28]

We now know that notwithstanding the Bush administration's official policy of letting the Europeans clean up their own backyard, Washington played a direct role in aborting the February 1992 Lisbon agreement for an ethnic division of Bosnia and Herzegovina that would have given Bosnian Muslims 44% of the territory and control over all but 18% of Muslim population[29]. The subsequent Owen-Stoltenberg tripartite division rejected by the Bosnian Muslim parliament at the end of September 1993 would have left the Muslims in control of slightly more than 30% of territory and without sovereignty over their narrow access corridor to the Adriatic.

The EC recognized Croatia and Slovenia on January 15, 1992,

Bosnia and Herzegovina on April 6. The US followed with recognition of all three breakaway republics on April 7. These Yugoslav successor states were accepted as members of the United Nations on May 22, 1992.

Lessons of Yugoslavia for Post-Communist Balkan Security

First, in the international political economy of the 1990s, security is interdependent and indivisible. There is no such thing as sovereignty in the classic sense.

Second, there is no savior out there. EC, now EU, members were divided and it is more likely that continued differences over Bosnia and Kosovo will Balkanize the European Union than that its members will get their act together.

The UN embargo leaked worse than a sieve. In implementing the UN self-defined mission, there were bureaucratic squabbles between UNPROFOR Commanders in the field and former UN Secretary General Boutros Boutros-Ghali.

NATO's out-of-area policy vis-a-vis Bosnia and Herzegovina was tied to its members who were also divided, and to the U.N. where there was major ambivalence. The Russian representative sent a letter insisting on Moscow's right of consent in terms of air strikes[30].

NATO's partnership for peace could not be much comfort for Romanian President Emil Constantinescu after his all out campaign to mobilize Romanian popular support for membership in the first round of NATO enlargement in July 1997. Nor will demands focused on the hard choices involved in economic reforms for being included in a projected second round improve his democratic coalitions' chances of staying in power. Still more serious, this did not translate into any support from Washington for President Sali Berisha's hard pressed government during the Albanian anarchy following economic melt-down precipitated by failed pyramid schemes in the fall of 1996 and early 1997. Indeed, the UN mandated multinational forces sent in to protect humanitarian aid did not include American troops, were not under NATO control, and left after the 1997 summer elections that turned the government over to Albanian socialists potentially with even more authoritarian tendencies than the much maligned Berisha. This was all notwithstanding our October 1993 military cooperation agreement with Albania.[31]

Third, in or outside of the former Yugoslavia, minority populations will not be secure unless they develop workable political/economic relationships with majority populations. Specifically, Croats in Croatia will not be secure unless the human and civil rights of the shrunken Serbian minority are protected and a genuine working agreement is implemented in regard to Eastern Slavonia. Croats and Muslims in Bosnia will not be secure as long as Mostar remains a divided city plagued by low level violence that could escalate to drag Zagreb into another shooting war. Bosnian Serbs are made less not more secure by the expansion of SFOR's mission to include active support of Bosnian Serb President Biljana Plavsic and her followers in Banja Luka against her one time mentor former President Radovan Karadzic in Pale. Equally, unless democratic Serbs want to become prisoners of an impoverished dictatorship cut off from Europe in order to hang onto the territorial gains of civil war, they must come to see their security as dependent as much on protection of the human and civil rights of Kosovar Albanians as of Serbs and Montenegrins in Kosovo. Meanwhile, Macedonians and Albanians living together in the newly independent Macedonia cannot be secure unless something is done to deal with the tensions involving demands for Albanian language higher education, public jobs and local governmental autonomy for Albanian majority communities. This is particularly dangerous because it would be political suicide for any politician to make concessions before the next Parliamentary election set for 1998 and by then it may be too late to keep the peace.[32] The same is true of Romanians and their Hungarian minority; of Bulgarians in relationship to their indigenous Turkish minority.

Unless one is willing to accept the fundamentally pessimistic conclusion that in the post Cold War world Gorbachev's call for *demilitarizing, democratizing* and *humanizing* of international relations[33] is not likely to become the Balkan reality for the foreseeable future, Southeast European politicians, policymakers, soldiers, and populations must let go of the "old thinking" that for centuries pitted Balkan peoples against each other. All too often the frustration and insecurity of transition to the brave, new world of democracy and the market erupt against one another in senseless, violent, scape-goating of traditional enemies.

This is the road to another Bosnia. A shared, peaceful future requires "new thinking" of politicians and military commanders alike. It requires a new concept of collective security that is measured not in the currency of military power but by diplomatic skill and commitment to conflict containment. In circumstances where troops increasingly define their loyalties by national origin, military leaders must insist upon professionalism or risk not just declining resources, but the collapse of military discipline and military establishments. During the delicate process of depoliticizing armies, the survival of post-communist democracies depends as much upon restraint and negotiating skills of military leaders as upon political development and democratic norms in the civilian sector.

Above all, politicians and military leaders in the post-communist Balkans need patience to wait out the nationalist fever that is a symptom of post-communist euphoria and frustration. The politicians need to tell voters economic/military realities; to stop substituting nationalist circuses for bread. Military leaders need to help officers and soldiers accept the hard choices imposed by political/economic imperatives.

Fourth, this goes beyond an East European Balkan country-specific or regional problem. To tell it like it is and survive politically these politicians must be able to deliver economic performance instead of rhetoric. If international financial circles do not come up with more than platitudes, any East European policy-maker who can do the job will sink like a stone. The flood of refugees that will engulf neighboring countries if these politicians continue to seek legitimacy by playing the national/ethnic card is a security nightmare for the New Europe, East and West alike.

The European Union, NATO and the Clinton foreign policy team need to consider the implications of the anonymous Bosnian general who predicted that if the Bosnian Muslims could capture the munitions factory at Vitez without Bosnian Croats blowing it up, they could fight on for another five years.[34] The bottom line is that there can be no

European security separate from security for peoples of the post-communist European Balkans. Such security requires a political solution to the Yugoslav wars of secession. It also requires Western investment and trade policies that level the playing field for Balkan exports rather than ducking the expanded competition of emerging market economies.[35]

Notes

1. This chapter draws upon and expands my earlier research dealing with security in the post-communist Balkans: "Balkan Triangle: Washington, Moscow, Belgrade," in Sharyl Cross and Marina Oborotova, eds., *Prospects for American-Russian Cooperation in the Post-Cold War Era (Greenwood, 1994) 153-168.* *"Bosnian Muslim Views of National Security"* with Francine Friedman in Constantine Danopoulos and Kostas G. Messas, eds., *Crises in the Balkans: Views from the Participants* (Boulder, CO: Westview Press, 1997) 93-112. "Ethnonationalism and the Disintegration of Yugoslavia," in Winston A. Van Horne, ed., *Global Convulsions: Race, Ethnicity and Nationalism at the End of the Twentieth Century* (Albany: State University of New York Press, 1997) 161-180. "Partije, armija i bezbednost u istocnoevropskims balkanskim drzavama," (Parties, Armies and Security in the East European Balkan States) in Zlatko Isakovic, ed., *Vojske i promene u evropskim socijalistickim zemljama (Armies and Transition in European Socialist Countries,* Belgrade: Institute for International Studies, 1994) 65-83. "State Cohesion and the Military," in Jill Irvine, Carol Lilly and Melissa Bokovy, eds., *State-Society Relations in Yugoslavia, 1945-1992* (New York: St. Martin's Press, 1997) 61-78. "Stumbling into War: Collapse of the Yugoslav Alternative, " in Zoltan Barany and Ivan Volgyes eds., *The Legacies of Communism in Central and Eastern Europe* (The Johns Hopkins University Press, 1995) 267-288. "The Yugoslav Army: Trauma and Transition," in Constantine Danopoulos and Daniel Zirker, ed., *Civil Military Relations in Soviet and Yugoslav Successor States* Boulder, CO: Westview Press, 1996).

2. Mikhail Gorbachev. *Perestroika: New Thinking for Our Country and the World* (New York: Harper and Row, 1987).

3. *The New York Times* (July 13, 1989).

4. On July 1 the Political Consultative Committee went out of business pending ratification by parliaments of member states. *The New York Times* (July 2, 1991).

5. By the end of May 1992 there were increasing calls for tightening "the economic noose" against Serbia, comparisons of inaction in defense of Bosnia and Herzegovina to those who looked the other way as Hitler began his march in Munich 1938. See *The New York Times* May 21, 1992 editorial "Shame in Our Time, in Bosnia" featuring Bosnian Foreign Minister Haris Silajdzic' plea that world inaction while his country was turned into a slaughterhouse was "a disgrace for Humanity."

6. Daniel N. Nelson. *East European Security in the Wake of Revolution* (University of Missouri-St. Louis Center for International Studies, Occasional Paper No. 9112 (December 1991) 2-3.

7. *The New York Times* (March 23, 1992). Note that Albanian socialists lost not for lack of privatization, but because giving back the land did not bring about the rise in living standards that had been expected.

8. See Miranda Vickers and James Pettifer. *Albania: From Anarchy to a Balkan Identity* (London: Hurst and Company, 1997) and Elez Biberaj. *Albania in Transition* (Boulder, CO: Westview Press, 1998.)

9. Eric A. Nordlinger. *Soldiers in Politics: Military Coups and Government* (Englewood Cliffs: Prentice-Hall, 1977) 15-19. Nordlinger's model is refined from the totalitarian model of Morris Janowitz, *The Military in the Political Development of New Nations: An Essay in Comparative Analysis* (Chicago: University of Chicago Press, 1964) 4.

10. This section follows line of analysis taken in my discussion of search for security in " and the Market in East Central Europe: The Hard Choices," in Gary D. Wekkin, et.al. eds., *Building Democracy in One-Party Systems: Theoretical Problems and Cross-Nation Experiences* (Westport, CT and London: Praeger, 1993) 153 ff, subsequently expanded as a full-length chapter "The Yugoslav Army: Trauma and Transition" in Constantine P. Danopoulos and Daniel Zirker, eds., *Civil-Military Relations in the Soviet and Yugoslav Successor States* (Boulder, CO: Westview Press, 1996).

11. George Modelski. *The Communist International System* (Princeton, NJ: Princeton University Center for International Studies Monograph, 1960) 45.

12. Michael Roskin. *The Rebirth of East Europe* (Englewood Cliffs, NJ: Prentice Hall, 3rd Edition, 1997).

13. See Peter F. Sugar and Ivo J. Lederer. *Nationalism in Eastern Europe* (Seattle: University of Washington Press, 1969).

14. *The New York Times* (July 30, 1993).

15. Ivo Andric. *The Bridge on the Drina* (New York: New American Library, 1960) 322.

16. *The New York Times* (May 26, 1992).

17. *The New York Times* (January 21, 1994).

18. The Foreign Minister of Republic of Serb Krajina, Slobodan Jarcevic, flatly denied that Croatia could sign agreements for Serb Krajina. See Richard H. Ullman, ed., *The World and Yugoslavia's Wars* (New York: Council of Foreign Relations Book, 1996) 70-72.

19. For an expanded treatment of the following section see Robin Alison Remington, "Yugoslavia: The Road Away from Europe, " in Teresa Rakowska-Harmstone and Piotr Dutkiewicz, eds, *On the Road Back to Europe: East Central Europe* (Bloomington, Indiana: Indiana University Press, 1999.)

20. In my view, the first year of the Yugoslav transition began after Tito died in May

1980. However, for purposes of this analysis, I have focused on the impact of the collapse of Communist governments in the neighborhood and the end of the cold war on the already increasingly sectarian power struggle underway prior to 1990. With regard to the army this section draws upon my earlier study of the failure of the Yugoslav army to make the transition to a multiparty system, Robin Alison Remington, *Yugoslav Soldiers in Politics: On the Road to Civil War* (University of Missouri-St.Louis Occasional Paper 9109, October 1991).

21. See John R. Lampe, *Yugoslavia as History, Twice there was a country* (New York: Cambridge University Press, 1996).

22. Joseph C. Harsch, "Back to the Future in the Balkans," *The Christian Science Monitor* (January 29, 1992).

23.See Stephen Engelberg, "Carving out a Greater Serbia," *The New York Times Magazine* (September 1, 1991). Even if one believes that Engelberg's sources are suspect and had their own agendas, subsequent events support the general thrust of his analysis.

24. Quoted by Milicia Stamatovic, "The Future Lies in Democracy," *Politika: the International Weekly* (6-12 April 1991) 2. In fairness there is no evidence to confirm popular rumor that U.S. Secretary of State James A. Baker,III encouraged Markovic to use military means to hold the country together during his June 1991 visit to Yugoslavia.

25. Who gave orders to whom and who was responsible for what remains very unclear. Prime Minister Markovic said flatly on Belgrade television that his order had been exceeded. The army insists that it was acting in accordance with decisions of the government and the presidency; that politicians must take their share of responsibility, *Narodna Armija* (Belgrade) (July 6, 1991). Subsequently in a closed session of the Federal Executive Council that leaked within days Markovic went on to accuse the army of acting on its own in Slovenia, *Vreme* (Belgrade) (September 23, 1991) 5-12.

26. In fact Belgrade BBC had cited this theory from the British press even before it was taken up as a Serbian rallying cry. Belgrade Television, June 28, 1991. In the post-mortem of the EC recognition of Croatia and Slovenia this theory was elaborated. "The united Germany of today is not the same as the West Germany of yesterday....New structures already operating within the European Community. Actually Germany and Italy are developing their alliance; on the other hand, they have brought into accord their interests regarding the division of Yugoslav territory. The same interests and motives are involved as those that brought about the establishment of the Rome-Berlin axis on the eve of World War II." Mirko Ostojic, "Breaking Up of Yugoslavia," *Review of International Affairs*, vol. XLIII, no. 1001 (February 5, 1992) 7.

27. Text of EC "Declaration on Yugoslavia," (Brussels 17 December 1991) in *Review of International Affairs* (Belgrade) vol. XLII, no. 998-1000 (December 1, 1991) 28. See

also Predrag Simic, "Europe and the Yugoslav Issue,'" *Review of International Affairs* (Belgrade) vol. XLIII, no.1001 (February 5, 1992) 1-5.

28. See Patrick Moore, "Ethnic Cleansing in Bosnia: Outrage but Little Action," *RFE/RL Report* Vol. 1, 34 (28 August 1992) 1-7.

29. David Binder's analysis in *The New York Times*, August 29, 1993 quotes from then U.S. Ambassador to Yugoslavia, Warren Zimmerman, as saying that these days that agreement does not look so bad.

30. *The New York Times* (January 24, 1994).

31. *The New York Times* (October 21, 1993).

32. Author's discussions in Skoplje, October 13-17, 1997. See, Barnett R. Rubin, ed. *Toward Comprehensive Peace in Southeast Europe: Conflict Prevention in the South Balkans.* Report of the South Balkan Working Group of the Center for Preventive Action (A Twentieth Century Fund Book, 1996).

33. Mikhail Gorbachev. *A Road to the Future: Complete Text of the December 7, 1988 United Nations Address* (Santa Fe, NM: Ocean Tree Books, 1990) 30-31. See also, Daniel L. Nelson, "Balkan Insecurities," in Andrew A. Michta and Ilya Prizel, eds., *Post-Communist Eastern Europe: Crisis and Reform* (New York: St. Martin's Press, 1993) 85-110.

34. *The New York Times* (October 21, 1993).

35. *The New York Times* (January 23, 1994).

5.
Romania and the Struggle for New Directions

Arthur W. Helweg

The end of the 1980s was a decisive period of tumultuous changes for the Soviet Union and Eastern Europe. With Mikhail Gorbachev coming to power in 1985, policies of *glasnost* and *perestroika* were instituted. These policies, combined with the cutting of Russia's military budget, allowed greater freedom of speech and self determination for people in the Soviet Union and her satellite countries. The end result was a series of events that brought an end to the Cold War by the disintegration of the USSR and the Soviet bloc. In 1989, Poland had her first free elections since the Communist[1] takeover. Also in that same year, Hungary, East Germany, Czechoslovakia, Bulgaria and Romania cast off the yoke of authoritarian rule and demanded democracy.

It was a time of optimism and euphoria for both East and West. Democracy, capitalism, private ownership and free markets were perceived as panaceas for the poor standard of living in the Eastern bloc countries.

The momentous changes were not generally predicted; those who foresaw the disintegration of the USSR and her satellites were ignored.[2] Events happened so fast that policy makers and planners did not know how to respond. A year later Jeffrey Sachs, the Harvard economist who is touted by some as "the most important economist in the world,"[3] stated that "the book on development has to be written as we go along."[4]

Lack of knowledge did not prevent Western experts on economic, political and social development from arguing their theories and dogmatically deriving their solutions. At first glance, the situation of the Eastern bloc countries seemed unique in modern history. In East and West, there was general agreement with intellectuals like Sachs, who argued that the experiment with communism had failed and the solution was to develop a free market with private ownership.

Immediately plans and policies were developed to convert Eastern bloc countries from a centralized political and economic system to one emphasizing democracy, free market and private ownership. The World Bank, International Monetary Fund, and aid policies of western countries like Germany, Britain, France and the United States were not only geared to promote the principles of democracy, free market and privatization, but to do it suddenly. Jeffrey Sachs advocated "shock therapy," arguing that the change must be immediate because public and private enterprise cannot coexist. The Shatalin Plan was proposed in Russia which outlined a complete shift from communism to capitalism and private ownership in 500 days.

Now that the euphoria is over, the ideology of the West is being tried. How the results are interpreted depends on who is doing the evaluation and the data used. Those who use broad economic statistics, such as the Gross National Product (GNP) and currency stability on the international market, point to successes in countries like Poland, as they did in earlier years with economies like Brazil, which are now failing. However, the people in almost all the Eastern bloc countries, including Russia, feel their quality of life has declined since 1989.[5] The casual observer in cities like Bucharest will see an increase in available food in the summer and more foreign luxury products in the stores, but a closer examination shows that productivity is dropping, the middle class is declining, the gap between the rich and poor is increasing and most people feel their quality of life has declined.

It is time to evaluate the policies imposed on Eastern Europe and the countries of the former Soviet Union by the West. To understand what is happening, I will briefly focus on the international context, evaluation of the free market and privatization programs, using Romania as a case in point.

The data on Romania focuses on social processes and perceptions rather than statistics because 1) statistical indicators do not always indicate the quality of life of the average populace, 2) development programs often fail because the culture and perceptions of the people involved are different from those of the implementers, and 3) peoples' perceptions are what people respond to, not necessarily what is actually happening. Also, the manner in which an outsider interprets a situation may differ markedly from the perceptions of the local populace. And, the local populace behave according to their impressions.

My analysis of Romania is based upon a year of intensive research while living in that country during 1991/92 and subsequent visits in 1993, 1994, 1996, and 1997. Although my focus is on Romania, it must be kept in mind that the countries and regions under discussion vary tremendously. Thus, further research will be needed to determine the degree of relevance of the Romanian situation to other nations.

International Context

Events since the Second World War impacted Western response to the balkanization of the East. Shortly after World War Two, the United States became the dominant world power in the West. Under the strong influence of the US Secretary of State John Foster Dulles, the US promoted an ideology at home and abroad that communism was a threat to the world and it must be contained. Often, the propaganda, especially during the Reagan Presidency, cast the communist countries as evil and wanting to take over the world to subjugate all people to their devilish design. This ideology promoted the formation of alliances like North Atlantic Treaty Organization (NATO) and Southeast Asian Treaty Organization (SEATO). It was partly responsible for justifying the successful Marshall Plan that was instrumental in rebuilding Western Europe after the Second World War.

United States ideology argued that there were universal ethical, economic, political and social systems that should be employed by all nations; and, those who were not adhering to the capitalist/free market/private property position were not only against it, but were evil. It took the form of religious fervor, a "civil religion."[6] The issues were political, social and economic, but the behavior was similar to a religious movement, working to not only convert others to its cause, but resorting to force to bring others into its ideological realm, as was paramount during the crusades and various holy wars throughout history. It was not conversion to a religious view that people were advocating, although in some groups democracy and Christianity seemed synonymous; the world was divided into two ideological camps between nations advocating democracy/free market/ private ownership versus communist/centralized planning/public ownership. What is interesting is that alliance and identification was based on what governments claimed to be, not what they actually practiced. Some of the most oppressive and authoritarian regimes of South America and East Asia, such as South Vietnam, claimed to be anticommunist and democratic. And, they were considered free democracies.

From the American perspective, there was no neutrality, a nation was either in one camp, that is pro-West, democratic and good, or communist, anti-West and evil. Countries like India, which took a neutralist policy, were classified as communist. The Soviet Union and China, at least up to the time of President Nixon, were perceived as one and the same in that they were both communist and part of the international conspiracy to promote and conquer societies emphasizing democracy, even though they often had conflict between them. From the ideological view of the United States, there was no compromise or differentiation.

In the Eastern bloc countries, similar propaganda was being waged concerning the debilitating results of capitalism and the superiority of communism. State-controlled movies, television and radio emphasized the unemployment and violence of American society. Children in school were taught communist ideology and social programs were instituted to eliminate hierarchy based on wealth, heritage and knowledge.

Thus, with the collapse of the Soviet Union, it seemed to both sides of the Iron Curtain that the capitalism, democracy and emphasis in private ownership of the West was superior. Reformers in the East and West set out to bring about a reformation to conform to Western ideas.

Transition from Communism to Capitalism--Some Thoughts

The recognized authority on economic development, Jeffrey Sachs, not only advocates "shock therapy"[7] to jolt economies of the former Eastern bloc countries to stability and viability, but he argues that public and private sectors cannot coexist. Thus, public sector enterprises must be immediately shifted over to the private sector, which must also operate on a free market system. He uses the analogy of a country shifting from a right-hand drive traffic system to a left-hand drive traffic system. It has to be done suddenly. You cannot have trucks change one day and cars the next. But, what has experience taught about free market and private enterprise systems? Also, is the traffic analogy valid? Can a sudden shift be implemented?

The Free Market

In theory, Sachs's argument is very logical; but, does it work? Human behavior is not always rational, at least according to Western thinking. The first question to ask is, "Has Sachs's view been tested?" The answer is "yes." In general an unregulated free market:

> 1)...responds to the tastes of those who can pay, the privileged minority. Left to its own devices, the market simply mirrors inequalities in wealth and income. We must not delude ourselves into thinking that it registers the needs and wishes of all people.
> 2)...the market is...blind to the social and resource costs of the production engine it is supposed to drive.
> 3) It leads to the concentration of economic power.[8]

There are many case studies that support the above; one of the more prominent is Brazil. According to Francis Moore Lappè,[9] a development economist, Brazil did everything right. They followed the economic theories of Milton Friedman of the University of Chicago. They borrowed heavily, developed industrially and soon had excellent economic indicators. Yet, in spite of having some of the highest paid executives in the world, the tuberculosis rate, poverty level and rate of sickness in Brazil is among the highest in the world. Brazil's economy has reached a perilous state. The situation of Brazil is not unique: there are many instances that parallel Brazil's experience.

Is Sachs correct in saying that private and public ownership cannot exist side by side? The answer is "no." The United States, one of the biggest advocates of the free market, is a case in point. When companies like the Chrysler Corporation were about to go bankrupt, the United States Government rescued them and awarded them with massive loans. Companies like Boeing are kept viable by being awarded defense contracts, a form of public assistance. And many institutions and groups, like the American farmer, although remaining private enterprise, are heavily subsidized and regulated by the United States Government.

In actuality, one should look at the United States to determine what did happen when a totally free market was instituted. During the turn of the century, when there was little or no regulation of enterprise, the rich got richer and poor got poorer. Once an individual or company reached an advantage over others, they used their power to exploit the others. A good example is Standard Oil. It became so big and powerful that any business starting to compete was immediately crushed. Generally, Standard Oil sold gas next to a competitor at a loss, as other parts of the corporation countered the loss by their profits. In this way, a competitor was immediately crushed and Standard Oil raised prices to recover losses. General Motors (GM) was so powerful that it bought or crushed the competition to maintain a monopoly. In some cases GM bought out entire companies or inventions. In other cases GM pressured government to pass laws that limited public transportation, so people would buy automobiles.

As social injustices became apparent, laws were passed to regulate the market so that competition would be fair. Companies like Standard Oil had to relinquish their monopoly by divesting their holdings. Laws were implemented to regulate the market so access would be fair. Next, an infrastructure[10] was instituted to enforce regulations. The United States Interstate Commerce Commission (ICC) is an administrative body charged with enforcing the federal laws regulating trade and communications between states within the country. A cursory knowledge of American history at the turn of the century reveals that the free market system did not work even in the United States until sufficient regulations and an adequate infrastructure were in place to insure that the market would work for the benefit of the society as a whole. In actuality the United States and Western Europe are trying to impose an economic system on the Eastern bloc countries that even they do not adhere to.

Criteria for a Free Market

Sachs argues that for free markets with private ownership, five conditions have to be met:

1) It must be realized that there is no third way, private and public ownership cannot coexist.
2) A legitimate government with political and social stability must be in place.
3) Market experience with the West is crucial.
4) There must be skilled managers in the system.
5) A sufficient infrastructure, with banks, lawyers and accountants must be in place.

To examine each of these conditions more fully, the following should be considered:

Coexisting of Public and Private Enterprise.

Governments like India have had private and government-owned industries that compete with each other. There is disagreement as to whether this was the best policy for India. But, industrial conglomerates headed by families like the Tatas and Birlas and hotel chains like the Taj and Oberoi groups have not only survived but have become international competitors.

However, the bigger issue has to do with government control and interference in industrial development. Japan and the Minidragons of Asia, Malaysia, Singapore, South Korea, Thailand, Taiwan and Hong Kong have heavy government involvement and investment in private enterprises. Central control and investment are often essential for economic growth. The Air Bus developed by England and France is competitive and successful because of government investment in the project. In fact, it may be coming to the point where even enormous companies like Boeing do not have sufficient resources to compete in research and development with subsidized projects like the Air Bus. The point is, however, that developing economies cannot compete without substantial central and/or foreign investment and centralized direction and administrative support.

Second, many essential services may be needed which are not profitable for private enterprise to enter. These can range from unprofitable air line routes to enterprises like the Tennessee Valley Authority (TVA) built during the depression. There is a time when the center has to step in and become involved, either in doing the endeavor or providing sufficient stimulus for private enterprise to accomplish the task. Either option is a central-government controlled enterprise.

Legitimacy

Institutions that demand loyalty are based on the perception of a society. Majority rule and freedom of expression do not necessarily create legitimacy; it is based on tradition. The United States had over two hundred years to establish a system that the population considers legitimate.

It was tradition that kept President Nixon, as Commander in Chief, from having the military arrest Congress when he was being threatened with impeachment. It is tradition that enables Britain to function based on the Magna Charta, in itself a brief, general document. These countries have had several hundred years of isolation from foreign involvement to establish these traditions. In countries like Romania, the meaning of democracy has not been established; and, minority groups such as the Hungarians, Gypsies or Germans perceived majority rule as a tyranny of the majority. In such a case, the end result may be social upheaval. Majority or democratic rule does not ensure legitimacy for any community. To some, democracy may mean anarchy; to others, it may be more centralized control. The meaning of democracy and freedom varies from culture to culture and nation to

nation.
Also, an economic system cannot develop unless there is a degree of political and economic stability. A viable economic system cannot exist if the society is continually interrupted by revolutions. A money-based economy is senseless if the inflation rate is so high that the people have no faith in the currency. A business cannot operate if it is continually being robbed due to lawlessness. There must be political, social and economic stability for the country to progress.

Experience with the West
Since the West is the primary supplier of capital, customers and aid to Eastern Europe,[11] it is imperative for those societies wanting to develop a free market to know the culture, banking, legal, accounting, marketing, and business practices of the West. They have to be able to negotiate, sell, analyze and deal with the West. Experience in business and cultural processes are crucial for this. Such knowledge was essential for the development of Japan and the Minidragons. It is· essential for the former Eastern bloc countries also. At present, due to the isolation imposed during the Cold War, the number of people in Eastern Europe with Western experience are limited.

Skilled Managers
Competent managers are crucial. There has to be a segment of the population which is skilled in leading and motivating employees, organizing economic activity and marketing on the local and international levels. Some societies obtain such a cadre from the educational system where there are programs to train students in business, management and manufacturing. Others have a traditional segment of the population composed of families, ethnic groups or classes that have been performing these activities for generations. However it is obtained, there must be a managerial class skilled in business and manufacturing who can take the leadership in developing these sectors of the economy.

Infrastructure

Infrastructure is a broad term which stands for supporting structures and talents necessary for economic development to take place. Sachs emphasizes banks, lawyers and accountants. But it is, of course, much broader. Markets cannot operate unless there are means to get goods to them. Thus roads and vehicles may be part of the infrastructure needed for a free market to exist. A business cannot compete equally with another business if one has a telephone and the other does not. Thus, having a viable telephone system may be crucial for having a free market to operate. Infrastructure can also include a modern banking system and government regulations and laws to allow the importation of spare parts and many other items.

A free market cannot be free unless all have equal access and the rights of all are protected. Infrastructure such as laws, regulations and enforcement systems also have to be in place for a free market to operate so that there is freedom for all. Components for an infrastructure that enables a free market to operate are enormous; the country that does not have a sufficient infrastructure cannot have a free and equitable market.

Motivation

Besides the above criteria set forth by Sachs, I would add one more, "motivation." People in the society have to have a reason to work. Money is not a sufficient motivator. People have to feel there is purpose and meaning in what they do. Unless there is a cultural framework that provides a context for participants to see meaning and purpose in what they do, they will not do the task well. Force and money are not enough.

The question still remains: can a sudden change to a free market, with emphasis on privatization, bring about positive change in the former Eastern bloc countries? Should such a change even take place? Looking at the Romanian case can give indications toward an answer.

Romania: A Case Study

Located on the Black Sea in Southeastern Europe, Romania has a population of 23,397,000 (1991 estimate). Ethnically, it consists of Romanians, 89%; Hungarians, 7.9%; Germans, 1.9% and Gypsies.[12] The geographic area is 91,699 square miles, slightly smaller than New York and Pennsylvania combined. Its population density is 225 people per square mile, but 53% of her population is urban. Romania claims a 96% literacy rate and an economy that produces steel, metals, machinery, oil products, chemicals, textiles and shoes. Romania also has a thriving tourism industry.

Historically, Romanians claim the geographical regions of Bukovina, Moldova (which includes Besserabia), Wallachia, Transylvania, Banat, Oltennia and Dobrudja as their homeland. But, under Soviet Union domination, some of these areas were divided and given to other countries; in the case of Moldova, it was divided and the Republic of Moldavia was created as a separate Soviet republic from part of the region.

Today, Romania, like other countries, is trying to forge a new direction, but there are various conflicts as to what they are expected to do and what they can do. Since the 1989 revolution, Romania has been going through the process of nation building. The process involves the development of political and economic institutions to insure national security and social stability.[13] To do this, they are pressured by the West to form a democratic political structure with an emphasis on a free market and privatization. However, they are also pressured to make these radical changes suddenly. Can this work? And, if it does work, is it good for the country or society? First, let us apply the criteria for a free market based on privatization to Romania.

Privatization

Countries like Romania are told by Western advisors that there is no third way, that public and private ownership cannot coexist. This advice is almost impossible to follow. Factories, refining companies, farmland and equipment, were under state control. How is this all to be divested equitably to the people? In the case of Romania, several processes of privatization can be identified. Vouchers which were issued to the citizens equally divided up the assets, but the redemption of these vouchers was confusing to the citizens. Should they retain them as an investment or should they redeem them for cash as soon as possible? And, with the high inflation rate, is their worth quickly evaporated? Many citizens, including educated ones, are so confused by the voucher system that they consider it worthless.

The second consideration is the actual disposition of property. Should it be awarded to those who owned it before the revolution, or should it be sold to the highest bidder? Is it right for the people who have been living in a house or farming the land for the past forty years, thinking it was theirs, to be immediately dispossessed, especially if the claim on the real estate is by a person who now lives in an urban area and will probably never return to that property? If urbanites are granted agricultural land, productivity is sure to decrease for the owners will not have the knowledge to maximize agricultural production.

Those who feel they are treated unjustly can go to court, but legal fees and the credibility of the legal profession make such endeavors questionable. Just the divestiture of public assets can be a time-consuming process, especially if no one has the money to buy government-run enterprises. Often foreign companies are not interested because Romanian technology is outmoded and inefficient. Thus, selling off the enterprise itself poses problems.

Local people do not have the capital to invest, even to buy shares in a company where they work. Under the former communist system, it was difficult, if not impossible, for a person who was not a high-ranking party member to accumulate investment capital. One might rise and obtain perks, power and influence, but money was only for those who did things illegally or who were high party officials. Unless foreign investors are interested in inefficient and obsolete technology, no one will invest so an enterprise can privatize.

Consequently, to privatize, Romania may have to either give away what others do not want, or sell it to foreigners or former communist officials. Either solution may not be the best. In selling to foreign companies, Romania loses control of her most profitable enterprises to foreigners; in selling to former communist officials, economic power goes into the hands of the former high communist officials. It is the second process that is happening in the former Eastern bloc countries--former Communist Party officials have the money and contacts to gain or maintain positions of authority and control in the new democratic system.

Legitimacy in Romania

Romania does not have a democratic tradition. Historically a type of feudal society has dominated, with an aristocratic elite and merchant class governing over a subservient peasant strata. Romania was a monarchy in the later 19th and early 20th centuries. The idea of a democratically elected parliament is recent. Thus, the country has not had time to develop a tradition to determine legitimacy. Some feel that if they did not vote for the ruling party, it is not legitimate. Minorities such as the Hungarians feel that they have no chance. For minority communities, the present government is not legitimate for them.

With the casting off of Soviet power other minorities seek independence. Thus, the Gagauz of Moldavia, a region of only twelve villages, declared themselves an independent nation in 1992. They argue that they are now "grown up" and no longer should be subservient to the government in the Moldavian capital of Kishinev. Who has the right to self determination? What the Gagauz did was consistent with Woodrow Wilson's Fourteen Points for the right of a people to have self- determination.[14] Whose vote should be considered in the majority? What or who decides if the government is legitimate? These are all questions that took decades for countries like the United States and Britain to answer; they are being asked in countries like Romania and other former Eastern bloc countries. However these countries have neither the tradition or yet the opportunity to work out an answer for themselves, one that suits their cultural, social and historical framework.

Experience with the West

It is difficult to understand how a people think differently from us, when they have not had experience in a western style market economy. Those indoctrinated in a Western market system think primarily in terms of efficiency and maximizing profits. Organization, hiring of personnel, acquisition of technology, marketing and managing are all done with the idea of either improving efficiency or maximizing profit. Under the centralized communist system, a different thought pattern developed. Managers were political appointments. Thus, a manager of an enterprise thought in terms of rising in the party apparatus. A manager was concerned with creating jobs, implementing job security, and providing benefits for his workers, such as housing. The position was used to obtain patronage from those below and to obtain contacts and give patronage to those above. Production was not according to need or market, but to post good statistics so that one could boast about production levels. Whether the items produced were sold or used was often immaterial. It was the productivity statistics that were important.

With the revolution in 1989, the managerial segment of most industries did not change. Even today, those in high managerial positions in industry, as well as workers, do not fully comprehend how to fit into the competitive world market. For too long their market was assured by the Council for Mutual Economic Assistance (COMECON) structure. Operating in a competitive atmosphere was alien to them.

In 1991 interviews of plant managers who were often managing outdated, inefficient operations, they assumed a western company would come and buy the concern and it would become profitable. They had no concept of the enterprise not being desirable, or if it was purchased, that making it profitable would entail updating technology or firing workers. By 1993, however, some of these misperceptions were changing.

Workers also do not comprehend a system where they may lose their job. For forty years employment has been assured by the state. Many now are at an age where they realize that new employment is not a viable option if they are terminated. But, instead of working harder to make the operation efficient, they often think in terms of sabotaging the operation so that the state will reclaim it.

Skilled Managers

The managerial segment of the population, whether it be in business, finance or industry was virtually eliminated under the communist regime. When the communists took over the homes and enterprises of business people, they were quickly confiscated and the people turned out. Often, the children of the intelligentsia were inhibited from going to the university. Those in positions of authority were deprived of their position and/or assets; their children were also prevented from taking the place of their parents in the economic sector. The goal of the Communist leaders was to glorify the workers and make the society less hierarchical, except for Communist Party members.

Before the Second World War, Romania had a relatively strong economy. Bucharest, the capital city, was known as the "Paris of the East." The authoritarian communist government turned out to be one of the most oppressive in Eastern Europe. The aristocratic, business and managerial segments of the population were actively attacked and deprived of their assets and the ability to use their knowledge in the development of Romania's economy. What in the past were positions based on ability, class, and assets were turned into political appointments.

While the business and managerial class were being actively eliminated, contact with the West was cut off. Literature concerning the behavioral and social sciences and business management were not allowed into the country. Thus, even those who wanted to learn about personal management and economic theory could not do so. Teaching in the universities was dominated by what the Romanian Communist Party validated as Marxist-Leninist doctrine.

The result was not only the elimination of a whole class of business and managerial people, but that this class was prohibited from rising again and any knowledge in these fields was actively fought and not allowed to enter the country. The new communist leadership were uneducated peasants and workers who were loyal party members. The goal was to gain power and use it to personal advantage. And, since the economy was tied to the Soviet bloc, efficiency and market mentality were not the means by which one gained power; it was through political maneuvering in the Communist Party apparatus.

The problem of lack of contact with the West and a market economy was most notable in the governmental bureaucracy. When companies came to look at economic opportunities in Romania, the members of the bureaucracy did not know how to talk with them, what they were interested in seeing or what information they needed. They often could not obtain the reliable information needed, and did not know how to negotiate. Initially, the feeling was that western investors would come in and buy anything and everything for any price. The common feeling was that the United States would bring in a lot of capital and make everything right with little or no effort on the part of the Romanians.

After the 1989 revolution, there was no business, industrial or entrepreneurial class to step in and help the economy start developing. There were exceptions, but for the country as a whole, these segments of the population did not exist. This was a strong inhibitor to the economic and political stability of the country.

Infrastructure

Without business, industrial and managerial experience, the creation of an infrastructure is almost impossible. Banks are needed but cannot develop because they are state controlled and the people in positions of authority do not know the needs of business and industry nor how to serve them. For example, the National Bank of Romania in 1993 was happy that they had a surplus, but instead of using that surplus to ease credit, they used the profits to repair streets in Bucharest. Because of the high and unpredictable inflation rate, they charged a 70 per cent interest rate to off-set the high inflation. No starting business could pay such charges.

Like bureaucrats, Romanian bureaucrats think in terms of the survival and maximization of the power of their institution rather than the purpose it should serve. Also, competent lawyers, accountants and managers were absent both in the private and public sector. Under the communist system professions dealing with business and finance were scorned. Students were encouraged and socialized into majoring in engineering or the hard sciences. If subjects concerning finance and business were offered, they were taught in a manner that promoted the Communist Party.

However, infrastructure is more than just skilled people. It is institutions such as proper schools, it is facilities such as roads and telephones, it is a governmental and economic bureaucracy that supports and regulates. But a revolution tears down existing structures. In addition, Romania did not have these well established before the revolution. People do not know how to proceed or know the rules governing ordinary political and economic behavior. The revolution eliminated old rules; the new ones are not yet developed.

Last, there has to be a moneyed sector in the population that has capital to invest. Knowledge and capital are both necessary. The traditional families and people performing such functions were eliminated under communist rule. The only moneyed segment of the population after the 1989 revolution were former communist party officials and illegal entrepreneurs. The former communist party members have the capital and contacts to use their money to advantage. Thus, in Romania, like many other countries of the former Soviet bloc, former communist party officials now have a stronger hold on economic and political power than ever before--all under the guise of capitalism and democracy.

Motivated Work Force

Western reports typically view former Eastern bloc workers as lazy and not motivated. However, very little is said as to why workers seem to lack the "work ethic" found in the West. Sachs points out that the process the Eastern bloc countries are going through now is unlike anything experienced in recent history. There are two possible parallels. One is the experience of colonized people when they achieved independence; the other is the description set forth in George Orwell's *1984*.

Postcolonial societies had to contend with their community and culture, on both the group and individual level, being destroyed. As in colonial societies, or plantation economies, people were forced or enticed to leave their rural communities to settle in urban areas. This was the case in Romania. The country industrialized rapidly, agriculture was collectivized, and people, especially the younger generation, were enticed or forced to move into urban apartment houses, which were built in the pattern of what can be termed "prison modern" architecture. The apartment buildings, by design, did not facilitate interaction of the inhabitants. That factor, combined with the threat of the Securitate (Secret Police) having informants everywhere, inhibited people from developing communities of support and cohesion. A community and culture did not develop. What happened was the creation of suspicious and autonomous individuals who were paranoid and anomic.

Without community development, the enculturation of a value system that would provide a way for a people to achieve meaning and purpose in life was not possible. Thus, things like having pride in one's work, or doing a good job for god, country and society, were not present. People thought only in terms of themselves.

The social structure had been destroyed. The managerial, business, professional and intelligentsia were systematically demoted into unskilled professions and their children placed at a disadvantage for getting a university education. People performing menial tasks, such as unskilled factory work and street sweeping, were paid better than doctors and accountants. Thus, when independence came, and international companies entered Romania, there was much worker discontent when professional and financial people were now better paid.

There was little or no relationship between hard work and rewards, although even Marx and Engels in the *Communist Manifesto* argued that there has to be a relationship between work and rewards. Under the Romanian communist system that did not exist. A person could work very hard on the job, but generally that had little to do with promotion. Promotions and authority were political. Job security was assured, no one was fired, and the values of loyalty to the community were destroyed. What arose was a whole population that emphasized doing as little as possible in their job. The only criteria was that they show up for work. Once they were there, they wanted to "beat the system" and anyone who worked hard was pressured to conform to the behavior of others, that is, do as little as possible.

Thus, it is not surprising that one multinational had numerous problems when it bought two local Romanian companies. First, the workers were disappointed because the company did not repaint and clean up the buildings immediately, and second, did not raise their salary by a third, although many foreign companies had done that. The company was upset when they found out they could not fire people, although later they discovered a loophole whereby they could terminate workers. When this was communicated to the employees, they immediately began to sabotage the company. The employees reasoned that if the operation was not profitable, the state would buy the enterprise and they would again have job security.

When the company started paying accountants and financial experts higher salaries, the workers in the manufacturing section were dissatisfied because they had been the higher paid. Employees had no concept of market determination. And when employees in one company, which had not been computerized and was less efficient, found out that they were paid less than an efficient computerized operation, they held strikes, for they felt that they were doing the same job and should be paid the same wage.

Pilfering was also a big problem. It had been common practice and it was difficult to stop. Since analysts were not familiar with Western companies, they did not know how to provide information in a manageable, meaningful way to the Americans who were running the operation. Older workers resented and sabotaged the efforts of younger workers who were more easily indoctrinated into the new philosophy.

Of course, the problems were not just present in the factories. The younger population who left the villages might be unemployed in the cities but they did not want to return to their villages. The agricultural population is now dominated by old people who will soon be dying off without knowledgeable people to replace them.

Implications

In this cursory treatment of the situation in Romania, the

implications are numerous. I would like to focus on a few:

First, the free market coupled with privatization in and of itself cannot solve the problems of the former Eastern bloc countries. Every successful economy to date, whether it be the United States, Japan, Korea or Malaysia, has had a high degree of governmental involvement in the economic development of the country. Malaysia did it by attracting foreign investment, Korea by giving favored treatment to a cartel, Japan, with the Ministry of International Trade and Industry (MITI), by creating an environment for Japanese industry to develop and expand at home and abroad. Thus, the involvement of the central government is crucial, the issue is how. An unregulated free market with privatization is not enough.

Second, a whole new infrastructure has to be created. Everything from roads to an educational system that creates managers and peoples sufficiently educated in the social and behavioral sciences so that people can be understood, communities can develop and workers can be motivated.

Third, more is involved than just monetary investment and technology. The crucial factor is the people issue. Societies like Germany, Korea and Japan were able to retool and develop very rapidly, in part because the people had a vision of a society, a culture that had not been destroyed. Romania, and many other Eastern bloc communities, have either never had this or it was destroyed under communist rule. Thus, the emphasis has to be on training people, educating the governmental bureaucracy, and informing the public about issues like democracy, privatization and free market. The public needs to be informed as to what these things are, how to deal with them and what to expect.

Fourth, foreign advisors, whether economists, political scientists, business people, or technicians must know the totality of the problems being faced by former Soviet bloc countries. They must know how and what the local people think, how they behave, and why they do what they do. Advisors must think in terms of a package, not in isolated solutions such as privatization and free market. Societies and cultures are systems, but market and privatization are not the all pervasive prime movers.

In my third month in Romania, I was living in a dwelling, as were most Romanians at the time, without heat and hot water. I was chilled to the inner most parts of my body. The weather had been below freezing for several weeks, and the warmest place was in the subway. Like many around me, I had only bread, potatoes and pork to eat, which was all that was available on the market.

One day I went to interview a member of USAID. As I walked into his clean warm office, it felt like I had gone to heaven. However, my view of "heaven" was shattered when the first sentence shot from his lips saying, "These Romanians must realize that if they are going to develop, they are going to have to make some sacrifices." What came immediately to my mind was, "I wonder if he would say that if he lived like I was living now, or was living like the average Romanian was living now, or if he had sacrificed for the last 40 years for his children, only to now hear an American advisor say that they must sacrifice more." Would that advisor have such an attitude if he really knew what the Romanians were going through?

Notes

1. The term "communist" as used here is not the pure form advocated by Marx and Engels in the *Communist Manifesto*, but an authoritarian system implemented by Russia and her satellite countries. It was not pure communism.

2. For scholars who perceived these events, see Daniel Patrick Moynihan in *Pandemonium: Ethnicity in International Politics* (Oxford, New York, Toronto: xford University Press, 1993) and Ernest Gellner, *Soviet and Western Anthropology* (New York: Columbia University Press, 1980) and Ernest Gellner, *State and Society in Soviet Thought* (Oxford and New York: B. Blackwell, 1988).

3. Peter Passell, "Dr. Jeffrey Sachs, Shock Therapist," *The New York Times Magazine* (27 June 1993) 52.

4. *World Net,* aired on September 25, 1990.

5. For example, see Andrew Soloman, "Young Russians Defiant Decadence," *The New York Times Magazine* (July 18, 1993).

6. The term "civil religion" stems from the phenomenon of political and economic ideology taking the fervor of a religious crusade; people, communities and nations work to convert or win others to their particular belief. Often proponents expound an ideal rather than a real application of their point of view. It is ethnocentrism in its most extreme form.

7. His views are set forth on the Public Broadcasting (PBS) program *World Net*, aired on September 25, 1990. See also Jeffrey Sachs, *Developing Country Debt and Economic Performance* (Chicago: University of Chicago Press, 1989) and Jeffrey Sachs, *Peru's Path to Recovery: A Plan for Economic Stabilization and Growth* (Washington, D.C.: Brookings Institute, 1991).

8. Francis Moore Lappè and Joseph Collins. *World Hunger: Twelve Myths* (New York: A Food First Book, Grove Press, 1986) 77-84.

9. *The Politics of Food*, a television program produced by the Public Broadcasting System (PBS) in the United States. For a more detailed but critical evaluation of a free trade and free market system, see Frances Moore Lappè and Joseph Collins, "The Free Market Can End Hunger" and "Free Trade is the Answer," *World Hunger: Twelve Myths*.

10. "Infrastructure" refers to the supporting mechanisms needed for a program to succeed. Making television available is of little value if people are not trained to repair them and spare parts are not available. The training of repair people and making spare parts available are examples of infrastructure. Infrastructure can be both a regulatory and a supporting mechanism. Having the means to prevent a company from exploiting

workers is a regulatory function. Having schools to train repair technicians is a support system, both are considered infrastructure.

11. To date, Japan has not been a major investor in the former Eastern bloc countries.

12. Although Gypsies are few in numbers, animosity against them is very strong.

13. Although national security and social stability are general goals, what these mean and the addition of other criteria vary from country to country.

14. Moynihan, *Pandemonium: Ethnicity in International Politics.*

6.
Romania's First Steps Toward Privatization
James K. McCollum

Romania emerged from its 45 years of communism with almost all productive enterprises in the hands of the government. This is, of course, the same situation that prevailed in all of the former communist bloc nations and each of them has had to devise a plan to "privatize" the state-owned enterprises to allow them to become part of a free market system. Each of the former communist nations has handled the problem in a different manner. None of them had a viable model to follow for privatization, since there has never been such a large number of enterprises in state hands that needed to be converted to the private sector.

Previous examples of privatization were scarcely applicable to the state-controlled economies of the former communist bloc. Great Britain had nationalized its steel industry under a labor government as late as 1976, only to have that industry returned to private hands under the conservative government upon its return to power. There is little to be learned from this example, however, because the British had an active securities market, hard currency, and hordes of investment capital that could be ploughed into the denationalization of the industries, three attributes that the former Soviet satellites and the former Soviet Union lack.

Chile's adventures into socialism under Premier Salvador Allende involved much more of the national economy than in Great Britain, but the socialist condition was quickly erased with the Allende assassination in 1973. In all, 470 companies, producing 24 percent of the added value to the economy were privatized after the downfall of socialism.[1] Thus, the institutionalization of the socialist command economy had not become imprinted on the Chilean economy to the extent that it had on the former Communist-party socialist states and was easily eliminated by the Pinochet dictatorship. Again there are no major lessons to be learned for the former Soviet bloc.

First, to break away from communism, Poland began with a wide-sweeping privatization plan aimed to rapidly remove the government from the business of competing with private enterprises. That rapid privatization did put many enterprises into private hands, most of them were those of foreign investors. The new owners' desires for efficiency brought about widespread unemployment as the new management eliminated many redundancies and over employment. After a year of the program, the social cost of rapid privatization became too great to sustain and the Polish government slowed the process.[2]

Czechoslovakia began a privatization process that consisted of selling vouchers to investors which would allow them to own shares of government enterprises. This plan worked slowly toward moving state-owned enterprises into private hands and perhaps has more promise for privatizing without painful social repercussions.[3] Russia also began selling vouchers in October, 1992, but initially little interest was generated.

In Romania, there were about 12,000 state-owned enterprises that could become privatized. Most of these enterprises began during the 45 years of communist rule and thus clearly belonged to the people of Romania. A relatively small number were in existence before the communists nationalized them in 1948 and there were competing claims of ownership for these enterprises. In 1990, the Romanian Parliament passed laws to begin the privatization process for some of the 12,000 enterprises and for the agricultural holdings. The process has progressed rapidly for agriculture, but more slowly for industry and commerce.

Romania's privatization is different from that of other former

Soviet bloc countries and may yet be workable. The privatization plan in Romania has been called "A program of unprecedented scope," but the results thus far have produced little movement. By mid-October, 1992, only two entire companies had gone into private hands. Thus the process, which is not expected to be completed before the end of this decade, is in its infancy and fell behind the government's schedule almost immediately.[4]

The Situation Before the Communist Takeover

Romania had a primarily agrarian economy prior to World War II. It had undergone a land reform program after World War I and much of the land was in small parcels which were owned by peasant farmers. The high productivity of the agricultural sector earned the title "Breadbasket of Europe" for the nation.

Some industry had been established prior to the communist takeover, employing only ten percent of the labor force in 1940;[5] it was relatively insignificant compared to agriculture. However, there were some innovations in the industrial sector. Romania had developed an aircraft industry and its fighter planes were used against the Soviet Union when Romania, alongside the Germans and Hungarians, invaded the Soviet Ukraine in 1941.

The nation's private industry also made locomotives, rail cars, and rails for its railways in the 1930's. Additionally, the petroleum industry was well developed and had provided most of the petroleum fuels for the Nazi war machine from 1940 to 1944. Mining of metallic ores was also a major economic asset to the Romanian economy prior to the communist takeover in 1948.[6]

Except for the petroleum industry, these nonagricultural pursuits were not well developed prior to the communist takeover. Most of the nation's work force was engaged in agriculture.

Situation During Communist Rule

Industrialization was increased under the communists, first by President Gheorge Gheorghiu-Dej, then at a much more rapid pace under Nicolae Ceausescu. Ceausescu wanted Romania to be self-sufficient in industrial outputs as well as in agriculture. In order to achieve this aim, he forced peasants to move out of farming villages and into cities where heavy industry was being established. The nation's steel-making capacity was expanded and it developed factories to make such items as trucks, tractors, automobiles, earth moving hydraulic machinery, electrical machinery, and machine tools.

For example, at the time of the Romanian Revolution in December, 1989, there were three types of automobiles being made in Romania, the Dacia, the Oltcit, and the ARO. The Dacia was made under licensing agreements with Fiat of Italy or Renault of France; the Oltcit under licensing agreements with Citron of France; and the ARO was an original design. The Romanian government also had entered into a licensing agreement with Mann of Germany and was manufacturing a truck named the Roman.

One of the biggest industries in Romania prior to the revolution was in the fabrication of rail cars. Romanian rail cars were purchased and employed throughout the Soviet Union in addition to being used on the Romanian rail network. Rail car sales provided much needed international exchange within the COMECON economic alliance.

The clothing industry was well developed in several cities throughout the country. With its large harvest of wool from Romanian sheep, knitted goods were a natural outgrowth. An electronics industry was flourishing by 1989, producing the poor quality television sets that presented the daily two hours of broadcasting that was devoted to the activities of Nicolae and Elena Ceausescu, the "he and she" exploits. Little other programming was allowed.

While the industrial buildup was occurring, Romanian farms were collectivized. Romanian state planners believed that by collectivizing agriculture, more farm labor could be released to work in the cities while agricultural outputs would also increase. The increases in farm outputs did occur, but were at a rate which did not match the population increase. Ceausescu designated agricultural outputs as major sources of foreign exchange to be used to fund his grandiose building projects and as the population increased, due to Ceausescu's policy against birth control without commensurate increases in food availability, the population's hatred of the dictator became markedly intense.

Post-Revolution Moves Toward Privatization

On December 23, 1989, one day after Nicolae and Elena Ceausescu fled from Bucharest, the newspaper *Scinteia Poporului* announced in a front page article that the forces who had toppled the Ceausescu government had "declared firmly for socialism, for the people's ownership and honest socialist principles untinged by the adventurist spirit and political demagogy of the Ceausescu clan."[7] The article claimed that the path of the Romanian people would be that of "purified socialism." It appeared that the National Salvation Front (NSF) which quickly emerged to take control of the leaderless nation intended to follow a form of socialist *perestroika* similar to that of Mikhail Gorbachev in the Soviet Union. This initiative would seem to be expected of the NSF leader, Ion Iliescu, who had long been a communist party functionary and had been demoted by Ceausescu in the 1970s, but had been a protege of Gorbachev while studying in the Soviet Union.

The NSF proposed to restructure the national economy on the criteria of profitability and efficiency and to eliminate centralized direction of the economy. It also intended to promote free initiative and competence in all of the nation's economic sectors.[8] In a January 4, 1990 speech, Prime Minister Petre Roman reported that as a result of the policies of the previous regime the Romanian economy was in a state of profound crisis and that the priority of the government would be to get the economy out of the crisis state and to start satisfying the immediate needs of the people. No shock therapy of immediate privatization was envisioned at that time, but rather, a gradual changeover without large scale dislocations would occur.

The NSF leaders were troubled by the low productivity in the economy, a state that was partially due to shortfalls in energy and raw materials. Other factors were also recognized as major contributors to the low productivity: poor work habits and labor unrest.[9] Thus the major focus of the government was to make the existing enterprises more effective by improving their leadership and getting the work force to put forth better efforts.

After the May 20, 1990 election in which Iliescu won 85% of the popular vote and the NSF won 67% of the votes for parliament seats,[10] Prime Minister Roman moved quickly to put an economic reform plan into place. On June 28, he presented a program for parliamentary approval that envisioned more rapid changes than the NSF campaigners had put forth.[11] Roman's remedy for the damage caused by the communist regime was to move most of the state enterprises into the private sector. The immediate goal was to remove the enterprises from the oversight of the central government and to give the enterprises responsibility for generating profits and accountability for their performance. The first step was not to be privatization, but semi-autonomy for the individual enterprises. The program was initiated in the Romanian Parliament by Law Number 15, "Law on State-Owned Enterprise Restructuring," in August 1990. Under that law, the companies that clearly should operate without government support or direction were separated from those that either could not operate without subsidies or should have close government regulation, or both.[12]

The first category of enterprises was called "commercial societies" or "joint stock companies" and they were required to form their own boards of directors. They were removed from the control of their respective government ministries and began to act semi-independently under their directors even though they still belonged to the state. Approximately 6,000 state enterprises were in this category at the outset. A second group of enterprises was curiously designated as "regie autonomes" (a term borrowed from the French) which translates as "self sufficient companies." They were also semi-independent, but most were not privatized. Included in this group were the traditional government monopolies of most European countries: the postal services, radio and TV stations, railroads, symphony orchestras, opera companies, and defense industries. Additionally, Romania had as regie autonomes the coal mines, oil wells, and energy distribution enterprises.

Law Number 15 also established the National Agency for

Privatization (NAP) which was created to oversee the conversion of the state enterprises to private ownership. The law required the commercial societies to undergo an evaluation and to turn over securities to the National Agency for Privatization, which represented 30% of their established capital, and NAP would use this amount to issue shares of stock worth 5,000 lei each to all Romanian citizens 18 years of age and older after December, 1990. No such stock issuance was accomplished in the mode specified in this law.

In November 1990 Law No. 31, "Company Law," was passed by the Romanian Parliament allowing the establishment of privately held companies. Private companies could be partnerships, joint-stock companies, or limited liability companies. This law was a formalization of an earlier law promulgated by the provisional government, Decree Law No. 54/1990, which had first allowed the formation and operation of private enterprises. In accordance with these laws, more than 300,000 private enterprises were in operation in Romania by May 1992 with more than 6,000 having investments of foreign capital.[13] A subsequent law (No. 58) in August 1991 decreed the transfer of 30% of the value of the commercial societies into five Private Ownership Funds (POFs). These POFs were owned by the Romanian citizens: one share of each of the funds was granted to every citizen who was 18 Years of age on December 31, 1990. Thus the stock issuance under Law Number 58 changed the implementation method, though not the intent, of getting 30% of the value of the commercial societies into the hands of the citizens.[14]

The remaining 70% of the valuation of the commercial societies was to go into a State Ownership Fund (SOF) whose directors were charged with selling these holdings to any and all investors, foreign and domestic, until the SOF no longer had anything to sell. In late 1992, the provisions of Law Number 58 was slowly being implemented. The POF certificates were available for acceptance by the citizens in late May, 1992. Boards of Directors had been appointed for the five POFs and the SOF by September, 1992. Each of the 5 POFs has a geographical region where it owned 30% of all of the commercial societies. A commodities exchange had been formed in Bucharest and the next step could be a stock exchange.

A report of the National Agency for Privatization of November, 1992, provided details of the actions accomplished under Law Numbers 15, 31, and 58. The report showed the number of commercial societies to be privatized as 6,280, with a 1991 book value of 1.5 trillion lei (about $250 billion at the 1991 exchange rate). The report stated that the figure for book value was inaccurate because it was not the same as market value and that the valuation was set at different times for the different enterprises.[15]   However, if we look at the figure that was presented, 30 percent for the Private Ownership Funds would be 450 trillion lei ($75 billion) to be divided among the 16.5 million shareholders. Thus, each shareholder was to get a certificate worth about 27,273 lei or $450.

At about the same time as the issuance of the NAP report, the commodities exchange had been formed in Bucharest. The introduction of a stock exchange would enable the SOF to sell its holdings in the marketplace.[16]

The five POFs were being organized along industrial lines with headquarters located in different sections of the country. The POFs with their designated industries were as follows:

POF I Arad:	Wood Processing; Non-Ferrous Metals
POF II Becau:	Textiles and Clothing
POF III Brasov:	Naval Transport; Fishing; Tourism and Catering
POF IV Bucharest:	Glass and Ceramic Goods; Construction Materials; Cosmetics; Pharmaceutical
POF V Craiova:	Electronics and Electrotechnics; Footwear and Leather Goods

The commercial companies in "critical" industries were spread among the five funds. These industries: ferrous metals, machine building, chemicals and petrochemicals, financial services, and insurance; were designated as "critical" industries because of the difficult financial situation they were in and due to their importance to other activities. The reasons given for dividing them as equally as possible among the POFs were those of spreading the risk, avoiding one POF being dominated by such industries, and increasing the opportunities for restructuring.

An Administrative Council of seven members appointed by the government had the responsibility of managing each of the POFs. This council supervised the trading of POF certificates and publicized the market value of their respective POF certificates. When sufficient profits were shown by a POF, its council would award dividends to POF certificate holders.

Other Law 58 provisions called for early privatization of 0.5 percent of the commercial societies (30 companies) by December 31, 1991. This date arrived with no companies privatized. Administrative procedures such as audits of enterprise evaluation were very late in their creation and thus the sell-off of these enterprises could not take place.

The legislation also allowed for the sale of "assets" of commercial societies. Assets were "stand alone" segments of larger enterprises, such as a restaurant in a hotel, or a grinding mill at a farm cooperative. The assets were to be sold in auctions conducted by NAP. Several of these auctions did take place in 1992, resulting in the establishment of approximately 1133 new private companies. A total of 6000 assets had been put up for sale, but there was much criticism of the auctions.[17] Some were by secret bid and allegations were made that the highest bidder was not the winning bidder in many cases. It was widely believed that some assets were sold at bargain prices to individuals who had influence with NAP and that foreign bids were not accepted.

Most of the assets sold were from Domestic Trade (671), with Tourism and Catering having sold 281, Manufacturing 63 and Miscellaneous.[18] The total amount of the proceeds from the auctions as of November, 1992, was 10 billion lei ($23 million).[19]

Another provision of Law Number 58 allowed employees and managers of state-owned companies to purchase ten percent of their company's stock at a ten percent discount. By September, 1992, two companies, the Ursus Brewery in Cluj and the Vranco knitting wear factory in Focsani, had been completely privatized with the employees and managers purchasing a significant amount of the shares in both enterprises.[20]

In other legislation, Law Number 35 of April, 1992, the "Foreign

Investment Law," guaranteed foreign investors that their holdings would not be nationalized except in national emergencies and that foreign investors could repatriate the dividends earned from their investments. Foreign investors were exempted from taxation on their investments in most economic activities for five years. For extractive industries the tax exemption was for 3 years and for tourism activities for 2 years.[21]

Was the framework effective? Initially, it was not. The shares of the POFs became available for distribution in late May, 1992, but nobody knew what companies were to be placed in which fund and there were no boards of directors established for the POFs or the SOFs. Street vendors were observed offering the POF certificates for 2,500 lei (about seven dollars) and by November, 1992, less than 4/5 of the eligible population had claimed their certificates. It was hoped that this transfer would have an electrifying effect on the Romanian economy as the citizens were given part ownership of the nation's enterprises, but this was not the effect at the outset. Throughout 1992, the nation's economy staggered along with decreased productivity and increasing inflation and unemployment. Inflation was at ten percent per month by the end of 1992.

With the formation of the SOF Board of Directors, some new initiatives were contemplated. An SOF Board member stated in December, 1992, that the SOF would hold auctions for small state-owned companies beginning in January, 1993. He defined small enterprises as those with fewer than 500 employees. Within the year, medium sized enterprises would also be auctioned off. In the SOF's plan, the proceeds from these sales would be used to modernize the larger enterprises to make them more productive.[22]

Other Economic Factors

Many troubles of the Romanian economy could not be solved immediately by privatization and some Romanians believed it was a "trick" or a smoke screen to make them believe they were getting something worthwhile. Other problems included that of equity for former owners of enterprises or property that had been expropriated by the communist regime. The legislation was implemented slowly in 1992 to compensate them for their losses in the nationalization of 1948. A judge's ruling on the matter stated that legislation was unnecessary and that former owners could simply reclaim their property. By the end of 1992, it was still questionable as to whether this solution was workable. Many former property owners indicated that they were afraid to simply try to evict the present occupants of the disputed property and would rather have a piece of legislation to specify the rules of reclamation.[23]

Other pressing problems needed to be addressed. The overworked banking system was in need of an overhaul to improve communications and with that, the ability to transfer funds. Even with a 1990 decree that authorized the activities of private banks, by March, 1992, only fourteen commercial banks were operating in this nation of 23 million people. The dearth of financial institutions was a bottleneck to the granting of loans and honoring financial investments. Checking accounts were non-existent and the country was trying to do business in the modern world with a "cash economy".[24] Of course, as long as the Romanian lei was not convertible into hard currency, serious delays would occur in international transactions. Ingenious Romanian business people were dealing with these problems at that time through barter systems and three-way deals.

Prior to November, 1991, many businesses had large dollar accounts in Romanian banks. Suddenly they found that all of their dollars had been converted to lei by the central bank. The reason this measure was taken was because Romania's hard currency accounts had fallen to 1/4 of that recommended by the International Monetary Fund and the promised aid from the G-24 (the 24 most developed countries) had not yet been received.[25] After months of frustration to Romanian business managers, this problem was partially solved when the central bank president announced that after May 1, 1992, businesses could again have dollar accounts and would use 70 percent of the dollars that they carried in those accounts. However, there was still a long lag between the time that businesses deposited their payments on accounts and the time that they could use the money. Enterprise managers called it the "blockage."

Managers who had significant business with the West before

1988 said their three greatest needs were "the clause, the clause, and the clause", referring to the Most Favored Nation (MFN) status with the United States which former dictator Nicolae Ceaucescu renounced in that year.   Although the U.S. signed a bilateral trade agreement with Romania in May, 1992,[26] there was no reinstatement of MFN status when the national elections put the former communist, Ion Iliescu, back in office for another four years. Iliescu won in a runoff election in October, 1992, with some claims of election fraud lodged at the time of the elections.[27]

Meanwhile, Prime Minister Stolojan and the members of the government, particularly in the Romanian Development Agency and the National Agency for Privatization, were pushing to get privatization implemented as soon as possible.

Difficult times were in store for Romania whether privatization occurred or not.   Stolojan indicated in August, 1992, that he would close 100 of the unprofitable large enterprises by year's end, causing an unemployment increase, from   700,000 to over one million.   Stolojan believed that privatization would help the country recover more quickly than the state-continued ownership of the enterprises.   Poland's performance in 1992 tended to validate Stolojan's position as that country began operating successfully in the free market.[28]   This was also a validation of Kornai's belief that rapid restructuring will get the unneeded employees out of the large state enterprises and into commercial and service sector jobs where they are needed.[29]

While the October, 1992, election put Ion Iliescu back into the presidency for another four years and the fragmented parliament elected a like-minded NSF functionary, Nicolae Vacaroiu, as prime minister the move toward privatization did not diminish. Iliescu and Vacaroiu feared the social upheaval of rapid privatization, but they also desired the acceptance of Romania into the family of nations.[30]   They might slow the pace of privatization, but it is unlikely that the process would be cut to the point that it could not eventually succeed, as it apparently has in Poland.

Interviews of State Enterprise Managers

In interviews with managers in 67 state enterprises between April and September, 1992, the author was told that privatization is desired by all of the state enterprises. The average employment in these enterprises was 2,091. The largest was the Sidex, S.A. steel works at Galati with 38,000 employees and the smallest would be any of several hotels which employed between 30 and 50 people.

Generally, the top manager gave the responses for the enterprise and universally the managers were in favor of privatization. The benefits they expected to receive from privatization, from most frequently mentioned to the least, were: improved productivity, funds for modernization, and ability to provide incentives for employees. The only disadvantage mentioned was unemployment resulting from the need for more efficiency in a free market environment. On average, the 67 enterprises were employing 20 percent fewer employees at the time of the 1992 interview than they were at the time of the 1989 revolution. The managers estimated the time required to privatize their enterprise and the average of the 67 estimates would be 2.5 years. Some believed they could be privatized within one year. Others felt that the process might take as long as 5 years and there were many estimates between these extremes.

The managers enumerated the problems in the Romanian economy. Among them were: financial blockage, lack of raw materials, need for expansion of the banking system, need for foreign investment, need for the most favored nation status with the U. S., and others. All had faith, however, that Romania, with its abundant resources and well-educated work force would eventually be able to overcome these difficulties and perform well in a free market setting.

Summary

Almost all of Romania's enterprises were in state hands after the revolution that overthrew the communist dictator, Nicolae Ceaucescu. The National Salvation Front which took up the reins of government after the revolution attempted to retain a socialist economy, but was blocked by prime minister Petre Roman and other liberal NSF members who recognized that the nation's enterprises would be efficient and viable only after they had passed into private hands. Thus, a series of decrees and legislative acts were created by the Romanian government which set the stage for privatizing at least 6000 of the state enterprises. But, the Romanian government's timetable for privatization in the first years was not met; few state enterprises were in private hands at the end of 1992 although the process was continuing. However, 1133 former "assets" were transformed into private companies and were competing with the more than 300,000 newly created private companies. The competition from the private companies and the recognition that the survival of the enterprises was at stake provided the incentive to continue the privatization drive. Managers in state enterprises wanted privatization to occur as early as possible. They saw many benefits to privatization and continued to argue for it.

Notes

1. *The Economist* 7725 (1991).

2. Austrian Finance Minister, Keynote Address, Conference on Privatization, Vienna (February, 1992).

3. Mark Mowery, "Czechoslovakia: Good Start on Reform Improves Business Climate," *Business America* (April 1992) 20.

4. Jacques Neher, "Privatization: A Program of Unprecedented Scope," *Institutional Investor* (March 1992) 14-17.

5. Comisia National Pentru Statistica (1992). *Anuarul Statistic Al Romaniei* (Bucharest: 1991) 98-101.

6. Ian M. Matley. *Romania: A Profile* (New York: Praeger, 1970).

7. *Scinteia Poporului* (December 23, 1989) 1, 2.

8. "Comunicatul Catre Tara al Consiliului Frontului Salvarii Nationale," *Monitorul Oficial al Romaniei* (December 22. 1989) 1.

9. "NSF Holds Final Meeting Before Reformation," *BBC Summary of World Broadcasts* (Bucharest Home Service, Aired on February 3, 1990).

10. "Final Election Results," BBC Summary of World Broadcasts (Rompres in English, Aired on May 25, 1990).

11. "Petre Roman Presents Government Programme and New Ministers," BBC Summary of World Broadcasts (Bucharest Home Service, Aired on May 25, 1990).

12. Romanian Development Agency. *Law Digest for Foreign Investors* (February 1992) 7-11.

13. National Agency for Privatization (1992). *Privatization Programs in Romania* (Bucharest: November, 1992) 1-29.

14. *Wall Street Journal* (November 5, 1992) A-6.

15. National Agency for Privatization. *Privatization Programs in Romania* (Bucharest: November, 1992) 13.

16. *Wall Street Journal* (November 5, 1992) A-6.

17. Gheorghe Zaman, Director of Economics, Romanian Academy, Interview (December 14, 1992).

18. Barbu Mihaescu, Director, Technology Marketing, Electrical Engineering Institute, Interview (August 27, 1992).

19. National Agency for Privatization (November, 1992).

20. Barbu Mihaescu, Director, Technology Marketing, Electrical Engineering Institute, Interview (August 27, 1992).

21. Romanian Development Agency. *Law Digest for Foreign Investors (Bucharest: June, 1992)* 115-124.

22. Zaman Gheorghe, Director of Economics Section, Romanian Academy, Interview (December 14, 1992).

23. Gary Humphrey, "Romania: Bump Starting the Economy," *Euromoney* (September-October 1991) 6-8.

24. Jacques Neher, "Banking: Expanding to Meet New Needs," A Special Sponsored Section. *Institutional Investor* (March 1992) S 18-19.

25. _____, "Romania: A New Course for the 'Nineties," *Institutional Investor* (March 1992) S 3-6.

26. "Eagleburger Signs Agreement," *Nine O'clock* (Bucharest: May 28, 1992) 1.

27. Ion Cristoiu, "O Noua Iluzie Spulberata," *Lumea Libera Romanesca* (October 28, 1992) 1.

28. Barry Newman, "Vital Signs Point to Poland's Recovery," *Wall Street Journal* (October 22, 1992) A-10.

29. Janos Kornai. *The Road to a Free Economy: Shifting from a Socialist System* (New York: W. W. Norton & Company).

30. George Flowers, Chief of Economic Section, American Embassy, Bucharest, Interview (December 10, 1992).

Part Three

Other Post-Communist Countries

7.

Poles in the Newly Independent States of Lithuania, Belarus and Ukraine:
A Case Study of Inherited Past and Uncertain Future
Z. Anthony Kruszewski

"Polonia", the Polish minority in the newly independent republics of Belarus, Lithuania and Ukraine, is a residue of the 1386-1795 rule of the Polish-Lithuanian Commonwealth over the territory now encompassing Latvia, Lithuania, Belarus and two-thirds of the contemporary Ukraine[1]. Forty-six percent of the pre-1939 Polish Republic's territory is also included in that area.

These Poles were reduced from their former status as members of the ruling group to a subject and oppressed minority by punitive Tsarist policies that followed the nineteenth century Polish uprisings, the 1917-22 Soviet Revolution and War Communism, the Stalinist terror of 1936-38, the post-1936 mass deportations to the interior of the USSR and post-World War II border changes and population transfers.

The Polish interwar autonomous regions, schools, theaters and cultural activities[2] were completely destroyed by the Stalinist terror, except in Lithuania where the reactivation of the schools and cultural activities was permitted after World War II. The large Polish minority, one to two million strong, has been rapidly losing its native language. Until Gorbachev's *glasnost*, the Poles, along with the Jews and the Germans of the USSR, were the largest minorities singled out for such treatment. The collapse of the Communist system and the independence of the Baltic republics, Belarus and Ukraine brought about the revival of sociocultural activities and a quest for national identity among the titular nations of these states and their minorities.

The Poles within the borders of the former USSR have lived there at least since the thirteenth and fourteenth century and are mostly the descendants of the waves of Polish colonization that were triggered by the Polish-Lithuanian Union of 1386. Recent research suggests, however, the presence of the Polish colonies in Lithuania and the Rus' prior even to the thirteenth century.[3] Those Poles were in all likelihood descendants of prisoners of war captured by the Lithuanians and Ruthenians in the numerous wars that predated the union, which the latter was supposed to prevent in order to face the challenge of a new common enemy (which appeared on the coast of the Baltic in 1228), the Teutonic Knights. The subsequent Polish colonization of the areas in question followed a much earlier wave of compulsory Polish settlement. The far-reaching immigration of Polish peasants and nobility who received land grants from the Polish rulers resulted in a considerable and marked transformation of many parts of that territory.[4]

Their numbers grew in spite of the demographic setbacks after each war and the ensuing depopulation. The Polish population peak was reached toward the end of the eighteenth century during the partitions of Poland between her three rapacious neighbors--Russia, Prussia and Austria. Russia received the bulk of both the population and the territory of the old Polish-Lithuanian Commonwealth. The nineteenth century Polish uprisings, especially those of 1830 and 1863, were brutally suppressed by the Tsarist government. The reprisals were of great importance for the future status of the Polish population. Confiscated Polish landed estates were allocated to Russian generals or sold to the Russian upper classes. Those changes in land ownership markedly altered the position of the Polish community.[5] Although small peasant holdings were not greatly affected (the peasants generally did not participate in those uprisings *en masse*), there were notable exceptions; the dispossession of many vast Polish land holdings turned the balance of power in the countryside in favor of the Russians.

Finally, the Soviet revolution not only eliminated all remaining Polish estates but also affected the Polish peasants during the collectivization campaigns. Most of the land then owned by the Poles was but a fraction of original holdings given by the Polish kings and native aristocrats to the Polish settlers during the period between the fourteenth and seventeenth centuries. Loss of land effectively undercut the Polish position in the Borderlands and *de facto* closed that chapter of history by terminating their political and social domination in those territories. It is estimated that there were over five million Poles in the Borderlands before the Soviet Revolution. With their political and social power gone, there would occur the first exodus of upper classes from the Borderlands, the Polish "*Kresy,*" toward other ethnic parts of Poland.[6]

The Soviet Revolution was followed by the re-establishment of independent Poland. As a result of the Polish-Soviet War of 1919-21, areas now known as Western Belarus and Western Ukraine were allocated to Poland under the Treaty of Riga of 1921. Under that treaty a transfer of over 1.2 million Poles from the Union of Soviet Socialist Republics (USSR) was authorized and completed. A drastic reduction of the strength of the Polish population, in the areas east of the border established at Riga which became part of the USSR, left only 863,300 Poles in that area by 1931.[7] Educated Poles in general (but especially the former petty nobility, bourgeoisie and middle class) left for the new Poland. This strengthened the Polish presence in the *Kresy* area left to Poland but irrevocably weakened the strength of the Polish communities in the USSR.

A total sociopolitical restructuring of that community by the new Soviet government followed. Besides industrialization and agricultural collectivization there was also an attempt to build a new Polish-Soviet intelligentsia of worker/peasant origin to replace the educated classes which left for Poland.

Autonomous Polish areas, according to the Leninist nationality principles, were established. One such area was in the Ukrainian Soviet Socialist Republic (SSR), in the Zhitomir area, west of that city--with the town of Dolbych/Markhlevsk as a center--and was named the Markhlevski Polish Autonomous *Rayon*. The second autonomous *rayon* was west of Minsk, capital of the Belarussian SSR, with the town of Koydanov/Dzerzhinsk as center, and was named the Dzerzhinski Polish Autonomous *Rayon*; the latter was just a few miles east of the Polish-Soviet 1921-39 border.[8] That those two regions were purely Polish warranted a special political-administrative treatment, although Polish minorities were to be found all over the Ukrainian and Belorussian republics and in a few other parts of the Russian SSR.

In implementing the Leninist nationality principles, two institutions of higher education for the training of the teachers were established in Kiev and Minsk. Those capital cities also boasted Polish theaters and other sociocultural organizations. A fully developed Polish high school and grade school system was set up in the localities where there were at least ten Polish-speaking students. A Polish language daily, *Mlot* (Hammer), was published in Minsk, Belorussia, in the 1920s.

These measures were aimed at creating a new Communist-oriented Polish intelligentsia in the USSR. The overwhelming (over 80%) proportion of the Polish minority in the USSR, until 1939, were peasant in origin. Under communist rule they were remolded socially and economically, not very differently from all other segments of the Soviet society. Anti-Polish biases did exist, due to the centuries-old Polish sociopolitical domination of the areas described, but was officially frowned upon. The initial post-revolutionary terror was directed, ironically enough, by Felix Dzerzhinski, a Polish nobleman and close friend and associate of Lenin, primarily against the remnants of the former leading classes.

All this was to change during the 1930s Stalinist purges and terror against the society at large. By 1936 both Polish Autonomous regions were abolished and a large part of the Polish community was either expelled or forcibly resettled in the interior of the Russian republic or in Kazakhstan.[9] All the Polish sociocultural institutions and organizations were closed by 1939.

The Ribbentrop-Molotov Pact of August 23, 1939, which divided

Poland between the USSR and Nazi Germany, brought into the USSR not only Ukrainians and Belorussians but also some 3,500,000 to 4,200,000 Poles as well.[10] The two figures suggest the difficulty of assessing the size of the Polish community there. The first is based on the religious criterion of the Roman Catholic faith, according to the 1931 Polish census. Although the census was subject to manipulation by the Polish authorities, the Belorussian and the Ukrainian citizens of pre-1939 Poland often feared being classified as non-Poles, so it would be realistic to extrapolate and accept 3,800,000 as the size of the Polish community in the pre-1939 Eastern Poland annexed by the USSR.[11]

That figure was increased by the inclusion of the Bialystok area in the 1939 Soviet borders and the influx of refugees from the Nazi-ruled part of Poland. The sizeable Polish communities in Lithuania and Latvia and the Romanian provinces annexed in 1940 by the USSR should also be included. Hence we arrive at a possible minimum of over 5 million + 0.9 million (old Polonia) + 250,000 in Lithuania + 60,000 in Latvia + 65,000 in Romania + 3,000 in Estonia[12] + undetermined numbers of refugees from Nazi-occupied parts of Poland (possibly 100,000 to 200,000).

The Polish minority in the annexed Eastern Polish *Kresy* was able to retain most of their schools and cultural organizations, although obviously Communized in form and context, until the Nazi attack on the Soviet Union in June of 1941. They were, however, brutally decimated by a series of deportations in 1940 and 1941 which affected at least 1.2 million Poles in the areas annexed by the USSR in 1939, some 32% of the total.[13] Although it is impossible to assess precisely the numerical scale of those deportations and the death toll which followed in Siberia, the interior of Russia, and the Central Asian republics, it is accepted that at least half of them died there. Those losses associated with prison terror, executions and wholesale deportations of various professional groups *in toto* account thus for at least 12% of the pre-1939 Polish population of Eastern Poland occupied by the Soviets.

Hence those losses percentage-wise do equal the losses inflicted on the Poles under Nazi-occupation (c. 3 million of the 24 million).[14] Whereas the latter have been fully documented by scholars since World

War II, until 1988 the losses of the Eastern Poles due to the Stalinist
terror were documented only in the West. The collapse of Communism
in Poland in 1989 permitted documentation of the history of
deportations, the Katyn Forest Massacre, and the status of the former
Soviet Polonia.

As if such a decimation were not tragic enough, those Eastern
Polish territories also suffered losses at the hands of the Nazis who
occupied the area for three years (1941-1944). Hence, the Polish *Kresy*
were brutalized by both totalitarian oppressors of World War II--the
Nazis and the Stalinists. Furthermore, instead of liberation, that
community was subjected to the ultimate disaster, the loss of their
homes after the end of World War II. The population transfers affected
some three million Eastern Poles by 1958.

The initial wave of transfers from the territories of the Lithuanian,
Ukrainian and Belorussian republics in 1944-1947 affected over 1.7
million Poles who were resettled in the Western Territories newly
acquired from Germany under the Potsdam Treaty of August 1, 1945.
The migration forced by the westward shift of Soviet borders, which
were now to include 46% of the pre-1939 territory of the Second Polish
Republic, caused tragic human hardships. It split many families as the
older generations often opted to stay in order to save their homes, while
the children were more inclined to move into Poland within her new
borders. The difficulty of making such a harrowing decision is
documented by the fact that the number of those initially registered for
the transfer was larger by 50% than the number of people who actually
left for Poland.[15]

The people who opted for transfer also lost *de facto* contact with
their families who remained within the USSR, as the new border
became almost impenetrable until the advent of *glasnost* in the late
1980s. Until 1989 the entire 1200 kilometers of new Polish-Soviet
border had only two border road crossings and three railroad
crossings.[16]

In spite of the losses during the Stalinist and Nazis terrors and the
population exchanges, at least 750,000 Poles live in Lithuania and

Belarus, according to the 1989 census figures, but it is probably at least twice that many, mostly in the areas which formed the pre-1939 territory of the Polish state. Because of the violent nature of the Polish-Ukrainian nationalist confrontations almost all the Poles from the Western Ukrainian areas fled to Central Poland before 1944 or transferred out after World War II.[17]

Hence, the Poles living today in Ukraine are the tragic remnants of the pre-1939 Soviet Polonia who somehow escaped the 1936 expulsion to Siberia and Kazakhstan. They now live east of the prewar Polish-Soviet border in the Zhitomir, Vynnitsa and Khmelnitski *oblasti*. The distribution of the Polish minority in Lithuania and Belarus is, however, still reminiscent of the pre-World War II situation, in spite of the effect of the postwar population transfers. The Poles still live in a stretch of territory from the border city of Grodno to Daugavpils on the Dvina in Latvia.[18]

The Polish population of the USSR is overwhelmingly rural, except for a large urban concentration in Vilnius (Wilno) of over 100,000 Poles, who form some 19% of the city's population. Ironically enough, it almost equals numerically the prewar Polish population of Wilno, which was 126,000.[19] The only other sizable Polish urban population is that of Grodno, Lida, Lviv (Lwow) and Zhitomir (the last city is within the pre-1939 borders of the USSR).

The total number of Poles in the USSR officially decreased from 1.38 million in 1959 to 1.1 in 1980.[20] But, those figures are a result of manipulation and pressure, especially *vis a vis* the "undesirable" minorities. This is fully documented by the latest issue of the *Soviet Encyclopedia* which does not provide specific data nor the distribution by *oblast* of the Polish community in its major area of settlement in the Belorussian SSR, as if to hide the fact that the area around Grodno and Lida (two major cities) is still overwhelmingly Polish.[21]

Such data is beginning to be published in the Polish press and the area of Grodno is shown on the map of the former USSR as being more Polish than the area west of the post-World War I Curzon Line, inside Poland and beyond the border, which was supposedly drawn on ethnographic lines.[22] Such an admission, on the Soviet map, questions the rationale used to set the 1945 Polish-Soviet border.[23]

There are very few post-World War II descriptions of the Soviet Polonia, either from Soviet or Polish sources. The paucity of Soviet sources does suggest Soviet uneasiness about the fate of the Poles in the USSR. After 1989 the Polish government broke its silence over the fate of the Soviet Poles.[24] The beginning of a veritable flood of contacts, discussions and publications can be dated from the visit of General Wojciech Jaruzelski in Vilnius/Wilno after his meeting with Soviet Secretary General Gorbachev in 1986.

In contrast, all contacts with the Western "Polonians" were not only encouraged but propagandized and very often subsidized by the Polish Communists. That attitude had been always denounced by the Polish and "Polonian" leaders in the West as irresponsibly hypocritical, without a similar policy directed toward the Soviet Poles. Since 1989 that duplicity has been removed.[25]

Now, for the first time in half a century the Soviet Poles were allowed to come to Poland to study at the Polish universities (they were always excluded from the Soviet-Polish student and scholar exchanges), visit their families and come as tourists. Likewise, the Poles are visiting Poland's new neighbors, areas which have been largely off limits to them since the end of World War II (except for main transit highways and railroads). The sudden influx of visitors (some seven million entered Poland from the East in 1992) from both sides resulted in the opening of new highway border crossings--two each into Lithuania and Belarus and more promised. This new transborder traffic reached the point of being a mass phenomenon, resulting in a series of agreements which would also facilitate the rescue, conservation and protection of the Polish cultural heritage in the former Polish Eastern territories.

In spite of the drastic political changes, the fate and very survival of the Poles in the East as a group is still basically endangered. The Poles, while being the second largest population, still suffer from the results of past national policy discrimination. The Polish autonomous *rayons* were never reactivated. Likewise, no schools, theaters or Polish organizations were allowed outside of Lithuania until *glasnost*, except in the Lviv area of Ukraine, where two Polish schools were also allowed to open in the Lviv/Lwow area after the Polish community there pushed for the expansion of the Polish schools.[26] The Polish minority, next to the Jews and Germans, was the only million-plus community subjected to de-nationalization. Those three groups were the only communities of their size which did not benefit from Soviet federalism and which did not enjoy some administrative autonomy in the Soviet federal system. Of these three groups, even during *glasnost* the Poles fared the worst of all at the hands of the Soviet Government. After 1958, the Poles were not allowed to migrate to Poland while Jews and Germans were selectively allowed to exit.

Poles in the former USSR had the lowest percentage (15%) of native language speakers of all large Soviet nationality groups.[27] This data might still be a result of manipulation, but it documents the fate of the Polish community within the USSR. The almost total lack of schooling in the Polish language is considered to be the overriding element in the rapidly progressing denationalization of the Poles in the former USSR. The nearly total disinterest in the past of the Polish Communist regime on that issue, until a few years before the collapse of Communism, largely deprived the Poles in the USSR of even meager support for educational materials in the Polish language.

That situation was described as critical in the Polish press. The policy reversal by the Polish government since 1988 allowed new initiatives to be undertaken, to rescue the Soviet Polonia from Russification and rapid assimilation. The summer of 1989 saw a first: a visit by Polish scholars from the USSR at the Third Meeting of the Scholars of Polish Extraction in Warsaw and the appearance of Poles from the USSR at Polish universities. A political taboo had been finally broken and an open Polish-Soviet dialogue on those issues began.[28]

The rebuilding of the Polish cultural life in the former Eastern Polish area began in earnest after the collapse of Communism. The rebuilding has been receiving impetus from the Lithuanian Poles who have been providing both their experience and some educational materials to the Poles in other areas. But in some areas (Belarus and Western Ukraine) local authorities often still try to prevent reorganization by delaying the permits for the opening of Polish schools, clubs or sociocultural organizations. Attempts have been made to deny the very existence of the Poles, by advancing the argument that those in question are not Polish but Lithuanians, Belarussians or Ukrainians, who happen to speak Polish.[29]

In Belarus, attempts are also being made to deny the very existence of Polish ethnic areas, which in the past were officially reclassified as non-Polish ones. Pressures are still applied to prevent the opening of Polish-language classes, which by law must have a minimum of ten students; administrative pressure is often used to scare away parents attempting to enroll the tenth child. The reopening of Polish language church services in the Roman Catholic parishes, which had been destroyed, is proceeding slowly yet persistently. A recent analysis demonstrated the existence of some 250 Roman Catholic parishes in the *Kresy* reestablished through the relentless efforts of local Poles.

Generally the quest to reestablish the local parishes of the Catholic church is by far the most effective weapon in the rebuilding of Polish spiritual and sociocultural life in the former Polish Borderlands. It is largely due to the time-honored criterion, a Catholic equals a Pole, as perceived by the Belarussians and Ukrainians. Religious activity is also apparently still seen as less challenging and more "neutral" in the eyes of the local leaders.

The rebuilding and reorganization of the Catholic parishes is often linked with the reopening of churches (some of considerable historic value) dating back to the sixteenth century. It helps parishioners to obtain permits when the petitions are couched in the language of the cultural preservation of the buildings which have fallen into disrepair and ruin or been used as warehouses. In such cases the repairs are done spontaneously by the community. The rebuilding is often achieved in a relatively short time considering the universal shortage of building materials in the former USSR. All such materials and labor have been donated. The descriptions of such activity suggest the existence of vast untapped human and material resources which are being used in the interest of rebuilding the communities.

The slow but steady growth of Polish Catholic organized life is hampered by the very lack of Polish-language parish priests. The few local Polish-language priests are often in their seventies and eighties. The others, an overwhelming percentage, were trained in the only remaining seminaries, the Vilnius Catholic Seminary, with Lithuanian as the language of instruction, and the Riga Catholic Seminary with instruction in Russian.[30] Most new priests serving newly reopened parishes are graduates of the Riga Seminary, even if they are of Latvian or German nationality. Additionally, priests from Poland are sent there with approval of Poland's eastern neighbors.

In the Vilnius seminary compulsory fluency in the Lithuanian language, although useful in the training of the future priest for the Lithuanian parishes, is a real barrier for the students of other nationalities. There is also a growing conflict about the reintroduction of Polish in the reopened Lithuanian and Belarusian parishes.[31] The lack of Polish-language priests, who were mostly killed during the Stalinist terror or emigrated or died in the intervening years, forms a real barrier to reestablishing Polish religious and cultural life. But, in spite of such problems there is a relatively rapid regrowth of Polish life.

The role of the church parish in the reorganization of Polish life cannot be underestimated. The church parish traditionally functioned as the pillar of such activity, which was one of the reasons for its destruction at the hands of the Communist security authorities in the 1940's. Hence, the importance of the current nationality struggle in those areas.[32] The struggle over liturgical language is also waged within the Catholic church between Lithuanians, Poles and Belarussians. Poles who themselves now speak Ukrainian or Belarussian at home generally insist on liturgy in Polish and are perceived as Poles by their neighbors.

Thus, the Catholic church played a key role in Polish national revival in the old *Kresy* and functions as an anchor for all the other cultural and educational activities in the villages. Conversely, reopening the Polish language schools and cultural organizations is almost impossible without the reopening of the church and reintroduction of Polish language services. The lack of Polish language priests has been remedied with the help of the Polish Catholic hierarchy in Poland, which obtained the necessary permission from the newly independent states to allow priests from Poland to function in the territories in question.

The well-publicized pastoral visit in 1988 of the Polish Primate Joseph Cardinal Glemp to Belarus, where he made an extensive visitation of the Polish parishes, was historically momentous. Glemp was the first Polish head of the Catholic church in 50 years to be allowed to make such a visitation. He also had meetings with the local Orthodox church leaders, the first such high level ecumenical meetings between Catholics and Orthodox. Obviously this was approved at the then highest Soviet governmental level.[33]

It is necessary to stress the connection between the denationalization of the Soviet Poles and lack of Polish-language schools since the increase in the percentage of native language use, now about 15%, cannot be achieved without rebuilding the Polish schools. That problem has, however, several potentially explosive dimensions (i.e., different attitudes towards minorities at various levels of government in the newly independent states). Pitting various nationalities against each other in competition for scarce public resources arouses their quest to preserve their respective linguistic sphere of influence. Unfortunately, it also falls in line with the "divide and rule" syndrome of past Soviet nationality policy.[34]

The other aspect, as explained to this author during research trips to Lithuania, Belarus and Ukraine, is the fact that the use of the Belarussian language in the schools, especially in the cities, had been previously suppressed; use of Ukrainian in Kiev, Kharkiv and the Donbass region was severely restricted by the immigration of the Russians and by administrative restrictions.

Further growth of the Polish language undoubtedly will create severe problems for Belarussian and Ukrainian officials, who see the revival of a Polish minority language to be at their own expense. Such feelings have already brought forth a long- ignored language conflict between the Lithuanians and Poles in the Vilnius (Wilno) area, which has been bitterly argued in the Polish and Lithuanian language press and in radio and at Lithuanian political meetings. For the first time since the days of the independent Lithuanian republic, that issue has appeared full blown. Books describing such past tensions in the early 1940s have also appeared.[35]

The reemergence of ethnic and linguistic conflicts and tensions, exacerbated by the civil war in the Caucasus, spread to a less publicized arena. While the collapse of Communism has undoubtedly allowed for a redressing of many discriminatory practices *vis a vis* the Polish minority in the former USSR, it also has reopened many interethnic conflicts and issues which were formerly carefully hidden from public view. There is an air of urgency in the attempts being made to find an interethnic accommodation, in order to bring tolerance to an area that exacted such a human toll and brought misery and hatred.

The revival and return of the organized Polish cultural, religious and educational life makes for the normalization of policies after nearly half a century. It is both a great opportunity and a challenge for the Polish, Belarussian and Ukrainian nations. Likewise, most of the discussions, which are ongoing in the mass media and organizations, are generally far less nationalistic and emotionally charged than previously.

There is, unfortunately, still a tendency to revive old historical grievances, especially between the Poles and the Lithuanians. Lithuania, alone among the seven states bordering Poland, refused to sign a comprehensive treaty with Poland, demanding that the latter should include in it an official condemnation of General Zeligowski's occupation in Vilnius in 1920. The Polish side remembers the clashes between the Polish underground Home Army (1941-1944) and the Lithuanian Nazi-organized police and army units, which participated in pogroms. Likewise, they remember the Lithuanians who responded that in both cases they were protecting their national identity. The post-Communist tensions between both nationalities center on the privatization of land, a mainstay for the Polish minority's existence, which is complicated by the Lithuanian refusal to honor pre-World War II Polish deeds and documentation. The role of the old Polish-Lithuanian Commonwealth (1386-1772) is viewed negatively by Lithuanian historians who blame it for the loss of Lithuanian identity and the

Polonization of the elites.

The positive diplomatic stand of Poland in accepting the present borders, not supporting the separatism of the Polish minority and eschewing any territorial claims should undoubtedly serve to remove tensions over time. Those positions are based on the premise that both nations need each other in full partnership. Once European standards are implemented fully for the Polish minority, guaranteeing its cultural, economic and linguistic rights, the internal tensions are bound to lessen between both nationalities.

It remains to be seen if present generations can avoid the nationalistic pitfalls of the past and thus contribute to a historical breakthrough in an area of Europe which has not been known for such a positive approach. Currently, however, many old prejudices and positions are being reenacted as the Wilno Poles, ironically enough (because of their Slavic linguistic background), sided initially with the Russians against the Lithuanians fighting for their own national revival. The predominantly Polish Vilnius rural and Salcininkai districts, however, voted 57% and 53% for Lithuanian independence in the poll-plebiscites held in February of 1991.[36]

Are we facing more of the same errors from the past? Or, is it an opportunity to close the sordid chapters of nationalist tragedies once and forever for the sake of a better joint future for the Poles, Lithuanians, Ukrainians and Belarussians without any thought of national domination over each other? A historical opportunity is unexpectedly available for the present generation to fashion a better future, for all people who love that part of Europe, so steeped in the past.

Appendix
The Polish Minority in Lithuania: General Data (1993)

Polish Population over 250,000 or 7% of Lithuania.

Poles comprise 19% of the population of Vilnius and are a majority of population of the Vilnius rural and Salcininkai regions, i.e. 63% and 81%, respectively. In Sviencienis region the proportion is 29% and Trakai 24%.

There are 128 schools in Lithuania teaching Polish to 11,000 students. That number is growing. A new Polish school is being built in Vilnius. In 24 other institutions Polish is also taught in the weekend courses, while 484 students received instruction in Polish high schools in 1990/91 - some of them in Vilnius are technical, pre-medical and educational ones. Poles studying at the Lithuanian colleges and universities numbered 2,500; since 1989 additional Poles also were allowed to attend Polish universities. Vilnius Pedagogical Institute offers Polish Language and Literature. The number of Polish college graduates has been growing since the 1970's. In the last twenty years it has grown by a factor of 4.5 but the Poles are still placing last (according to education) among the Lithuanian minorities.

Some 13 Polish organizations have been formed since 1988 and 10 papers and journals are appearing in Polish. Warsaw TV is being re-transmitted in Vilnius and surrounding areas inhabited by the Poles. Furthermore, Lithuanian TV and radio has a daily information program and special Sunday program in Polish.

The Polish Minority in Belarus: General Data

Polish minority officially comprises over 400,000 or 4% of Belarus population, but those figures are probably only half of the actual ones. In contradiction there were no Polish schools allowed since 1947/48 and some 100 are now in the process of formation but none has a building of its own. Dozens of Polish organizations have been formed (e.g. Central Union of Poles in Belarus with headquarters in Grodno where a Polish home was recently built for them by the Polish "Wspolnota" organization from Warsaw; Polish Scientific Association in Minsk etc.). Some 70-100 Roman Catholic churches have been offering services in Polish. The Union of Poles planned to build four buildings for Polish schools in Grodno, Lida, Baranowicze and Slonim.

The Polish Minority in Ukraine: General Data

Polish minority comprises some 250,000 or 0.5% of Ukrainian population. Those figures based on old 1989 Soviet census should probably be doubled. At present there are only two Polish High Schools (with their own buildings in Lviv) and a number of them in the process of formation (e.g. Gorodok in Podolia). Dozens of Polish organizations are being formed. The Union of Poles in Ukraine, with headquarters in Lviv has some 27 branches all over the western and central Ukraine. Some 200 Roman Catholic churches are offering services in Polish. The situation of the Polish minority varies greatly between the Western Ukraine, where there are many Ukrainian-Polish tensions, and central Ukraine outside the pre-World War II Polish boundaries where Polish-Ukrainian relations are relatively good. It is there where some 2/3 of the Poles live. In Western Ukraine the Polish population numbers 70,000-80,000 with less than 20,000 in Lviv.

Sources: Author's summer 1993 research trip throughout these three states (some 1,500 miles by car).

Notes

1. Heinz Quirin and Werner Trillmich. *Westermanne Atlas Zur Weltgeschichte* (Braunschweig: Georg Westermann Verlag, 1963) 139.

2. *Rocnik Polityczny i Gospodarczy 1936* (Warszawa: P.A.T., 1936) 1160.

3. T. Manteufel, ed., *Historia Polski* (Warszawa; P.W.N.: 1958-1984) vols. I-IV, 562.

4. Ibid., 589-593.

5. A. Lewicki, J. Friedberg. *Zarys Historii Polski* (London: S.Z.P.Z. Publishers, 1947) 317-322.

6. *Maly Rocznik Statystyczny 1939* (Warszawa: G.U.S., 1939) 52.

7. *Rocznik Polityczny*, op. cit., 1160.

8. Ibid.

9. Krajowa Agencja Informacyjna, "Kazachstan: Przesiedlency I Ich Potomkowie," 11, 1478; 3, 4-20 (1989), *Dziennik Zwiazkowy* (Chicago) "Polacy W Kazachstanie: 7/14-15/89. Ambassador Yuli Kvitsinski, a Soviet Pole and the Soviet negotiator on nuclear disarmament, is by his own admission a son of an engineer, who in the 1930s "emigrated" to Siberia.

10. Z. Anthony Kruszewski. *The Oder-Neisse Boundary and Poland's Modernization: The Socioeconomic and Political Impact* (New York: Praeger, 1972) 49-53.

11. Ibid.

12. *Rocznik Polityczny*, op. cit., 1160.

13. Julian Siedlecki. *Losy Polakow w ZSRR w Latach 1939-1986* (London: Gryf Ltd., 1988); Jan T. Gross. *Revolutions from Abroad* (Princeton: Princeton University Press, 1988) 194-195.

14. *Maly Slownik Historii Polski* (Warszawa: W.P., 1967) 478-479; *Wielka Encyklopedia Ika Encyclopedia Powszechna PWN Polska* (Warszawa: PWN, 1967) 67-72.

15. Kruszewski, op. cit., 13-14; 49-53.

16. Z. Anthony Kruszewski, "Border Problem Solving in the Communist World: A Case Study of Some European Boundaries" in Oscar J. Martinez, ed., *Across Boundaries* (El Paso: Texas Western Press, 1986) 191-200.

17. Kruszewski, *Oder-Neisse*, 51-53.

18. *Atlas Narodov Mira* (Moscow: Akademia Nauk SSSR, 1964) 16.

19. *Rocnik Statystyczny*, op. cit., table 33, 38.

20. *Great Soviet Encyclopedia* (New York: Macmillan, 1983) vol. 31, 246.

21. Ibid., vol. 3, 613.

22. *Atlas Narodov*, op. cit., 16.

23. See also the school atlas published in the 1930's in Poland by Prof. E. Romer, a world-famous Polish geographer (E. Romer. *Powszechny Atlas Geograficzny* [Lwow: Ksiaznica Atlas, 1934]) 56.

24. Krajowa Agencja Informacyjan, "O Zmianach Programowych i Strukturalnych Towarzystwa Polonia," 17, 1484; 4, 25-5, 1 (1989).

25. Ibid.

26. See "Przebudzenie" in *Politika* 30, 1682 (Warszawa, July 29, 1989) 12.

27. *Slownik Geografii ZSSR* (Warszawa: W.P., 1974) 714.

28. Krajowa Agencja Informacyjna, "Polonia Radziecka-Naturalnym Pomostem Miedzy Polska A ZSSR," 8, 1475 (Feb. 21, 1989); Ibid., 6, 1473 (Feb. 7, 1989).

29. Przeglad Wiadomosci Agencyjnych, 188 (1989), as quoted in *Nowy Dziennik*, "Po I Zjezdzie Zwiazku Polakow Na Litwie," (New York, June 22, 1989) 4.

30. P. Lida, "Parafie Rzymskokatolickie Na Bialorusi I Ukrainie W 1988 Roku-Obsada Personalna, in *Zeszyty Historyczne*, 88 (Paris, 1989) 123-144.

31. Ibid., 140.

32. Ibid., 143.

33. The pastoral visit was extensively covered in the Polish press, which also reprinted an interview.

34. In Lithuania, Poles are blamed for preferring to study in Russian rather than in Lithuanian schools, if not attending the Polish ones.

35. P. Lossowski. *Litwa A Sprawy Polskie 1939-1940* (Warszawa: PWN, 1985); K. Podlaski. *Bialorusini, Litwini, Ukraincy* (Bialystok: Versus, 1990); M. Iwanow. *Pierwszy Narod Ukarany Polacy W. Zwiazku Radzieckim 1921-1939* (Wroclaw: PWN, 1991); T. Gawin. *Ojcowizna*, Fundacja in T. Goniewicza, Grodno-Lublin, 1992; *Mniejszosci Polskie i Polonia W. ZSSR* (Wroclaw: Ossolineum, 1992); J. Orchmanski, *Historia Litwy*, 3rd ed. (Wroclaw: Ossolineum, 1990); *Polska, Polacy, Mnejszosci Narodowe* (Wroclaw: Ossolineum, 1992).

36. Lithuanian Information Center news release, Brooklyn, New York, Feb. 10, 1991.

8.

The Polish Road to Self-Government

Joanna Regulska

The Path Toward Decentralization

The introduction, in postwar Poland, of the principle of uniform state power meant the fundamental restructuring of political and economic relations. For local government it meant the loss of autonomy and incorporation into the hierarchical system of power and decision-making process. Municipalities became an integral part of the people's council; their property was nationalized and their administration began to serve as an extension of the communist central government, duly fulfilling its directives.

Repeated political crises in Poland during the forty-five years of totalitarian rule almost always resulted in new government legislation pertinent to local government. The state apparatus and political leadership believed that by introducing new legislation and thus providing the society with the sense of change, they could avoid addressing issues of autonomy, democracy and self-determination. Thus, the 1945-48 period of establishment of the Communist regime was reflected in the 1950 "Territorial Agencies of the Uniform State Authority Act" which declared the end of local autonomy and defined a new status for the people's councils[1]. The 1956 crisis that brought Gomulka to power was reflected first in the 1958 Act and subsequently in the 1963 Act. The further expansion of central administrative power and autonomy of individual sectorial departments (horizontally subordinated to specific Ministerial offices) was the key element of the 1958 amendment. Although the purpose of this addition was to strengthen central control and hierarchical linkages, the evidence that this goal was achieved was minimal and the 1963 amendment picked up the issue again. This time the fear was that the local councils were losing political prestige and, therefore, needed to be given a greater role in the decision-making process. By providing the council's committees with special status, the central administration achieved greater control of local affairs and most importantly, drastically restricted council ability to decide local priorities for themselves.

The tensions of the 1968-70 period laid the foundation for the ill-conceived administrative reform of 1975, which by creation of a larger number of units at the local level and the elimination of the middle range of the administrative tier, was supposed to improve the efficiency of administrative management and to increase public participation. In effect, however, due to the principal of "unity of power" it allowed the further penetration of society by the state instruments of control (military and police) and finally facilitated the imposition of martial law in 1981.

The 1983 legislation is considered by some as an important step towards the advancement of decentralization through increased authority of people's councils and of their independence.[2] The theory was not, however, translated into practice: it only repeated the old paradox, "we are free to do more, but can do less," and only added to the already deep social dissatisfaction. The retention of administrative barriers, lack of resources, and contradictions between new and old legislation were not viewed by local authorities as an expansion of their power and effectiveness. Although the new legislation obliged the people's councils to adhere to social consultation, the failure to establish democratic mechanisms for such a process, *a priori* restrictions on the timing of such consultation and the lack of democratic elections precluded the development of public participation as a powerful tool.

The final pseudo attempt to restructure central-local relations took place in 1988, when, as a part of the so-called "second stage of reform," people's councils were supposed to obtain greater discretionary power in financial and economic matters, including the ability to raise their own revenues.[3] They were also scheduled to undertake a variety of obligations to provide certain services. Communal property again became a subject of debate with the proposal to restore communal ownership lost in the forties. The relevant legislation was to be approved in 1988 and implemented on January 1, 1989. This, however, did not take place. The events of the summer and fall of 1988 moved Poland onto a new political trajectory.

In the autumn of 1988, after a series of nationwide strikes, led by Lech Walesa's Solidarity, the regime of General Wojciech Jaruzelski decided that it had no chance of reforming the economy. It opted for what was called the "historic compromise," the introduction of opposition into the system. In December 1988, the "Citizen's Committee of Lech Walesa" was established. The actual terms for the introduction of the opposition into the system were worked out in "Round-Table" discussions in February 1989. The debates took place in three large subcommittees: 1) political reforms; 2) social and economic policy and 3) trade union pluralism. The subgroup on local government, led by Professor Jerzy Regulski, later a Senator and Undersecretary for Local Government Reform in Taduesz Mazowiechi's government, negotiated under the first theme. The opposition program concluded, from past failures, that only fundamental reform could bring back genuine local self-government. Its philosophy reflected unhappiness with the lack of democracy, social dissatisfaction and political bankruptcy of the regime. It stressed that:

1. the centralized political system and overdeveloped state administration, backed by monopolistic political power, caused previous reforms to fail;
2. the past changes reflected the objectives of internal governmental policies and not the public interest;
3. political weakness of local government was, among other things, derived from nondemocratic elections and the absence of public support for local councils;
4. restricted legal reforms would be insufficient to bring a change.

The program presented during the "Round-Table" demanded several fundamental changes. However, the goal of negotiations was not to produce yet another blueprint, in this case for the reemergence of local self-government. The intent was to change the nature of the state itself. The opposition side made it clear that the purpose of the debate was to remove all barriers and allow subsequently elected and appointed professionals to shape the scope and the content of the local government reform.[4] The outlined program argued for:

1. the abolition of the constitutional principle of uniform state power: local councils should represent local society and be free from hierarchical dependencies;
2. a new democratic electoral law;
3. communes to be recognized as legal entities with ownership rights;
4. a stable and controllable system of local budgets and financing, free of arbitrary decisions introduced by central administration;
5. a limitation of state interference in local affairs, by abolition of all central administrative regulations;
6. transfer of local state administration to communal control;
7. freedom to establish inter-communal associations, to advocate local interest in central government;
8. the right to judicial appeal against decisions made by state (central and regional) administration.

The outcome of the negotiations was far from satisfactory.[5] Agreement was reached in the areas of electoral law; ownership rights; local financing (partially); limitation of central state interference, and the right to organize inter-communal associations although only at the regional (voivodship) level. No specific calendar for the implementation of those points was set. Furthermore, no progress was made on key issues, essential to the overall success of the reform: the abolition of uniformity of state power; the transfer of state local administrative responsibilities; the establishment of a clear financial subsidies system for a five-year period and the freedom of local government to established national associations.[6] This unwillingness of the regime to reform intergovernmental relations should be seen in a larger context of willful ignorance of the political and administrative decentralization that had taken place. The government was too frightened to provide local councils with power to determine their own needs and priorities. The regime did not dare allow the creation of local political lobbies. The Jaruzelski regime resisted once again the attempt to entrust political power to civil society.

Post-1989 Local Government Reform

The June 1989 parliamentary elections and the establishment of the first non-Communist government in the summer of that year initiated widespread political and economic reforms. Local government reform was viewed as an essential element of the overall change. Between January and May of 1990, seven pertinent pieces of new legislation were signed by the President. Two of them were most significant for the future of local self-governance in Poland: the "Local Self-Government Act," cleared by the Parliament on March 19, 1990, and the "Local Government Duties and Powers Act," passed on May 26, 1990. The first set the overall structure of the local government, and the second established the division of responsibilities between local governments and state administration.

Local Self-Government Act

The eleven chapters of the Local Self-Government Act outlined the scope of activities and tasks which each municipality (*gmina*) can perform.[7] Furthermore, it defined the municipality's authority, ownership rights, and established their financial independence. Albeit restricted, the Act also contained provisions about the freedom to establish associations and inter-communal (inter-*gmina*) agreements. Finally, the Act discussed the role and status of the second tier of elected officials, the Voivodship Assembly, and the overall boundaries of supervision by regional and central authorities.

The Local Self-Government Act was of significant importance. By legally establishing the *gmina* as a local self-governing community, the Act provided the *gmina* with the power to govern its own resources and to make independent decisions; in short, to determine its own needs and priorities. The Act stated that "the scope of activity of *gminas* shall embrace all public matters of local significance that are not reserved by law for other units... and unless otherwise stated, the settlement of all matters rests with the *gminas*."[8] The Act was very specific about the tasks falling under the local jurisdictions and included virtually all spheres of community needs. The Act did not stipulate, however, which of these tasks were obligatory, which were delegated by the central government and which were the responsibility of the regional level. These issues were to be decided in the Local Government Duties and Powers Act.

The power of Polish municipalities extended beyond pure provision of services, as local authorities were allowed to engage in economic activities by establishing and owning commercial and industrial enterprises (a principle subsequently abolished). In addition, they owned the assets of such services as water and sewage systems, low-cost housing, and other public utilities. In this manner, the central state abandoned the socialist notion of regional equality and gave implicit legitimacy to uneven development.

In terms of the structure, the *gmina* council size varied between 15 members for the smaller units of no more than 40,000 inhabitants to as many as 100 members for jurisdictions of over 200,000 inhabitants. Councilors served a four-year term. The council had the right to appoint all standing and ad hoc commissions and could ask non-council members to serve on them, providing that at least half of the membership was composed of council members.

The *gmina* council elected from its membership a Board composed of four to seven members. The administrative officer, the mayor and deputies were members of the Board and could be chosen from outside the council. In the case of the administrative officer and mayor, they were elected by secret ballot, by absolute majority and in the presence of two-thirds of the council members. The deputies were elected by the council at the request of the mayor.

The Local Self-Government Act also provided the framework for financial arrangements. The municipalities were responsible for setting local budgets on the annual bases. The revenues were drawn from a variety of sources including: taxes, government grants, incomes derived from charges and loans, earnings from rents, lotteries and special events. The exact proportion in which each source contributed to local budgets was not however included in the Act. The lack, at taht point, of a clear delimitation of fiscal powers that were supposed to be devolved to the local level subsequently gave rise to continuous power struggles between central and local authorities.

The Local Government Duties and Powers Act

The Local Government Duties and Powers Act (often referred to as the Competence Act) defined the areas of responsibilities falling under the jurisdiction of the municipalities.[9] In addition, it laid the groundwork for separation of the decision-making power between the municipal level (elected officials) and the district level (appointed officials). The primary areas of responsibilities of local government were included: pre-school and elementary education (on a voluntary basis until 1994 and then obligatory); physical planning, land registry, land use management and property rights; building construction; housing management; public safety, highways and roads.

The Act also included provisions allowing for certain functions and powers to be delegated to municipalities by central government. The most significant were: civil defense; foster care; administration of sales and auctions of state property and land; and population statistics. Several other duties remained the responsibility of voivodships. These included: registration of properties; environmental protection and building inspection; determination of citizenship; car registration and driving license issuance.

In general, the approved legislation adhered to the principles of self-government adopted in western democracies and moved the Polish government towards a participatory democracy. Each municipality received a large degree of power. The challenge ahead was to learn how to exercise it. But, it is questionable if the new legislative framework did indeed allow for the full transfer of power to the local level. The issue of fiscal autonomy was one contested area. Another was the division of responsibility between local self-governing bodies and centrally-controlled regional and district administrations.

The Local Elections of May 1990

The May 1990 elections were a fundamental step towards reestablishing local self-governance. All citizens of Polish nationality residing in Poland who were at least 18 years old were eligible to vote. Only 42.27 percent executed their rights (Appendix A). The elections took place in 21,383 *gminas* and resulted in the election of 52,028 local officials. Over 147,327 candidates competed, a ratio of 2.8 candidates per seat. Women won 10.4 percent of the seats. Fifteen percent of candidates were women. The average age of women and men candidates, respectively, was 41 and 42.[10] One-third of the candidates were farmers, 15 percent were identified as industrial workers, 14 percent as technicians and 10 percent as teachers. Only 4 percent considered themselves civil servants with administrative experience and only a few represented technical sciences, with 3.9 percent being engineers. The majority of the candidates in urban areas had completed higher education and most frequently represented such professions as teachers, lawyers, economists, engineers, doctors and architects.[11]

The distribution of voting patterns results illustrate the unevenness with which the country moved through the political and economic transition during the first year. The areas where local society showed greater ability to mobilize and to organize its resources during the election campaign had higher turnouts. Similarly, areas with a greater number of candidates attracted more voters. Nonetheless, those results should not be uncritically interpreted as an early sign of positive change. A striking similarity could be seen when the turnout in local elections were compared with the results of the 1989 parliamentary elections. This uneven regional distribution reflected not only new, transitional trends but also old socio-economic and political patterns, both pre-World War II and those inherited from communism.[12]

Interestingly enough, in cities and towns with more than 40,000 inhabitants, where a proportional representational voting system was adopted, there were on the average 4.6 candidates per seat, while in smaller communities only 2.6 candidates per seat stood for election. This greater competition for seats in larger urban centers appeared to be a direct result of emerging pluralism on the Polish political scene. The National Election Commission reported that altogether over 350 parties participated in the election, including 80 organizations recognized as national political parties and 270 groups representing local parties.

Besides political parties, 660 organizations that did not perceive themselves as political entities supported candidates. In order to increase the chances of the candidates put forth by smaller and lesser known parties, several groups created coalitions and supported candidates on the joint list. By election day, 40 such coalitions were recognized, although often they were very fragile and their permanency was fluid. The most frequent alliance was between the Polish Social Democratic Union (PSDU) and the Polish Peasants Party (PPP), and the PPP and the Nationalist Party.

The organizations which supported the largest number of candidates included the Citizens' Committees, which stood behind Solidarity as well as behind the independent candidates (21.3 percent of candidates); the Polish Social Democratic Union (8.58 percent); the Polish Peasants Party (5.14 percent) and Social Democracy of the Republic of Poland (SDRP) (4.04 percent). The remaining 59.7 percent of the candidates were supported by a variety of smaller organizations, groups of citizens and coalitions.

The distribution of support among different organizations varied between small towns and villages, which had single-seat districts, and large, metropolitan areas that were multi-seat districts. Undoubtedly the character of the electoral ordinances, the majority system represented in the former areas, and the proportional system adopted in the latter case (in cities with more than 40,000 inhabitants) contributed significantly to this diversity. More importantly, however, it reflected the different stages in which rural and urban Poland found itself on the way to a pluralistic society. The greater visibility of a political scene and increased accessibility to a variety of domestic and international media were but only two important factors affecting the rapid awakening of political consciousness and of particular interests among different urban social groups.

This emerging political pluralism was reflected in the range of parties and groups supporting candidates in urban and rural areas. Except for the Citizens' Committees which supported the largest number of candidates in both cases (24 percent and 23 percent), the peasant movements represented by the Polish Peasants Party (8 percent) and the Solidarity-based Peasant Party (SPP) (2.5 percent) were respectively the second and third largest groups supporting candidates in rural areas. Candidates in urban areas originated in the main from the PSDU (9 percent); the Confederation for Independent Poland (CIP) (6 percent); the SDRP (5 percent); the PPP (5 percent) and several Christian Democratic parties (3 percent).

The turnout was considered low in comparison with Western countries but it was higher than the results of similar elections in other Central and East European countries. The turnout was generally higher in urban industrial areas (around 50 percent) than in rural areas (35-40 percent). The turnout in Warsaw was 43 percent and in Poznan and Gdansk, 50 percent. In general, southern Poland showed the higher turn-out, followed by border areas in the east and west (40 percent) and central Poland with the lowest participation of around 30 percent. In terms of political results, the candidates supported by the Citizens' Committees won overwhelmingly (41.4 percent of the seats). Independent candidates gained 38 percent of seats and were followed by PPP (6.5 percent) and SPP (4.3 percent). Other parties lost badly. The old regime structures such as SDRP won only 0.28 percent of the seats, but even new ones such as the CIP were hurt by winning only 0.1 percent of the seats. Hundreds of other parties and organizations were simply eliminated.

It is debatable if 42.27 percent should be considered as a low turn-out or whether the expectations of a 55-60 percent turnout were too high. Regardless of the answer, one may still question why people showed such a small interest in the first fully free elections. Many factors could be cited. Few, however, were mentioned enough to support the impression that their influences were decisive. The emerging tensions between Lech Walesa and Prime Minister Mazowiecki, the rail strike in northern Poland and overall rising economic difficulties unquestionably created a climate of uncertainty and disillusionment.

In addition, more deeply rooted skepticism and mistrust emerged. After 45 years of being denied the right to full expression and participation in governing of their country, people wanted immediate and deeply rooted change, but at the same time they did not perceive that it was up to them to take the leadership role.[13] The society was not ready to exercise the power provided by the new legislation. People did not grasp the importance of the election, nor did they realize the extent of power of the newly elected officials and the fact that by electing new local officials they would be able to break away with the old *nomenklatura* at the local level.[14]

This explanation essentially argues that society did not reach for the power provided by the new system. It implies a continued sense of powerlessness of the people. An opposite interpretation can be proposed, however. It can be argued that society did exercise its new power by interpreting it as a right to decide, and thus, exercised the right not to vote as well. In this context the absenteeism reflected acceptance of the new democratic rights.

Technical and organizational factors also affected participation rates. The failure to establish mechanisms for mail ballots, and thus the necessity for students, military and government personnel to travel to their place of permanent residence deterred many from participation.[15] The large voting districts, especially in the rural areas, also presented a barrier. On the one hand, they led to greater isolation of the candidates from the communities, on the other, with still limited availability of public and private transportation, many potential voters simply did not get to the polling stations. Finally, one may argue that the majority voting system adopted in the rural areas did not generate enough enthusiasm in an already pessimistic environment.

As much as these opinions and interpretations appeared on the surface to be diverse, they point to the difficulties encountered by Polish society and by the new Polish leadership during the period of transition. The conflicts between emerging political pluralism and the old remnants of the former monoparty system inherited from the communist state were acknowledged on the day of the elections. The question for both sides was how to build new economic and political structures while at the same time attempting to destroy the old one.

The Post-Election Road

The implementation of the newly designed system of local government was not without pain. The newly elected officials lacked experience in public administration and management. They lacked examples of how to implement decentralization and how to move from a centralized, totalitarian way of thinking into a system that required initiative and independent action by local leaderships. They were presented with the legacy of communist bureaucracy, with its inefficiency and apathy on the part of professional staff.

The difficulties were present not only at the local level. The government and its central administration had to relinquish some of the power. A struggle between the public administration sector, composed of officials appointed from the top, which preferred a semi-centralized system, and the self-governing sector, derived through local elections, which strove for transfer of power to the local level, emerged.

A year after the elections of 1990, the most visible tensions and conflicts could be identified in the following major areas:

1. in the establishment of an additional tier of state administration, below the voivodship level, composed of 250 districts. This new layer was charged with the power to oversee and to control many of the activities that had been recently passed on to the *gminas*; the employees of the districts largely represented old voivodship *nomenklatura* which was officially dismantled through the establishment of a local government. Nonetheless, delegitimized political power appeared to have control over the legitimized one.

2. in the division of responsibilities between districts (appointed officials) and *gminas* (elected officials). Local elected officials felt cheated because of the expansionary tactics of the district administration; the degree of power given to municipalities was being persistently narrowed down. This was interpreted as an attack on decentralization and as a clear unwillingness of the central state to relinquish its power.

3. in the division of property between *gminas*, state and private owners. Each municipality was required by law to conduct an inventory of properties on its territory. At stake were the future financial assets of the *gmina*, possession of which would have long-lasting financial repercussions for the economic stability of individual units.

4. in fiscal independence of municipalities. Legislation introduced by the

Ministry of Finance argued for the "centralist" solution and for a large degree of control over the establishment of tax rates and distribution of centrally-collected taxes and fees. The Ministry of Finance also sought to maintain control over allocation of grants and subsidies offered by the central government. Such an arrangement, however, meant little financial autonomy for the individual *gmina* and called into question the ability of local self-government to maintain autonomy.

The above areas of conflict illustrate the difficulties faced by the emerging Polish self-government. Many of these problems and issues have been dealt with in Western countries when they went through the process of restructuring their intergovernmental relations. What makes the Polish case and those of other Central and Eastern European countries different, is an attempt to simultaneously change the law, institutions and, most importantly, the behavioral patterns of the society.

This often-called "peaceful revolution," although desired by the people, met with resistance from political elites as well as from the society itself. While in the past many political leaders in Poland perceived decentralization as a threat to their central monopoly of power and central control, current officials often act as if they lack the trust that local societies can handle their own affairs. The belief is that the local council members are the most qualified to make decisions regarding community needs and the ways in which they should be met. In short, there seemed to be a reluctance to accept the ideology of local self-determination.

One year after the election people were also disillusioned. As a survey conducted in April 1991 indicated, people felt alienated and removed from participation in local affairs (Appendix B). When asked if they perceived that they had an impact on the affairs affecting their community, more than sixty-one percent responded that nothing had changed in comparison to previous communist local governments. Twelve percent indicated an actual decrease in their influence. Only 23 percent believed that a positive change had taken place.[16]

The new system of self-government did not initially manage to break the barriers between government and society established under communism. People indicated dissatisfaction and an increased sense that society's interests are the last to be addressed by local councilors.

Only 28 percent believed that newly-elected local council members were concerned with the needs of the *gmina* residents under their jurisdiction. An equal number (27 percent) believed that local leaderships defended primarily their own interests, the remaining 45 percent saw the interests of particular groups as the main focus of councilors' attention. Among the groups most frequently cited were Solidarity (10 percent); the Church (5 percent); the old communist nomenklatura (5 percent); the central government (2 percent) and other political parties (3 percent).[17]

By 1991 the society had yet to fully understand what self-governance means and what benefits it can bring for communities. It had to fully understand the extent of the actual powers held by newly elected local officials. At the same time the knowledge that many previous attempts to bring change had failed placed people in a "wait and see" position, not sure what transfer of power means in real terms. As one of the newly elected officials in a small town said "they gave us power, but they did not tell us what to do." One year after the first local elections Polish society had yet to embrace fully what self-government meant and what benefits it can bring.

A revised version of this paper was previously published in John O'Loughlin and Herman van der Wusten, eds. The New Political Geography of Eastern Europe, *Chapter 13, "Democratic elections and political restructuring in Poland, 1989-1991" (London and New York: Belhaven Press, 1993) 217-234.*

Notes

1. Jerzy Regulski, "Polish Local Government in Transition," *Environment and Planning C: Government and Policy*, 7 (1989) 423-444.

2. W. Zakrzewski, "Nouvelle loi sur le systeme de l'autogestion territoriale en Pologne" in *Federalism and decentralization* (Boulder, CO: Westview Press, 1987 and Fribourg, Suisse: Editions Universitaires, 1987); S. Zawadzki, "Decentralization and optimalisation of the local decision-making process (Poland)" in *Federalism and decentralization* (Boulder, CO: Westview Press, 1987 and Fribourg, Suisse: Editions Universitaires, 1987).

3. J. Chlopecki. *Przestrzen polityczna Polski: konflikt i zmiana* (Warsaw: Instytut Gospodarki Przestrvzennej, No. 28, 1990).

4. Jerzy Regulski, ibid., 423-444.

5. *Porozumienia Okraglego Stolu*, NSZZ 'Solidarnosc' Region Warminsko-Mazurski, Olsztyn (1989) 85.

6. Ibid., 87.

7. Dziennik Ustaw, Ustawa o samorzadzie terytorialnym (19 Marzec 1990) No. 16, 95.

8. Dziennik Ustaw, No. 16, Ch. 2: Art. 6 (1990).

9. Dziennik Ustaw, No. 34 (1990).

10. Office of the General Commission for Elections, "Sytuacja powyborcza w poszczegolnych regionach kraju," *Bulletyn* (May 30, 1990).

11. Ibid., (1990).

12. For a detailed discussion of spacial electoral patterns see Joanna Regulska, "Democratic Elections and Political Restructuring in Poland, 1989-1991," in John O'Loughlin and Herman van der Wusten, eds. *The New Political Geography of Eastern Europe* (London and New York: Belhaven Press, 1993).

13. Lech Walesa, Interview, *Rzeczpospolita* (May 30, 1990).

14. Zelzistaw Najder, Interview, *Rzeczpospolita* (May 30, 1990).

15. Jerzy Regulski, Interview, *Rzeczpospolita* (May 30, 1990).

15. Joanna Regulska, "Democratic elections and political restructuring in Poland, 1989-1991," 233; citing Centrum Badania Opinii Spolecznej (CBOS), *Wybory Samorzadowe*

'91 (Warsaw: 1991). For earlier CBOS preelection survey see Centrum Badania Opinii Spolecznej, *Wybory Samorzadowe '90 (Warsaw:1990)*, cited in Joanna Regulska, "Democratic elections and political restructuring in Poland, 1989-1991," 225.

17. Centrum Badania Opinii Spotecznej (1991).

9.

Elite Transformation in Post-Communist Eastern Europe:
The Case of the Disappearing Dissidents
Carol Skalnik Leff

The transitions from authoritarian rule in Central Europe presented a number of striking contrasts with those in other regions touched by the global "third wave" of democratization. Students of transitions from authoritarian rule in Latin America and Southern Europe depicted transitions based on strategic negotiations between authoritarian elites and their oppositions. To students of post-communist systems, what is perhaps most striking about this depiction is the profusion of groups and interests in the opposition: reassertive trade unions, intellectuals, human rights activists, party politicians of earlier democratic interludes, and alienated middle class and business supporters of the authoritarian regime. The spectrum is diverse, even cluttered, by contrast with the relatively stark landscape of East European politics, where decades of suppressed societal autonomy led to a dearth of organized opposition. There is broad consensus that the pivotal opposition role in the revolutions of 1989 was largely played by a small, often previously isolated, dissident minority.[1]

An inspection of the transition cases in East Central Europe reveals a second anomaly. Just as the scope of the opposition differs from the Latin American cases, so does its fate in the transition and consolidation period of the post-communist regimes.[2] In the Latin American cases, it was presumed that key opposition forces of the transition crisis would continue to play an important role in the post-authoritarian setting. Indeed, no stable regime would emerge if they did not. In Eastern Europe, by contrast, the political salience of the dissidents over the course of regime change marked a trajectory from counterelite, to agent of change, to political marginalization in the course of a few years. Far from forming the stable core of a post-authoritarian governing elite, dissident movements faced the twin disruptions of internal fragmentation, and external electoral/bureaucratic challenges of other political actors that frequently proved more adept than they in adapting to post-communist political environment. What accounts for this pattern, apparently so different from that of other "third wave" democratization efforts and indeed from our understanding of elite transformation in general?

The rapid emergence and departure of dissident elites from the center stage between the late 1980s and early 1990s appears to represent a deviant case of elite transformation. The following analysis traces the forces that shaped dissident participation in the three periods of the communist rule, transition and consolidation of post-communist regimes in Poland, Hungary and Czechoslovakia. Democratization theorists have debated the degree of constraint imposed on post-authoritarian regimes by the political and socioeconomic structures of the prior regime. There is a contribution to be made to the larger literature of democratization in thinking through the issue of authoritarian legacies, for the dissidents are in fact a specimen of the exotic fauna of European communism, and their travails and triumphs stem directly from that distinctive environment. To trace their trajectory is to trace the legacies of communist rule in an area of central importance--the problem of elite transformation.

Here, I will argue that the structuring of authoritarian politics (encompassing an experience that reaches back to the nineteenth century) conditioned the resources and strategies of opposition elites. This starting point, in turn, defined the political resources available to dissidents in the crisis of 1989, as well as their subsequent capacity to adapt to the new politics. It will then be possible to evaluate how the case of the disappearing dissidents speaks to the existing literature on elite transformation and to assess the way in which the broader dynamic of post-communist elite transformation relates to existing understanding of regime transformation in general. Central to this argument is the proposition that the twin anomalies that introduced this essay--the impoverished socio-economic base for opposition to communist regimes and the marginalization of the dissidents after their key role in the transition--are closely related, and can be understood in the context of how elite (re)credentialling works in periods of system change.

Theories of Elite Transformation

A strikingly consistent feature of existing conceptual frameworks for understanding elite transformation is their emphasis on change that emerges from confrontations over access and representation of important socioeconomic and institutional interests. The resultant reconfiguration of the political leadership is a result of shifts in the sociocultural and economic composition of political elites, a broadening, reconstruction or replacement of the "ruling class" in response to pressure to incorporate alternative socioeconomic interests. The literatures that deal with revolution, democratization and elite transformation appear to share this presumption, not rigorously validated in every case, that power is transferred or dispersed from the existing ruling elite to newly emergent socioeconomic forces that contest for power and access. Indeed, these are the terms in which elite transformation has been defined--as a change in the constellation of interests represented in the political leadership, an expansion or contraction of the socioeconomic and institutional base of power.

Scholars thus describe a gradual evolution of West European representative institutions and an expansion of the electorate that produced time-lagged shifts in the composition of political elites,[3] in response to socioeconomic changes that generated pressures for access to politics by new social forces. The literature on the "preconditions of democracy" that emphasized the correlation between democracy and economic development also accented the emergence of new socioeconomic forces whose interests would be served by incorporation into the political process through the broadening of the base of representative government and of elite recruitment. Regime transformation thus operated in conjunction with elite transformation.

In short, most theories of regime change and elite transformation assume the socioeconomic rootedness of contending forces as part of the dynamic of transformation, a rootedness that makes sense of the pattern of conflict. The current analysis does not challenge this understanding of elite transformation. In fact, the peculiarities of post-communist elite transformation, I would argue, reinforce rather than undermine the logic of existing approaches to elite transformation in other settings.

It is in this context, in fact, that dissidents pose a problem that is simultaneously a clue to their eventual "disappearance." True, none of the models of elite transformation posits the case of a facilitative counterelite who, after a central contribution to the launching of a political transformation, succumbs almost immediately to marginal-ization. Such a "transitional" elite may even be a bit melodramatic for the social sciences; it is too evocative of a Deus Ex Machina introduced at a "critical juncture" in the admittedly theatrical plot. Yet a dynamic of this sort is not at all alien to the logic by which the post-communist cases are commonly differentiated from those of other post-authoritarian transitions. Higley joins many others in noting the systematic (although variable) communist repression of autonomous organization outside the sphere of government control, and the subsequent attenuation or absence of a broader political civil society that could generate "pluralistic elite configurations that are normally regarded as prerequisites for democracy."[4] In other words, communist states are industrialized without generating autonomous societal institutions and interests. The absence of viable alternative organizational bases for opposition elites means that a crucial ecological niche is vacant in the political environment; this niche must be filled, at least temporarily, for regime transformation to occur, since mass mobilization alone is insufficient. Thus, the launching of a successful transition requires that if counterelites do not exist, they must be improvised. The subsequent durability of such a transitional elite is by this very fact very much in question. Precisely because the dissident elites who brokered the transition from communist rule are *not* firmly rooted in burgeoning socioeconomic and institutional interests seeking representation, they are also vulnerable to subsequent displacement. In this sense, they are the exception that proves the rules normally understood to define elite transformation.

Having offered a preliminary explanation of the apparent misfit between the analysis of previous cases and the deviant pattern of elite transformation in post-communist systems, I will now turn to a more detailed analysis of the Central European cases, starting with the dissident opposition role as it was initially defined under communism. The dissident community's political style and role expectations, as well as the "political capital" forged in this crucible, can then be traced through subsequent periods of regime transition and attempted consolidation. There are two substantive questions to explore here, the centrality of dissidents in the transition period and their marginalization thereafter. This argument follows the premise of analysts who have emphasized the transmission of legacies of prior regimes into changed political contexts. As Kullberg and others argue, institutional and socioeconomic legacies are not merely manifest in concrete structural terms, but are also embodied in the formative communist-era experiences and perceptions that pivotal elites bring to the new settings.[5]

Dissidents Under Communist Rule

Without exhaustively recapitulating dissidents' experiences under communism, I will try to define that experience in terms that will clarify their role in the subsequent transition and consolidation periods. This analysis is generally guided by the attempt to define the niche they occupied in the political ecology of the communist period--a niche shaped by dissident resources and regime response--and the problematic convertibility of these assets in a post-transition environment in which that ecological niche had vanished. The most relevant factors are the character of the communist regime itself, which, coupled with the broader traditions of intellectual mission in Eastern Europe, shaped the political orientation of the dissident counterelite, its composition and role perception. The prior positioning of the dissidents under communism shaped their subsequent assets and liabilities.

Under communism, dissidents faced an official elite recruitment structure that was both inclusive and closed. It was inclusive in the sense that all top positions in major social and political institutions were subject to party review and approval; it was closed in that sense, and also in the sense that party organizations that served as gatekeepers to elite status were themselves self-recruiting and self-perpetuating.

The weakness of the opposition, however, was not merely a function of the closed structure of elite recruitment and the repression of alternative political participation. Key socioeconomic forces that underpinned capitalist interest politics were not only demobilized, but eradicated in the state-controlled economy. The communist party-state both bureaucratized and eviscerated potentially autonomous interests. This is the context in which dissident politics developed.

The core of the East European dissident movement in the communist period was generally the intellectual community--in particular those grounded in the humanities.[6] Through 1989, modern East European politics had largely been authoritarian politics: under empire before World War I, under local interwar bureaucratic authoritarian regimes (except in Czechoslovakia), under fascism and communism. As Jacques Rupnik notes, "Intellectuals in East Europe have traditionally been an alternative elite, spokesmen for nations without a state in the nineteenth century; for nations without a voice after the second world war." [7] Timothy Garton Ash elaborates on this intellectual mission as "conscience of the nation" and "voice of the oppressed"--"the writer as priest, prophet, resistance fighter and *substitute* politician."[8]

This self-conscious mission and identity, forged under un-democratic or quasi-democratic regimes, was politically relevant in a number of respects, as we will see. The first question, however, is how this opposition differs from counterelites in other authoritarian regimes. After all, intellectuals are hardly an unusual component of opposition coalitions in other settings.

What is distinctive in the East European cases is the extent to which dissident intellectuals in the communist era stood virtually alone, and usually isolated, as regime challengers. In Vaclav Havel's famous essay, "The Power of the Powerless," he characterizes dissidence as an "existential and pre-political" effort to live in truth, an act that immediately places the truthful outside the boundaries of the regime's compact with citizens who are "living within a ritual lie." Dissidence, he says, is not a social role or an "unusual occupation" or "profession," political or otherwise. It is "primarily an intellectual attitude."[9]

Despite, or perhaps because of, the fact that they saw themselves as conservers of the state conscience and national identity, the dissident intellectuals consciously stood apart from society, possessing what Melvin Croan terms an elitist "ascriptive claim to the august status of guardian of the nation's destiny."[10] In a slightly broader context, Judy Batt refers to "the intelligentsia's sense of its special mission to speak for society" as "reinforcing the sense of politics as the elitist 'preserve of experts.'"[11] Indeed, dissidents later acknowledged the problems of emergence from their "dissident ghetto," a "communications problem or even some kind of intellectual elitism."[12] Jakub Karpinski speaks of inequalities and elitism in the opposition, the exclusionary process of defining who is "one of us."[13] Under communism, the ghetto mentality was a matter of self-preservation. The danger of betrayal even lent certain conspiratorial elements to the practice of underground politics, reinforcing an isolation that would complicate subsequent elite-mass linkages.

The insulation of the dissident from a wider social base stemmed therefore in part from a conscious removal from conventional politics. This stance was of course heavily reinforced by the communist constraints on autonomous social activity in general. The regimes willingly collaborated in the dissident's self-definition as standing apart,[14] giving it a profoundly negative spin that stigmatized dissident intellectuals as an alien and isolated force toadying to the West. The regime also perpetuated dissident isolation by close monitoring of all their contacts, in itself a significant deterrent to contact between ordinary citizens and these pariahs. The success of such efforts to frame the dissidents' principled distance from socialist society as a decadent and futile insulation from reality should not be underestimated;

in the peculiar psychological setting, there was an understandable popular tendency to feel guilty resentment at those who surpassed them in moral courage. Czech philosopher and Charter 77 activist Ladislav Hejdanek later summarized the atmosphere this way: "most people here have a bad conscience....They all knew that what we [the dissidents] said was correct, but they thought we were silly to say it so loudly."[15]

A second difference between communist dissidents and oppositions to other repressive regimes lies in their goals. Unlike the Latin American oppositions, for example, dissidents did not themselves aspire to conventional access to power; they made no special claims for their own inclusion in the political elite. Although dissident counterelites varied in organization, coherence and size, their primary concern had been to develop a metapolitical critique of the existing regime. They challenged the essence of the system itself, and would not have considered it a victory for the cause they espoused to achieve representation in that system. In this sense they were revolutionaries without a revolutionary strategy of seizing power.[16] They were in no sense a shadow government with detailed alternative policies and programs. Even in Poland, the locus of the broadest-based opposition movement, Solidarity participants would later emphasize this point. What was true for Solidarity was still more true for smaller and more isolated dissident groups.[17] They could "tell the truth to power," measure the regime against the yardstick of international human rights standards, or push for a measure of liberalization, but they could only "dream of Europe," and of a radically different political and economic orientation.

Failure to prepare as a governing elite was a pragmatic response to the communist context, where state repression defused such aspirations. It also was inherent in the self-definition of many dissidents as "individuals who do what they must and consequently who find themselves in open conflict with the regime,"[18] and who sought, instead of regime overthrow, the cultivation of a "second" or "parallel" society within which human dignity might flourish.

What distinguishes East European dissidents as an opposition elite is that they were blocked by self-definition and authoritarian repression from mobilizing broader socio-economic bases and from seeking power the way counterelites did in other dictatorships.

The character of dissident politics differed as much from conventional politics as did their objectives. The skills and resources dissidents later brought to post-communist democratization were forged in unconventional politics. The profile of an effective dissident has been defined in terms of eloquence, courage and a certain moral stubbornness that allowed the individual to speak the truth to power regardless of the consequences. The definition of "winning" was the refusal to be silenced. These are not the skills and victories of the practitioner of conventional politics. A number of commentators have noted this imperfect fit with the strengths of an effective democratic politician. Dissidence does not put a premium on the ability to compromise, or even necessarily to cooperate.

Even more centrally, much of the dissident community embraced an anti-political ethos that rejected "dirty politicking." In the face of regime repression, there was a logic to emphasizing intransigence over flexibility and stark morally unambiguous confrontations between humanity and "impersonal power."[19] In this stance, there was also an element of what Kullberg calls reactive or reverse patterning--we are not like "them."

And as for political responsibility, it surely had a different meaning in such a setting: the willingness to take personal responsibility for one's own acts, and to pay the consequences. In the last analysis one was primarily accountable to oneself and one's conscience, in consonance with dissident emphasis on individual human worth. This had survival value in an ideologically and programmatically diverse dissident community united primarily in opposition to the regime. Individual accountability resolved the problem of cohesion amidst diversity.[20] This is a rather different conception of political responsibility and accountability than is generally understood in democratic politics, where an effective politician may in fact behave responsibly when compromising beliefs, negotiating and achieving a "satisficing" result.

To say that dissidents operated essentially outside the political and economic power structure in communist states is not to say that they lacked resources. The East European intellectual tradition itself invested their challenge with historical and moral meaning, validating the determination to continue the fight, even when both the regime and the larger society seemed unresponsive. Moreover, the intellectual dissident possessed what Pierre Bourdieu has termed "social capital"--the educational investment each had made, and subsequently re-invested in the opposition effort in the currency of words and thought. Such social or human capital, of course, could well be a convertible asset in other regime settings.[21]

The defining features of the dissident counterelite sketched above can be understood only in the context of the authoritarian regime they confronted. The dominance by default of the intellectuals in this counterelite stems both from historical tradition and from the poverty of alternative socio-economic bases for resistance. The character of the regime, its pervasive penetration of society, also explains why most dissident communities remained profoundly isolated from a mass base, why the dissidents did not think in terms of seizing power, and why the focus on reclaiming authentic human identity through an embattled, "anti-political" effort to live in truth was paramount. All these features differentiate the communist counterelites from mobilized oppositions in other authoritarian regimes, just as it inhibited the relevance of their experience as an "apprenticeship for power."

Unlike many elite actors, the dissident's positional definition--a self-definition as well as a broader societal one--was contextually dependent on the existence of the regime. It is possible to abstract many types of elite from a regime-specific context. But the dissident's status is self-liquidating in the event of regime change. The dissident has defined an identity by opposing the authoritarian regime. If successful, the dissident is no longer a dissident. It is possible to speak of class or institutionally based elites such as labor union leaders as oppositional, and then to envisage their repositioning in defense of their interests in a subsequent political order, but it is a stretch of the very concept of dissidence to speak of it as pursuing its own interest in a normalized post-authoritarian order. What interests are these? While a given elite faction may *pursue* an opposition stance, dissidence *is* an opposition stance. [22]

The problem then arises: could such an elite make the transition from symbolic politics to real politics, reconfiguring itself and coping with the routine problems of governance at the same time?[23] The subsequent analysis attempts to pinpoint the overarching pattern of constraints and opportunities that shaped a "curvilinear" pattern of rising and then declining dissident cohesion and salience in the periods of transition and consolidation.[24] Dissident centrality to politics crested in the transition period, eroding in the complex environment of post-transition politics.

Transition: The Recredentialling of a Marginal Elite

By the late 1980s, the Central European communist regimes were well aware that they faced twin crises of performance and legitimacy, even if they were unable to effectively respond to those crises. In fact, these regimes needed a credible negotiating partner even to promote a reform program, much less a political transition. The Polish government felt impelled to negotiate with the illegal Solidarity movement in order to garner support for a serious economic reform which the regime was too illegitimate to implement alone. Defeated in its unilateral efforts to gain public validation for economic reform in the referendum of 1987, the party subsequently battled an outbreak of strikes in 1988 which it seemed could only be pacified by the engagement of Solidarity leaders in a new social contract. Initiating negotiations with Solidarity validated both the movement and the government. The legalization of Solidarity was the regime's concession; Solidarity in return reluctantly agreed to participate in elections that were so stacked in favor of the communists that Solidarity leaders feared that both its electoral participation and its subsequent parliamentary presence would legitimate the communist regime, tarnishing the opposition by implicating them in policies they were helpless to shape significantly. In retrospect, the scope of the Solidarity electoral victory in June 1989 tends to overshadow these original fears. It should not be forgotten, however, that the impetus that drove the regime into the so-called "roundtable" negotiations was the need to find, and then coopt, an opposition partner with credible credentials to speak for a broader public.[25]

In Hungary, the younger generation of communist leaders who displaced the aging Janos Kadar and his septuagenarian colleagues in 1988 had also concluded that successful economic reform necessitated political opening. These leaders deliberately built bridges to the opposition in an effort to build a stable consensus for the evolution of a more open system.[26]

In both Hungary and Poland, the emergence of a credible opposition force facilitated the striking of a basic transitional bargain. In Czechoslovakia, where mass protest triggered the terminal crisis, the movements that negotiated transition (Civic Forum, Public Against Violence) were improvisations, cobbled together in reaction to the swift pace of events. These new movements lacked organizational and decisionmaking structures or defined leaderships, possibilities that authoritarian repression and the ethos of individual accountability had constrained. In Czechoslovakia, it is difficult, even by mid-1989, to find in the dissident community a systematic effort to negotiate regime change, or even a sustained debate within the counterelite over strategies to achieve such a result. Indeed, the possibility of radical political change came as a shocking surprise to both dissidents and rulers alike, and necessitated considerable improvisation. (The absence of a clear sense of such a possibility is visible even in Poland, and accounts for communist and Solidarity miscalculations about the outcome of the June 1989 elections.)

Yet movement politics was necessary, for mass protest in itself does not transform political regimes. Demonstrations cannot produce detailed agendas, negotiating points, a program to which the beleaguered communist regime is constrained to respond. Even an authoritarian regime that has accepted its crumbling hold on power cannot surrender to, or negotiate with, a demonstration. A party elite forced to renegotiate the political bargain must have credible negotiating partners. In much of Eastern Europe, negotiation between wings of the party itself was no longer credible in the fall of 1989, even though the German and Bulgarian parties did try to temporize by throwing unpopular communist leaders to the wolves. The image is one of confused and demoralized officers on a noisy and disorganized battle field, searching for an enemy to whom to surrender. A pledge to seek free elections was more persuasive if there was a credible opposition to monitor and participate in the implementation of that pledge. A founder of the Hungarian Democratic Forum, literary critic Csaba Kiss commented "The government has often said it wants a dialogue. The question is, *Who will its partner be?*"[27] Hence the proliferation of long-term or eleventh-hour roundtable negotiations to orchestrate the opening of the system, to determine its timing and groundrules.

Given the prolonged communist control of the major socio-economic and political institutions, the credibility of the pledge to open the political system (and thus defuse popular unrest) therefore depended on the engagement of the major recognizably non-communist force, the dissidents. Their moral credibility was a political currency that reached its highest value in the transition crisis period. In the more liberalized societies of Poland and Hungary, the earlier emergence of opposition leadership made quite clear whose imprimatur might defuse the political and economic crisis. Yet, all communist regimes in extremis and beyond the hope of retaining power "needed" an opposition with which to validate the terms of transition.

The political fluidity of the crisis, then, generated uninstitution-alized, improvised mechanisms of elite recruitment for ad hoc extra-constitutional decisionmaking forums or roundtables. The credentials that gained dissident entrée to the negotiation table were legacies of the former regime: those of authenticity in anti-communist resistance --the demonstrable suffering of the uncompromising opposition politician who could speak for the larger suffering of society as a whole. Only in Poland did these dissidents have a broad popular base before 1989; but in other countries the politics of confrontation brought to the fore dissident spokesmen who were positioned to trade in their certified records of anti-communist resistance for the rights of spokesmen and negotiators. Their jail sentences, their banned manifestoes, their sacrifice of economic and personal security, all gave weight to their moral authority to negotiate a communist surrender. In such circumstances, dissidents were able to breach the frequent isolation of the earlier period to gain public support and harness the popular anger of mass protest to the politics of transition. This relatively novel dissident-mass link was often validated quite informally. The regime decision to accept the negotiating bona fides of the dissidents was conditioned in part by the spectacle of crowd approbation for the spokesmen of the Velvet Revolution, and by the widespread public observance of the short general strike they orchestrated, sending a message of dissident credibility with the public in Czechoslovakia. In Hungary, the swelling attendance at dissident-organized demonstrations and observances was a similar cue.[28] The argument that dissidents were necessary actors in these transitions, that they were the best available intermediaries in linking mass dissatisfaction to the process of regime change, is made with due respect for the variations in the strength of civil society in the region. The sequence of regional crises is not unrelated to the relative strength and coherence of the opposition, particularly since the more organized oppositions in Poland and Hungary provided the foundation for the earliest negotiated transitions, and ignited parallel (and more temporally compressed) efforts elsewhere.

The fact that dissident credentials to broker the transition were originally forged in a very different political setting would subsequently prove problematic in a number of ways that I will discuss shortly, but the expenditure of dissident political capital on the achievement of relatively peaceful political transitions was a stabilizing factor. This was the apex of dissident authority and popularity, their finest hour. Emerging from the first elections, dissident Hungarian, Czech, Slovak and Polish intellectuals formed the core of many of the new governments; their unconventional backgrounds charmed western journalists and excited scholarly attention. In Hungary, for example, the new Prime Minister was a medical historian, the head of the National Assembly a historian of nineteenth-century Hungary, the Minister of Defense an eighteenth-century agricultural historian, and the Minister of Foreign Affairs a diplomatic historian.[29] Playwright presidents, journalist prime ministers, and even psychiatrist Defense Ministers abounded. Would these figures survive the professionalization of politics?

It is important to recognize that the suddenness and comprehensiveness of the shift in political context taxed the adaptability of dissident movements. For one thing, even the politics of transition represented a decided role shift for the dissident opposition. During the transitional crisis, the radically changed situation put pressure on prior values when dissidents were called upon to negotiate with power, rather than to confront it. The dissidents, while retaining their sense of mission, no longer acted as dissidents from the moment they entered into transactions with party leaders and government officials. They were no longer "substitute" politicians, but real ones. They were called upon to cut a deal, to define specific, realizable objectives and find a workable formula to implement them. Apart from the understandable internecine battles over tactics and strategy, there were very real tensions over taking on such an overtly "political" role. Still, the dissidents were acutely aware of the need for someone to act in the crisis period, and equally aware that there was no clear alternative to their own engagement. As the Czech Civic Forum would later query in the elections of 1990, "If not us, then who?"

In some senses, the first elections, although launching a new competitive elite recruitment process, were a reckoning postponed. These elections were fought along the same faultlines that obtained in the communist period--a referendum on communism rather than a clear explication of the generally vaguely defined goals of democratization, marketization and return to Europe. These "founding" elections therefore preserved some of the anti-political unity ethos of the late communist period, and the relatively stark choice presented to the electorate did not yet adequately address the complex policy choices to come. The characteristic feature of these elections, therefore, was movement politics of broad, incipiently heterogeneous anti-communist coalitions with strong dissident representation. The post-election consolidation period would clarify the weaknesses of improvised movement politics as a permanent political approach.

Consolidation Period

If many dissidents were already uncomfortable with filling political roles during the transition crisis, it was in the post-crisis consolidation period that a distinctively dissident perspective proved most difficult to maintain. The romance of the stoker or amnestied political prisoner turned cabinet minister may have been assurance that the transition was not a trick, but it was also a mark of administrative and political inexperience. Prior resistance to the communist regimes had excluded these dissidents from conventional policymaking roles. Anti-politics had legitimated the transition, but could one govern anti-politically? Or, as Rupnik asks, "How easily can dissident intellectuals who were expert practitioners of moral indignation turn into professional politicians who can orchestrate the compromises of everyday political life?"[30]

Polish sociologist George Kolankiewicz notes that post-communist "governing elites were well endowed with moral authority, just as their predecessors had been bereft of it, but they were short on programs and perspectives for system reform."[31] Solidarity trade unionist Karol Modzelewski notes "Solidarity's complete lack of an economic program of its own" in 1989. He adds:

> We none of us....expected such a sudden collapse of the Soviet empire and of communism....No one thought of the economic policy the opposition Solidarity would have to adopt as the ruling party. It seemed impossible, and to propose unrealistic steps towards that goal would only end in fights.[32]

This crisis of governmental expertise was ameliorated in part by the retention of substantial numbers of bureaucratic carryovers from the former regime, monitored by a thinly spread layer of dissidents and non-party experts "parachuted in" at the top of the political hierarchy.[33] Younger party technocrats, blocked in mobility and policy innovation by the rigidities of the old system, were often quick to transfer loyalties. In Hungary, the transition itself was dubbed "the revolution of the deputy-department heads" in recognition of their receptiveness to regime change.[34]

The acceptance of transferred loyalty was the first major dissident compromise with the former elite. Those dissidents who accepted the practical value of collaboration with existing bureaucracy were vulnerable to assaults on their political integrity from less accommodating brethren and, even more, from beyond the dissident core altogether. Hence a Mazowiecki outflanked by Walesa on the decommunization issue in the prelude to the 1990 presidential campaign, or a Havel defending the contribution of excommunist Prime Minister Calfa to the Velvet Revolution shared a common vulnerability: liability to criticism as excessively cooperative with the representatives of the former communist regime.

These problems of governance are more subtle than may first appear, and are worth examining in the context of the erosion of the primary dissident credential--moral authority. It was, in many respects, a no-win situation. On the one hand, a posture of continued moral certitude could impair political effectiveness, appearing arrogant and uncompromising just when accommodation was essential. The martyred morality that had been a badge of honor in the transition crisis now became a liability. On the other hand, the adaptable dissident who proved amenable to compromise and adept at the infighting of "normal" politics also lost luster. As Irena Gross describes the plight of Polish intellectual dissidents in power: "they quickly lost their (recent) saintly aura by starting to quarrel in public...Now that they became authorities themselves, they called for restraint, for compromise--they who always called only for truth. The new elite became 'them' in a matter of months."[35]

There were specific legacies of the dissident experience in the relationship to former power holders that further undermined moral credibility. The debarment of former communist officials and informers from key positions in public life, known as "lustration," is a phenomenon that Klaus von Beyme characterizes as "negative elite recruitment."[36] It was a contentious issue that soon tarnished the former dissidents themselves. Martin Palous reports of his defeated dissident-based Civic Movement that it was "constantly being accused of being pseudo-communists or of being a movement harboring a majority of sixty-eighters [the reform communists of the Prague Spring]." [37]

Ironically and most importantly, it was precisely the dissident community that was most vulnerable to penetration by regime informers under communism. After all, who could be more usefully coerced or corrupted into collaboration than those with inside information on the regime's fiercest critics? The luster of the dissidents' anti-communist credentials was radically diminished by this revelation of police informants in their midst. Dissidents might justly complain that the "purest" citizens turned out to be those most politically passive and unheroic in the past, and they even interpreted the lustration campaigns as the revenge of the previously uncommitted for the guilt induced by the example of more courageous dissidents, who were a living reproach to general popular collaboration and passivity in the communist period.[38] However, the fact remained that the strongest political credential of the immediate transition period, the credential of prior resistance to communist power, was sullied by the lustration controversies, and by the larger resentments that attended them. A decredentialling process that targeted communist elites had caught the dissidents in its undertow. This was clearly a legacy both of the dissident position in the former regime as a security police target, and of residual popular resentment of those who had crusaded against, rather than acquiesced in, the authoritarian regime.

In summary, the moral capital that dissidents had earned under the communist regime--the moral credential that facilitated the transitions and brought dissidents to power and that constituted their unique entitlement--was quickly dissipated once the problems of governance took center stage, self-destructing in the exercise of power. Moral credibility had stemmed precisely from acting outside politics, and was difficult to transfer into the context of conventional politics. There was no good way to practice politics anti-politically.[39]

A second hallmark of dissident marginalization was the fragmentation of the movements forged in the crucible of 1989. In the spirit of accountability to individual moral visions that had characterized the earlier opposition period, movements began to pull apart schismatically. They lacked both the glue of organizational cohesion and the coherence of interest-based purpose that might derive from a defined socio-economic base. Despite its breadth of support in 1989, even Solidarity struggled with fractured linkages to the grass roots and with an identity crisis: was it a party, a trade union, or a governmental directorate? Solidarity's fragmentation was dauntingly clear in the divisive elections of 1990 and 1991. Civic Forum and Public Against Violence in Czechoslovakia divided within a year of the founding election of 1990. The catalyst may have been the deadlines of the electoral process, but organizational weakness and the internal divisions present embryonically before 1989 and enhanced by the policy clashes of governance, underlay the electoral dispersion. Dissidents had moved from isolation to the leadership of umbrella organizations too unwieldy to gel into a durable electoral constituency.

Scholars have frequently noted this tendency of movements to fragment after the unifying goal of unseating the communist regime had been achieved. As one Solidarity adherent admitted, "Solidarity owed the clarity of its vision to the nature of its opponent." [40] The vanquishing of the opponent inevitably weakened the cohesion of the movement. Walesa's failed 1995 presidential campaign against ex-communist Aleksandr Kwasniewski signalled that the evocation of the heroic past of the region's most powerful movement had lost its resonance for the new Poland. Indeed, the vanquishing of the opponent had destroyed the entire context within which dissidents had defined themselves, in which they had a definable, cohesive identity, and in which they had been the heroes of 1989. The disappearance of the common cause that had cemented heterogeneous outlooks unleashed contention and even vituperation among erstwhile allies, especially in Poland. Individual dissidents confessed to disorientation at the loss of sustaining community in the teeth of rapid change and changing role expectations. The counterculture of dissidence did not facilitate a smooth transition to governance.

Two further problems, each with antecedents in the opposition years, accelerated the erosion of the dissident position. The first is the previously-noted social isolation of dissident movements, even to some extent in Poland, the lack of strong linkages with a larger mass public, especially where the opposition ethos was more cosmopolitan than nationalist. Regionwide, dissidents thus had difficulty breaking out of their urban strongholds to woo the countryside.[41] Marked as urban intellectuals, the intelligentsia that provided primary energy to the dissident movement often found that the communists communicated more clearly than they in rural areas. The communist-era ghettoization of dissidents as urban intellectuals proved telling in the context of developing a mass base, as did of course the superior communist organizational network.[42]

Second, others who were quicker to recognize the mobilizing potential of effective party organization reaped electoral rewards.[43] To the extent that dissidents continued to adhere to the congenial spirit of a broad movement rather than to a more organizationally disciplined party, they adhered to a vision of non-hierarchical solidarity that had sustained them in opposition and that had proved effective in the "referendum" elections of 1990.

The continued embrace of movement politics thereafter might seem a rigid clinging to the ethos of unity that was more appropriate under the dissident conditions of the communist period. In practice, the logic of the dissidents was more complex than that. Asked one Polish Solidarity partisan: "why not have political parties right away? There are two reasons for not doing so... our job of securing the transition in Poland is not yet accomplished, and for this we need unity.... Furthermore, there has been such a dislike of the communist party as a political institution that the notion of the possibility of legitimate political power expressed through formal parties has been discredited."[44] Echoing the perception of voter repugnance for parties, Charter 77 activist Jan Urban noted that three quarters of Civic Forum supporters didn't want it to become a political party. The dissident leadership of 1990 regarded their movement as a "primary school" for politics and politicians in the initial period, after which it might refocus attention on regional or grassroots politics.[45] In short, the attempt to perpetuate a politics of unity was not merely nostalgia for earlier solidarity, but also a sober if misguided response to the perceived needs of the current situation and to the attitudes of the electorate. However, this vision suffered an institutional impairment in subsequent elections.

In Czechoslovakia, the issue of institutional form erupted in fall 1990, when divisions within the governing Civic Forum-Public Against

Violence coalitions first began to manifest themselves clearly. At issue in the Civic Forum was not only the vague issue content of movement politics (critics described it as politically "illegible"), but the organizational directionless of the movement. Vaclav Klaus (an economist without dissident pedigree) favored the Forum's reconfiguration into a structured membership party, an approach that sat badly with his ex-dissident colleagues;[46] his election as movement chair heralded the disintegration of the Civic Forum the following winter. Thereafter, each group followed the logic of the stance they had espoused during the period of movement dissolution. The electoral results are instructive. Klaus accelerated the construction of a more disciplined party; his Civic Democratic Party successfully contested the next round of elections in 1992, and has governed since that time. A primary vehicle of the former Czech dissidents was the Civic Movement (OH), which adhered to a looser format. The 1992 elections that brought Klaus to power also saw the erasure of the Civic Movement as well as virtually all of the most prominent Czech dissident politicians (and many Slovak dissidents as well) from the parliament. This electoral disaster occurred despite the continuing personal popularity and influence of key party notables (including, among others, the Czech Prime Minister Petr Pithart, and Foreign Minister Jiri Dienstbier).[47] Rather, it would appear that OH's under-organization as a movement was a prime factor in the defeat, as was the OH image as a party of intellectual notables.[48]

Taken together, this analysis of the special liabilities and positioning of dissidents in the post-transition period point to important reasons for the reduction of their exalted status after the crisis period passed, all of them rooted in their positioning in the former regime. In a larger perspective, however, it is also important to recognize that the key political positions were hardly uncontested. The opening of the system to electoral competition, and the demands of the new policy agenda, radically reconstructed the available recruitment channels and opened the system to effective rivals.

Three broad groups were effective competitors to the dissidents in asserting their claims to effective post-communist governance: the technocratic professionals, the ex-communists, and a more amorphous group, the nationalists. In the Hungarian case, Akos Rona-Tas appropriated the Szelenyi metaphor "parking orbits" to describe the location of those with political inclinations who had navigated the communist period by immersing themselves in social science and legal scholarship, journalism and other professions that permitted safely indirect address of political issues. He identified the roundtable negotiations in Hungary as the key opportunity for such incipient politicians to enter the political arena. His analysis has broader applicability. A key example of emergence from "parking orbits" would be Czech econometrician and now Prime Minister Vaclav Klaus. Those in parking orbits, therefore, entered politics *after* the dissident period, during the transition, but frequently possessed legal and economic expertise lacking among dissident intellectuals, who were concentrated in the humanities. Recruits from the "parking orbits" assumed increasing prominence in the post-transition period.[49]

The communists themselves also proved to have political and social capital to convert in the post-transition period. The initial electoral victories of dissident-based movements did not establish a permanent barrier against the return of reformed communist socialist parties to power. Former communist parties gained sufficient electoral support to play a central role in forming new governments in Hungary in 1994 and Poland in 1993. The former Slovak communist party, refurbished as the Party of the Democratic Left, served in an interim governing coalition in 1994. Obviously, reform communists found ways of recredentialling themselves through embracing the new agenda and emphasizing a programmatic commitment to the most popular component of the communist party, the social safety net.[50]

In short, the elite recruitment channels were relatively open to contestation by forces that were more numerous, better organized or better grounded than the dissidents. The dissidents primary distinguishing claims to power--the resource of moral capital--was dissipated not only by the process of political infighting but by the very act of participating in politics. Individual dissidents might adjust and converge with other political forces, but the dissidents as a political/anti-political community were virtually by self-definition subject to loss of identity and cohesion in conventional politics.

Conclusion

In this analysis, I have contrasted the central role dissidents often played in the period of transition from communist rule, and their declining centrality to the political elite of the consolidation period. Although individual dissidents clearly continue to play important roles in the new setting, it would appear that their temporary preeminence in East European politics was the product of a historical moment that maximized group cohesion and relevance to the political opportunity structure in a period of transitional crisis. The dissidents could not be said to have created that crisis, nor would they emerge from it as the new ruling class, by an act of simple elite replacement. Rather, the most effective dissident politicians were integrated into a larger body of new professional politicians by the process in some respects comparable to what Higley et al have characterized as elite convergence.[51]

While the "emergency" credentialling process of the transitional crisis period gave special value to the moral capital of dissidents, the subsequent period of fledgling governance offered new bases for acquiring leadership credentials and a more open arena for merchandising political skills and substantive expertise. In the changing political environment, dissidents lost their unique claim on power. The dissident "voice" of the communist period that was a critically important moral credential for engaging the communist regime in negotiations during the transition crisis became increasingly irrelevant, and even counterproductive, in the consolidation period.[52] Previous dissident ghettoization often left its mark in an elitist distancing from the dirty business of currying popular support for government policy innovati.[53] The insulation that had been armor in the communist period eventually became something of a strait jacket.

The sources of the new political elite are eclectic, drawn from the ranks of the retooled communist parties (social-democratized by conviction or circumstance), nationalist spokesmen, the professional "parking orbits" of prior regimes, and those dissidents whose organizational skills, pedigree and temperament fitted them to adapt to the changed political environment.

Let us review this analysis in the broader of context of elite transformation in periods of regime change. The comments of Kolankiewicz are worth citing at some length:

> A major defining feature of the first wave of political elites in the new democracies is that they came to power on the basis of their moral authority, rather than their economic or political resources....They were not the representatives of any new form of economic power, indeed they were merely the harbingers of just such a class. This form of elite ascendancy goes against the accepted pattern of domination and legitimation.[54]

Kolankiewicz underlines a central element of the distinction that gave the dissidents their leading position in the transition and subsequently eroded it: their contribution to engineering a transition that lacked defined actors rooted in recognizable socio-economic interests. The solution to the case of the disappearing dissidents is thus the solution to a murder mystery: who killed a civil society of relatively autonomous organization and interests? The constraints on the emergence of alternative elites positioned to contest power left dissident elites as a default option for brokering the transition. If not us, then who?

This very anomaly, however, deprived the dissidents of a durable class or interest-based politics with which to embed themselves in a new political order. To this extent, the post-communist dynamic deviates from the pattern of socioeconomically-based elite conflict that is so frequently the centerpiece of the analysis of regime change in other systems, and that deviation explains both the centrality of dissidents in the transitions and their travails in the consolidation periods--creating the phenomenon of the "transitional elite" insufficiently rooted in a social base to retain an intelligible identity in the post-communist order. In more typical cases of regime transition, the oppositional elites retain the capacity to mobilize political support precisely because of the socioeconomic power bases that earlier anchored their confrontation with the authoritarian regime.

Yet the process of post-communist elite transformation does share features recognizable in other settings of regime change, features that point toward a useful comparative research agenda. Elite recruitment processes in any given regime tend to be structured by the operational logic of that system, to produce a characteristic form of elite credentialling as well as characteristically relevant credentials. Regime change thus alters recruitment channels as well, and in the process produces structured patterns of elite recredentialling and decredentialling (exclusion or negative recruitment). In the final analysis, the peculiarities of the post-communist elite transformation do fit into the larger framework of elite transformation theory. They are a deviant case, not in disproving the premises of elite theories based on competing socioeconomic forces, but rather as a control case allowing us more fully to grasp the importance of such competing forces, and the consequences of their attenuation or absence. They are also part of a larger universe of cases in which the processes of elite recredentialling and decredentialling during regime change could profitably be explored.

Notes

1. The label "dissident" refers to the antiregime activist whose activities directly and publicly confronted the authorities with sins of omission and commission. Not included in this category are independent thinkers whose political conceptions ran contrary to the reigning orthodoxy, but who took no public stance, and frequently retained positions roughly commensurate with their training and abilities. In Czechoslovakia, for example, the freqently-jailed Charter 77 activist Vaclav Havel was a dissident; economist Vaclav Klaus of the Institute of Economic Forecasting, was not, despite his heterodox economic views.

2. The terms used here--transition and consolidation--come from the lexicon of democratization theory, developed in the examination of regime change in Latin America and Southern Europe in the 1970s and 1980s. Transition refers to the period during which an authoritarian regime collapses or negotiates a relinquishment of power. Consolidation refers to the period in which the rules of the new game are established and operationalized, understood to begin with the inauguration of a democratically constituted government through competitive elections.   See especially Guillermo O'Donnell and Philippe C. Schmitter, *Transitions from Authoritarian Rule: Tentative Conclusions about Uncertain Democracies* (Baltimore: Johns Hopkins University Press, 1986).

3. Robert D. Putnam. *The Comparative Study of Political Elites* (Englewood Cliffs, NJ: Prentice-Hall Inc., 1976) 173-182.

4. John Higley and Richard Gunther. *Elites and Democratic Consolidation in Latin America and Southern Europe* (Cambridge, England: Cambridge University Press, 1992) 13-37.

5. Judith S. Kullberg, "In the Ruins of the CPSU: Elites and Party Formation in Russia," paper prepared for the 1994 Annual Meeting of the American Political Science Association, New York, September 1994.

6. In Poland, the anti-communist opposition had a much broader base than the intellectuals. However, this was atypical elsewhere, and its significance in Poland is even open to question.

7. Jacques Rupnik, *The Other Europe* (New York: Pantheon Books, 1988, 1989), 213.

8. Timothy Garton Ash, "Prague: Intellectuals and Politicians," *New York Review of Books*, 12 January 1995, 36.

9. Vaclav Havel "Power of the Powerless," in Jan Vladislav, ed., *Václav Havel: Living in Truth* (London: Faber and Faber, 1986) 78.

10. Melvin Croan, "Lands In-Between: The Politics of Cultural Identity in Contemporary East Europe," *EEPS* 3:2 (Spring 1989): 185.

11. Judy Batt,   *East Central Europe from Reform to Transformation* (New York: Council on Foreign Relations Press,   1991).

12. Martin Palous, cited in "Discussing the Elections: The Czech Point of View: An Interview with Martin Palous and Petr Janyska," Radio Free Europe *RFE/RL Research Report* 1:26 (26 June 1992), 25.

13. akub Karpinski "Opposition, Dissidents and Democracy," *Uncaptive Minds* 5:2 (Summer 1992): 17-23.

14. The Polish novelist Konwiecki even played with the notion of a complicitous relationship between regime and dissident, each playing an increasingly scripted role in a metapolitical scenario of power ritually confronted and ritually defended. See especially his *A Minor Apocalypse*. More broadly, there is a perverse sense in which the regimes' intense scrutiny of dissident activity invested it with meaning: what we are doing must be important if it receives such attention and retaliation.

15. Cited in Mark Sommer, *Living in Freedom* (San Francisco: Mercury House, 1992) 49.

16. This is certainly the case to the extent that dissident intellectuals were marginal elites by choice. True, the Czech dissident playwright Vaclav Havel was marginalized from childhood because of his bourgeois antecedents; he even attributes his own detachment from the system to this experience. He is certainly representative of a group of dissident activists whose family history had a distancing effect; this includes even some whose parents were among the communist elites purged in the early 1950s. However, it would need substantially more evidence to argue that the dissident intellectuals were initially any more marginal to the communist system than were the intellectuals as a whole. Many intellectuals did in fact make an accommodation with the regime, exchanging conformity for a well-modulated "voice" (indeed the regime needed such intellectuals). See Miklos Haraszti, *The Velvet Prison: Artists under State Socialism* (New York: Noonday Press, Farrar, Straus and Giroux, 1987). Any argument that identifies the dissident intellectuals as marginalized simply because they are intellectuals thus fails to distinguish the accommodators from the dissenters.

17. The Czechoslovak dissident movement Charter 77, for example, explicitly disavowed the intention of presenting an alternative. See Charter 77, January 1, 1977, reprinted in Hans-Peter Riese, ed., *Since the Prague Spring: Charter 77 and the Struggle for Human Rights in Czechoslovakia* (New York: Random House, Vintage, 1979), 14.

18. Havel, 78.

19. Vaclav Havel, "Politics and Conscience," *Living in Truth*, ed., Jan Vladislav (London: Faber and Faber, 1986), 145.

20. The dissident communities embraced secular excommunists who retained socialist sympathies, strongly anti-communist religious believers, ardent nationalists and ardent cosmopolitans, environmental activists, countercultural experimenters, and a range of other diverse viewpoints. It was a community of commitment rather than of uniform values.

21. Pierre Bourdieu, "The Forms of Capital" in John G. Richardson *Handbook of Theory and Research for the Sociology of Education* (New York: Greenwood Press, 1986), 241-260.

22. It might be argued that revolutionary movements without a defined societal identity have in fact weathered the transition from opposition to power without losing identity. The Bolsheviki seized and held power, despite the dominance among their top leadership of marginalized cosmopolitan intellectuals in 1917. However, to conflate dissident elites with revolutionary counterelites is to misconstrue the character of dissidence, which did not define itself as a movement to seize power. Revolutionary elites such as the Bolsheviki operated within an organizational/institutional structure, the Leninist party. It was the party that seized power, and it was the party that lent continuity to the revolutionary elite. Indeed, in the absence of the party institutional vehicle, one could argue that the original core of Bolshevik intellectuals did not hold the power they seized, giving way a broader, more proletarian leadership under Stalin.

23. Rupnik, p. 270; George Szablowski and Hans-Ulrich Derlien, "East European Transitions, Elites, Bureaucracies and the European Community," *Governance* 6:3 (July 1993) 313.

24. The expression is adapted from the usage of Daniel V. Friedheim, "Bringing Society Back into Democratic Transition Theory after 1989: Pact Making and Regime Collapse," *East European Politics and Society* 7:3 (Fall 1993) 505.

25. Josep M. Colomer and Margot Pascual, "Polish Games of Transition," *Communist and Post-Communist Studies* 27:3 (1994) 275-294.

26. For an excellent and exhaustive analysis of the politics of the Hungarian transition, see Laszlo Bruszt and David Stark, "Remaking the Political Field in Hungary: From the Politics of Confrontation to the Politics of Competition," in Ivo Banac, ed., *Eastern Europe in Revolution* (Ithaca, New York: Cornell University Press, 1992) 13-55.

27. Cited in Bruce Shenitz, "Hungary Seeks Its Own Glasnost," *Nation* (9 April 1988)

497.

28. See especially Timothy Garton Ash, *The Magic Lantern*, (New York: Random House, 1990).

29. Akos Rona-Tas, "The Selected and the Elected: The Making of the New Parliamentary Elite in Hungary," *East European Politics and Society* 5:3 (Fall 1991) 357.

30. Rupnik, 270.

31. George Kolankiewicz "Elites in Search of a Political Formula," *Daedalus* 123: (Summer 1994) 143.

32. Karol Modzelewski, "What happened to Solidarity?" *Uncaptive Minds* 1:7 (Winter-Spring 1994) 71.

33. For a standard rationale for this expedient, see the interview with the parliamentary Fraction leader of Hungarian Democratic Forum, cited in Valerie Bunce and Maria Csanadi "Uncertainty in the Transition: Post-Communism in Hungary," *East European Politics and Societies* 7:2 (Spring 1993) 244.

34. Klaus von Beyme, "Regime Transition and Recruitment of Elites in Eastern Europe," *Governance* 6:3 (July 1993) 413.

35. Irena Grudzinska Gross, "Post-Communist Resentment, or the Rewriting of Polish History," *East European Politics and Society* 6:2 (Spring 1992) 148, 145 and 141.

36. Klaus von Beyme, "Regime Transition and Recruitment of Elites in Eastern Europe," 411. Von Beyme relates the intensity of negative elite recruitment policies, or lustration, to the type of regime change; in the less rigid communist regimes of Hungary and Poland that transitioned by way of high-level elite negotiations in the course of a gradual erosion of communist power, the subsequent communist purges were less severe. See 412-418.

37. Cited in "Discussing the Elections," 25.

38. Gross, 144. In Poland, Solidarity was even reproached for the Roundtable bargain that provided the initial breakthrough. Willingness to compromise was criticized as having delayed a more thoroughgoing transition such as those that occurred in neighboring countries.

39. This holds true in any political system. Outsider politics in US elections may be a winning strategy, but the outsider then becomes an insider, who begins to lose the

outsider credential with the public, or sacrifices political effectiveness, or frequently both.

40. Janusz Ziolkowski, "Roots, Branches and Blossoms of Solidarity," in *Spring into Winter: the 1989 Revolutions,* Gwyn Prins, ed., (Manchester, England, Manchester University Press: 1990), p. 53.

41. For a summary of the historical and contemporary significance of the rural-urban rift, see Batt, 48.

42. Specific voting patterns illustrate the point. In Czechoslovakia, OH recorded high support primarily in Prague [See Jan Obrman, "The Czechoslovak Elections," Radio Free Europe *RFE/RL Research Report* 1:26 (26 June 1992), 16.], and the Hungarian Young Democrats in Budapest.

43. On the general evolution of the post-communist party systems, see for example Herbert Kitschelt, "The Formation of Party Systems in East Central Europe," *Politics & Society* 20:1 (March 1992) 7-50.

44. Ziolkowski, 55.

45. Jan Urban, "Czechoslovakia: Power and Politics of Humiliation," in Prins, 124. See also Bronislaw Geremek, "Civil Society Then and Now," *Journal of Democracy* 3:2 (April 1992) 9-10.

46. See "Civic Forum and Public Against Violence Strive to Become More Effective," *Report on Eastern Europe*, 1:42 (19 October 1990), 9-14.

47. See Carlos Flores Juberias, "The Breakdown of the Czecho-Slovak Party System, " in Gyorgy Szoboszlai, ed., *Flying Blind: Emerging Democracies in East-Central Europe* (Yearbook, Hungarian Political Science Association, 1992) 156-58. Petr Pithart returned as a senator in 1996.

48. See "Discussing the Elections: The Czech Point of View," 24-25. Sensitized by such lessons, the Hungarian opposition Alliance of Young Democrats (FIDESZ), a movement originating in the late communist period, repositioned itself at its pre-election annual congress in April 1993 to consolidate its party structure and broaden its constituency and leadership by abolishing the former age limit. See Judith Pataki, "Hungarian Youth Party Comes of Age," Radio Free Europe *RFE/RL Research Report* 2:21 (21 May 1993) 42-45.

49. Akos Rona-Tas, 370-72.

50. See Jane L. Curry, "Elected Communists in Poland," *Problems of Post-Communism*

42:1 (January-February 1995) 46-50.

51. Michael Burton, Richard Gunther and John Higley, "Introduction: Elite Trans-formations and Democratic Regimes, " in John Higley and Richard Gunther, eds., *Elites and Democratic Consolidation in Latin America and Southern Europe* (Cambridge: Cambridge University Press, 1992) 1-37.

52. "Voice" is used here in the sense defined by A.O. Hirschmann. See especially his "Exit, Voice and the Fate of the German Democratic Republic: An Essay in Conceptual History," *World Politics* 45:2 (January 1993) 173-202.

53. For an intensive case study of Poland, see Adam Przeworski, Luiz Carlos Bresser Pereira and Jose Maria Maravall, *Economic Reforms in New Democracies* (Cambridge: Cambridge University Press, 1993), Part III. Moreover, early electoral success, to the extent that dissidents were able to achieve it, was not an unmitigated blessing. Such early victors could well become casualties of the volatility of electoral choice in the painful period of attempted economic transformation, where the pattern of electoral response has often been to reverse the verdict of the initial elections.

54. Kolankiewicz, 154.

Conclusions

The papers included in this volume all focus on some aspect of the transition from a communist to a post-communist state during the 1989 to 1991 period. In some cases the transition is set in an historical context and concentrates on a limited area of a country's development that contributes especially to the particular characteristics of that period; in other cases the transition is examined in the context of a particular political event, such as an election or a legislative program for privatization of public holdings. However, the political and economic upheaval that followed the sudden shift from communism is evident in each of the countries examined. The entrenched communist leadership did not simply fade away but perpetuated its power under the guise of new party names, new constitutions and restructured political and economic institutions. This scramble to retain power took different forms in the various East European states. Some power holders used military action and virulent nationalism, others elevated majority rights over those of minority populations, and many established control, and even ownership, over profitable public economic enterprises at the expense of the larger population.

In the case of Yugoslavia, the collapse of the state was accompanied by increasing ethnic tensions which were driven by various ambitious leaders. The fears frequently expressed in the writings of George Klein concerning open ethnic conflict were finally realized; the political cohesion of the nation was destroyed, ethnic groups were slaughtered, and much of the economy ceased to function. Authoritarian governments reigned supreme and continued to threaten the security of the entire Balkans. Similar examples of violent political strife during the transitional period can be found in former republics of the Soviet Union.

Romania began its transition from the communist to the post-communist period with violence, which culminated in the execution of its communist leader. However, Romania avoided civil war and held elections for the selection of new leaders from the communist leadership. Laws were passed for economic reform and an orderly direction was established. With pressure exerted from the West to copy their economies, and the common problem in Eastern Europe, that the privatization of public property initially benefitted the power elite, Romania continued to struggle.

The picture in Poland of rule by law under newly approved election legislation contrasted sharply with the chaos that ruled in much of former Yugoslavia. The prospect of moving toward a democratic society through local elections seemed promising, since Poland had been moving away from its former authoritarian government toward increased democracy over a longer period than other East European states.

The "nationality problem" or the problem of minorities either within the host state or in neighboring states is a common occurrence within the newly post-communist states. The determined tenacity of these populations to retain their own distinct cultures, whether it be the ethnic groups in Bosnia-Hercegovina or the diaspora Poles in Belarus and Lithuania, is always an issue worth further study. The easy declaration, even in the face of contradictory evidence, that ethnic hatred is historic and necessarily follows from the mere existence of different ethnic groups within the same state, needs to be treated with skepticism. A greater understanding and recognition of the deliberate exploitation of ethnic differences by the leaderships in order to drive the country toward particular political goals might help avert future ethnic conflict. The more recent works of George Klein concentrated on better comprehending this area of potential ethnic conflict in Yugoslavia. There is need for scholars to continue such studies and to challenge proclamations of the inevitability of ethnic hatred and conflict with evidence of the amiable ethnic relationships that exist and how that status is maintained.

Appendix A:

Maps

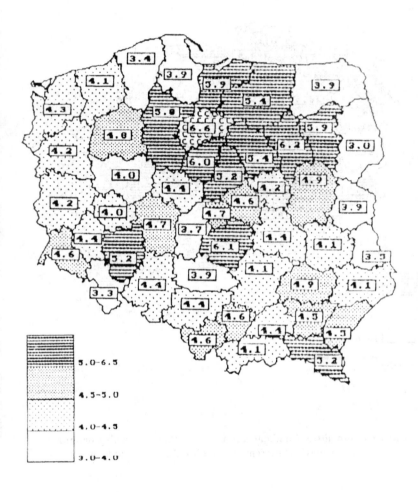

Map 1

Struggling with the Communist Legacy

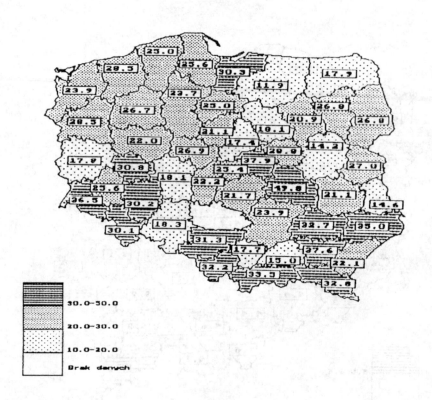

Map 2

**Citizen's Committees Candidates and Candidates of Citizen's Committee
"Solidarnosc" as Percent of Total Number of Candidates**

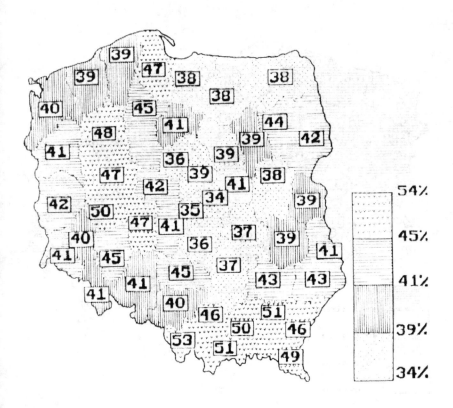

Map 3

Electoral Turnout

Map 4

Percent of Multiple-Mandate Districts with Four or More Party Lists

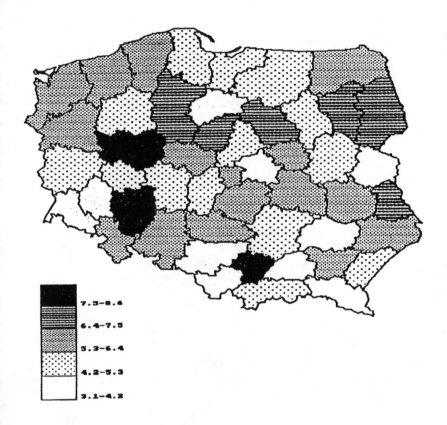

Map 5

Average Number of Lists Per One District in Multiple-Mandate Districts

Appendix B:

Charts

Question: How does this present council compare with previous councils?

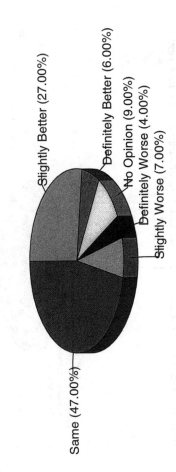

Comparison of Current Council with Previous Ones

Source: General Election Commission, 1991

Question: Has the influence of people like you changed after last years elections?

Did Not Changeg (61.00%)

Slight Decrease (7.00%)
Definate Decrease (5.00%)
No Opinion (4.00%)
Definate Increase (2.00%)

Slight Increase (21.00%)

Post-Election Changes in Individual Influence

Source: General Election Commission, 1991

Question: Has anything changed in your municipality over the past year?

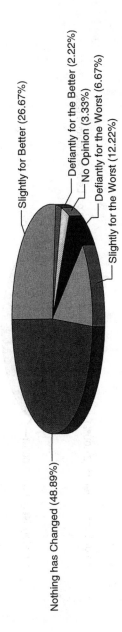

Slightly for Better (26.67%)

Defiantly for the Better (2.22%)

No Opinion (3.33%)

Defiantly for the Worst (6.67%)

Slightly for the Worst (12.22%)

Nothing has Changed (48.89%)

Municipal Change Over Past Year

Source: General Election Commission 1991

Question: What is your perception concerning the current GMINA council?

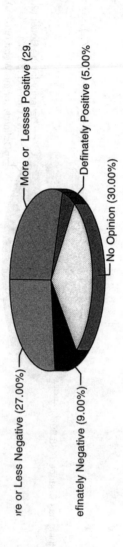

More or Lessss Positive (29.

Definately Positive (5.00%)

No Opinion (30.00%)

re or Less Negative (27.00%)

efinately Negative (9.00%)

Perception of the Current GMINA Council

Source: General Election Commission, 1991

References

Akos Rona-Tas. 1991. "The Selected and the Elected: The Making of the New Parliamentary Elite in Hungary, *East European Politics and Society*, 5, 3, Fall.

Amnesty International. Various reports from 1982 and after.

Andrejevich, Milan. 1992. "What Future for Serbia?" *Radio Free Europe*, RFE/RL Research Report, 1, 50, December 18.

Andric, Ivo. 1960. *The Bridge on the Drina*, Lovett F. Edwards, trans., New York: New American Library.

Anuarul Statistic Al Romaniei. 1991. Bucharest.

Ash, Timothy Garton. 1990. *The Magic Lantern*, New York: Random House.

_____. 1995. "Prague: Intellectuals and Politicians," *New York Review of Books*, 12, January.

Atlas Narodov Mira. 1964. Moscow: Akademia Nauk SSSR.

Austrian Finance Minister. 1992. "Keynote Address." Conference on Privatization, Vienna, February.

Banac, Ivo. 1984. *The National Question in Yugoslavia: Origins, History, Politics*, Ithaca: Cornell University Press.

Batt, Judy. 1991. *East Central Europe from Reform to Transformation*, New York: Council on Foreign Relations Press.

Belgrade Television. 1991. June 28.

Bell, John D. ed. 1998. *Bulgaria in Transition*, Boulder, CO: Westview Press.

Bicanic, Rudolf. 1938. *Ekonomska podloga, Hrvatskog pitanja*, Zagreb: Isdavac Vladko Macek.

Bilandzic, Dusan. 1985. Historija Socijalisticke Federativne Republike Yugoslavije, Zagreb: Skolska Knjiga.

Bokovoy, Melissa K, Jill A. Irvine and Carol S. Lilly. 1997. *State and Society Relations in Yugoslavia, 1945-1992*, New York: St. Martin's Press.

Bourdieu, Pierre. 1986. "The Forms of Capital." In John G. Richardson, *Handbook of Theory and Research for the Sociology of Education*, New York: Greenwood Press.

Bozic, Agneza. 1992. *The Rhetoric of Slobodan Milosevic and War on the Territory of Yugoslavia*. A Master's Thesis. Kalamazoo, Michigan: Western Michigan University.

Bruszi, Laszlo and David Stark. 1992. "Remaking the Political Field in Hungary: From the Politics of Confrontation to the Politics of Competition." In *Eastern Europe in Revolution*, Ithaca, New York: Cornell University Press.

Bunce, Valerie and Maria Csanadi. 1993. "Uncertainty in the Transition: Post-Communism in Hungary," *East European Politics and Society*, 7, 2, Spring.

Burdett, Anita L.P., ed., 1995. "Serbian Territorial aspirations in 1885, Translation of resolutions from a meeting of Serbians of Old Serbia and Macedonia, Belgrade, c. March 8, 1885." In *The Historical Boundaries Between Croatia, Bosnia, Serbia: Documents and Maps 1815-1845*, London: Archive Editions.

Burg, Steven L. 1977. "The Federalization of Socialist Yugoslavia: The Serb-Croat Conflict," *Publius*, 7, 4.

_____. 1983. *Conflict and Cohesion in Socialist Yugoslavia,* Princeton: Princeton University Press.

_____. 1988. "Elite Conflict in Post-Tito Yugoslavia." *Soviet Studies,* 38, 1.

Burton, Richard Gunther and John Higley. 1992. "Introduction: Elite Transformations and Democratic Regimes." In John Higley and Richard Gunther, eds., *Elites and Democratic Consolidation in Latin America and Southern Europe,* Cambridge: Cambridge University Press.

Calinescu, Matei and Vladimir Tismaneanu. 1992. "The 1989 Revolution and Romania's Future." In *Romania After Tyranny,* Daniel N. Nelson, ed., Boulder, San Francisco, Oxford: Westview.

Centrum Badania Opinii Spolecznej. 1990. *Wybory Samorzadowe '90,* Warsaw.

Centrum Badania Opinii Spolecznej. 1991. *Wybory Samorzadowe '91,* Warsaw.

Chopecki, J. 1990. *Przestrzen polityczna Polski: konflikt i zmiana,* Instytut Gospodarki Przestrennej, 28, Warsaw: Uniwesytet Warszawski.

Cifric, Ivan. 1984. "Savez komunista i seljastvo u socijalno-historijskom." In *Klasno-socijalna struktura Saveza kommunista Jugoslavije,* Vladimir Cvjeticanin et al, Zagreb: Globus.

"Civic Forum and Public Against Violence Strive to Become More Effective."1990. *Report on Eastern Europe,* 1, 42, October 19.

Cohen, Lenard J. 1977. "Conflict Management and Political Institutionalization in Socialist Yugoslavia." In *Legislatures in Plural Societies,* Albert Eldridge, ed., Durham: Duke University Press.

_____. 1993. *Broken Bonds: The Disintegration of Yugoslavia,* Boulder: Westview Press.

Cohen, Philip J. 1996. *Serbia's Secret War: Propaganda and the Deceit of History,* College Station: Texas A & M University Press. An excerpt of this work first appeared under the title "Holocaust History Mis-appropriated" in *Midstream*, a monthly Jewish review, published by the Theodore Herzl Foundation, 38, November 8, 1992.

Colomer, Josep M. and Margot Pascual. 1994. "Polish Games of Transition," *Communist and Post-Communist Studies*, 27, 3.

Comisia National Pentru Statistica. 1992. Bucharest.

"Comunicatul Catre Tara al Connsnilului Frontului Salvarii Nationale." 1989. *Monitoru Oficial al Romanniei*, December 22.

Cristoiu, Ion. 1992. "O Noua Iluzie Spulberata," *Lumea Libera Romanesca*, October 28.

Croan, Melvin. 1989. "Lands In-Between: The Politics of Cultural Identity in Contemporary East Europe," *EEPS*, 3, 2, Spring.

Curry, Jane L. 1995. "Elected Communists in Poland," *Problems of Post-Communism*, 42, 1, January-February.

Cvtila, Vlatko. 1991. "Tko je sto u armiji." In *Danas*, 568, 5.2.

Danas. 1988. Feb. 18. trans. in Joint Publication Research Service-EER (hereafter, JPRS) 88-033, Apr. 26, 1988, 43-45.

Dawidowicz, Lucy S. 1975. *The War Against the Jews, 1933-1945*, New York: Bantam Books.

Denitch, Bogdan. 1990. *Limits and Possibilities*, Minneapolis: University of Minnesota Press.

Demokracija. (Ljubljana, independent newspaper), 1989. Dec. 5.

Djilas, Milovan. 1969. *The Unperfect Society: Beyond the New Class*, D. Cooke, trans., New York: Harcourt Brace Jovanovich.

_____. 1977. *Wartime,* New York: Harcourt Brace Jovanovich.

Djilas, Aleksa. 1991. *The Contested Country,* London: Harvard University Press.

Duchacek, I. 1970. *Comparative Federalism: The Territorial Dimension of Politics,* New York: Holt, Reinhart and Winston.

Dyker, D. A. 1977. "Yugoslavia: Unity out of diversity?" In *Political Culture and Political Change in Communist State,* A. Brown & J. Gray eds., New York: Holmes & Meier Publishers.

Dziennik Ustaw. 1990. Ustawa o samorzadzie terytorialnym, 19 Marzec, 16, 95; 16, Ch. 2:Art. 6.

_____. 1990. Ustawa o podziale zadan i kompetencji, 26 Maj, 34, 198.

European Community. 1991. "Declaration on Yugoslavia," Brussels, 17 December 1991. In *Review of International Affairs,* Belgrade, XLII, 998-1000, December 1.

The Economist. 1991. 7725.

Eckstein, Harry. 1966. *Divisions and Cohesion in Democracy: A Study of Norway,* Princeton: Princeton University Press.

Elazar, Daniel J. 1971. "The Themes of a Journal of Federalism," *Publius,* 1, 1.

_____. 1987. *Exploring Federalism,* Tuscaloosa: University of Alabama Press.

Engelberg, Steven. 1991. "Carving Out a Greater Serbia,"*The New York Times Magazine,* September 1.

"Eagleburger Signs Agreement." 1992. *Nine O'clock,* Bucharest: May 28.

"Final Election Results." 1990. *BBC Summary of World Broadcasts.* Rompres in English, Aired on May 25.

Fischer, Mary Ellen. 1992. "The New Leaders and the Opposition." In *Romania After Tyranny*, Daniel N. Nelson, ed., Boulder, San Francisco, Oxford: Westview.

Flowers, George. Chief of Economic Section, American Embassy, Bucharest. 1992. Interview, December 10.

Fribourg. 1987. Suisse: Editions Universitaires.

Friedheim, Daniel V. 1993. "Bringing Society Back into Democratic Transition Theory after 1989: Pact Making and Regime Collapse," *East European Politics and Society*, 7, 3, Fall.

Friedrich, Carl J. 1968. *Trends of Federalism in Theory and Practice*, New York: Frederick A. Praeger.

"Funkioniranje jedinstvenog Jugoslovenskog trzista.".1988. *Jugo-slavenske Pregled* 32, 4-5.

Garasanin, Ilija. 1844. "Nacertanije." A long-term program for building the greater Serbia, 1844. Reprinted in D. Stranjakovic. 1939. *Kako je postalo Garasaninovo*. Spomenik SKA, XCI, Beograd.

Gawin, T. 1992. *Ojcowizna*, Fundacja, In T. Goniewicza, *Grodno-Lublin*.

Gellner, Ernest. 1980. *Soviet and Western Anthropology*, New York: Columbia University Press.

_____. 1988. *State and Society in Soviet Thought*, Oxford and New York: B. Blackwell.

Geremek, Bronislaw. 1992. "Civil Society Then and Now," *Journal of Democracy*, 3, 2, April.

Glenny, Misha. 1992. *The Fall of Yugoslavia*, New York: Penguin.

Goati, Vladimir. 1989. *NIN*, Oct. 8; JPRS-EER 89-126, Dec. 27, 1989.

Gorbachev, Mikhail. 1987. *Perestroika: New Thinking for Our Country and the World,* New York: Harper and Row.

_____. 1990. *A Road to the Future: Complete Text of the December 7, 1988 United Nations Address,* Santa Fe: Ocean Tree Books.

Gow, James. 1991. "Deconstructing Yugoslavia," *Survival,* 33, 4.

Grdesic, Ivan. 1986. "Interesi i moc: sadrzaj rada opcinskih skupstina u SR Hrvatska," *Politicka Misao,* 23, 1.

Great Soviet Encyclopedia, Vol. 31. 1983. New York: MacmMillan.

Gregory, Mary B. 1973. "Regional Economic Development in Yugoslavia," *Soviet Studies,* 25, 2, October.

Gross, Irena Grudzinska. 1992. "Post-Communist Resentment, or the Rewriting of Polish History," *East European Politics and Society,* 6, 2, Spring.

Gross, Jan T. 1988. *Revolutions from Abroad,* Princeton: Princeton University Press.

Gruenwald, Oskar. 1983. *The Yugoslav Search for Man: Marxist Humanism in Contemporary Yugoslavia,* South Hadley: J. F. Bergin Publishers, Inc.

Grupa Akademika SANU. 1988. *Nase Teme,* 33.

Gunther Richard and Anthony Mughan. 1993. "Political Institutions and Cleavage Management." In *Do Institutions Matter?* R. K. Weaver and B.A. Rockman, eds., Washington DC: The Brookings Institute.

Hall, Edward T. 1959. *The Silent Language,* New York: Doubleday.

Haraszti, Miklos. 1987. *The Velvet Prison: Artists Under State Socialism,* New York: Noonday Press, Farrar, Straus and Giroux.

Harsch, Joseph C. 1992. "Back to the Future in the Balkans," *The Christian Science*

Monitor, January 29.

Havel, Vaclav. 1986. "Politics and Conscience." In Jan Vladislav, ed., *Vaclav Havel: Living in Truth*, London: Faber and Faber.

_____ 1986. *"Power of the Powerless."* In Jan Vladislav, ed., *Vaclav Havel: Living in Truth*, London: Faber and Faber.

Hayden, Robert M. 1992. "Constitutional Nationalism in the Formerly Yugoslav Republics," *Slavic Review*, 51, 4 (Winter).

Higley, John and Richard Gunther. 1992. *Elites and Democratic Consolidation in Latin America and Southern Europe*, Cambridge, England: Cambridge University Press.

Hirschmann, A. O. 1993. "Exit, Voice and the Fate of the German Democratic Republic: An Essay in Conceptual History," *World Politics*, 45, 2, January.

Hopken, W. 1985. "Party Monopoly and Political Change: The League of Communists since Tito's Death." In *Yugoslavia in the 1980s*, P. Ramet, ed., Boulder: Westview Press.

Humphrey, Gary. 1991. "Romania: Bump Starting the Economy," *Euromoney*, September-October.

Huntington, S. P. 1970. "Social and Institutional Dynamics of One-Party Systems." In *Authoritarian Politics in Modern Society*, S. P. Huntington & C. H. More, eds., New York: Basic Books, Inc.

Iwanow, M. 1991. *Pierwszy Narod Ukarany Polacy W. Zwiazku Radzieckim 1921-1939*, Wroclaw: PWN.

Janowitz, Morris. 1964. *The Military in the Political Development of New Nations: An Essay in Comparative Analysis*, Chicago: University of Chicago Press.

Jovanovic, Batric. 1990. "The Albanization of Kosovo Supported by an Anti-Serbian Coalition," *Politika*, March 7; JPRS-EER 90-039, June 1, 1990.

Juberias, Carlos Flores. 1992. "The Breakdown of the Czecho-Slovak Party System." In Gyorgy Szoboszlai, ed., *Flying Blind: Energing Democracies in East-Central Europe* (Yearbook, Hungarian Political Science Association, 1992).

Karpinski, Jakub. 1992. "Opposition, Dissidents and Democracy," *Uncaptive Minds*, 5, 2, Summer.

"Kazachstan: Przesiedlency I Ich Potomkowie." 1989. Krajowa Agencja Informacyjna, 11, 1478.

Kitschelt, Herbert. 1992. "The Formation of Party Systems in East Central Europe," *Politics & Society*, 20, 1, March.

Kljajic, Radmilo. 1987. *Mladost*, Nov. 2. JPRS-EER, 88-009, Feb. 5, 1988.

Klein, George. 1970. "Yugoslavia--The Process of Democratization." In *The Changing Face of Communism*, Peter Toma, ed., Tucson: University of Arizona Press.

_____. 1971. "Worker's Decision-Making in Communist Countries," *Studies in Comparative Communism*, 4, 4, July-October.

_____. 1972. "Yugoslav Views of Social Conflict and Development." Presented at the Fifth National Convention of the American Association for the Advancement of Slavic Studies, March.

_____. 1973. "Yugoslavia: The Politics of an Institutional Crisis." Presented at the Southwestern Association for Slavic Studies, March 22.

Klein, George. 1975. "The Role of Ethnic Politics in the Czechoslovak Crisis of 1968 and the Yugoslav Crisis of 1971," *Studies in Comparative Communism*, 8, 4.

_____. 1976. "Detente and Czechoslovakia." In *From the Cold War To Detente*, Peter J. Potichnyj and Jane P. Shapiro, eds., New York: Praeger.

_____. 1976. "Environmental Protection and the Energy Crisis: Czechoslovakia,

Rumania and Yugoslavia." Presented at the Inter-national Studies Association in Toronto, Canada, February 26.

_____. 1976. "Self-Reliance and Yugoslav Ethnic Politics." In *Report: Self-Reliance and Solidarity in the Quest for International Justice*, Celigny: World Council of Churches, April 3-9.

_____. 1976. "Soviet Policy Options for Coping with Contemporary Political Problems in the Balkans." Presented at the Mid-west Slavic Studies Conference in Chicago, May 6-8.

_____. 1977. "Czechoslovakia: Views of the Bridge," *Problems of Communism*, 26, November-December.

_____. 1977. "Eastern Europe: Czechoslovakia, Rumania and Yugoslavia." In *The Energy Crisis and Environment*, Ch. 4, Donald R. Kelly, ed., New York: Praeger.

_____. 1977. "Workers' Self-Management and the Politics of Ethnic Nationalism in Yugoslavia," *Nationalities Papers*, 5, 1.

_____. 1978. "Charisma vs. Institutions." Presented at the Second International Symposium on Social Change in the Contemporary World at the Grand Valley State College, Grand Rapids, Michigan, April 10.

_____. 1978. "Social Deviance in Yugoslavia." In *Social Deviance in Eastern Europe*, Ivan Volgyes, ed., Boulder: Westview Press, Friedrich A. Praeger.

_____. 1978. "Yugoslavia." In *The Hungarian Revolution of 1956 in Retrospect*, Belak Kiraly and Paul Jonas, eds., Boulder: East European Quarterly.

_____. 1979. "The Czechoslovak Economy." In *Czechoslovakia: The Heritage of Ages Past*, Hans Brisch and Ivan Volgyes, eds., Boulder: East European Monographs.

_____. 1979. "Soviet Foreign Policy Options in the Contemporary Balkans." In *Soviet Policy in the Post-Tito Balkans*, Phillip A. Petersen, ed., Studies in

Communist Affairs, Vol. 4, Published under the auspices of the United States Air Force. Washington, DC.

_____. 1980. "The Changing Balance of Energy Resource Utilization in Czechoslovakia and Yugoslavia and Its Impact on the Environment." Presented at the Twelfth Annual Convention of the American Association for the Advancement of Slavic Studies in Philadelphia, November 5.

_____. 1980. "The Politics of Energy and Environment in Yugoslavia and Czechoslovakia." Presented at the International Studies Association in Los Angeles, March 19.

_____. 1981. "Politics and Environment in the Danubian Basin." Presented at the International Studies Association in Philadelphia, March 17.

Klein, George and Patricia V. Klein. 1972. "Some Approaches to the Problem of Ethnicity (Nationality) in the United States and Yugoslavia." Presented at the Sixth Annual Meeting of the Yugoslav Sociological Association, Portoroz, February 10-13..

_____. 1974. "The United States and Yugoslavia: Divergent Approaches Toward Ethnicity." In *Ethnic Dynamics*, Chester L. Hunt and Lewis Walker, eds., Homewood, Illinois: The Dorsey Press. Second Edition, Holmes Beach, Florida: Learning Publications, 1979.

_____. 1979. "Land Reform in Yugoslavia: Two Models." In *The Peasantry of Eastern Europe*, Vol. II, Ivan Volgyes, ed., Rural Transformation Series. New York: Pergamon Press.

_____. 1981. "Nationalism vs. Ideology: The Pivot of Yugoslav Politics." In *The Politics of Ethnicity in Eastern Europe*, George Klein and Milan J. Reban, eds., Boulder: East European Monographs.

Klein, George and Milan Reban, eds. 1981. *The Politics of Ethnicity in Eastern Europe*. Boulder: East European Monographs.

Klein, George and Peter Toma. 1979. "Ethnicity in the Politics of the Czechoslovak

Communist Party." Presented at the Annual Conference of the American Political Science Association in Washington, DC, August 31-September 3.

Klein, George and Milos Samardzija. 1971. "A Perspective View of Self-Management in a Socialist Context," *Studies in Comparative Communism*, 4, 3-4.

Kolankiewicz, George. 1994. "Elites in Search of a Political Formula," *Daedalus*, 123, Summer.

Kornai, Janos. 1990. *The Road to a Free Economy: Shifting from a Socialist System*. New York: W. W. Norton & Company.

Kostunica, Vojislav. 1988. "The Constitution and the Federal States." In *Yugoslavia: A Fractured Federalism*, D. I. Rusinow. ed, Washington, DC: The Wilson Center Press.

Kostunica, Vojislav, and K. Cavoski, K. 1985. *Party Pluralism or Monism: Social Movements and the Political System in Yugoslavia*, Boulder: East European Monographs.

Kruszewski, Z. Anthony. 1972. *The Oder-Neisse Boundary and Poland's Modernization: The Socioeconomic and Political Impact*, New York: Praeger.

_____. 1986. "Border Problem Solving in the Communist World: A Case Study of Some European Boundaries." In Oscar J. Martinez, ed., *Across Boundaries*, El Paso: Texas Western Press.

Kucan, Milan. 1989. "Jugoslovenski federalizam od speransa do razmisljana o novom Ustavu." In *Federal izam po mjeri i buducnosti*, Ciril Ribicic and Zdravko Tomac, eds., Zagreb: Globus.

Kullberg, Judith S. 1994. "In the Ruins of the CPSU: Elites and Party Formation in Russia." Presented at the 1994 Annual Meeting of the American Political Science Association. New York, September.

Lalovic, Dragutin. 1988. "Upotreba Jugoslavije." *Nase Teme*, 33, 1-2.

Lampe, John R. 1996. *Yugoslavia as History, Twice there was a country*, NewYork: Cambridge University Press.

Lang, Nicholas R. 1975. "The Dialectics of Decentralization." *World Politics*, 27, 3, April.

Lappè, Francis Moore and Joseph Collins. 1986. *World Hunger: Twelve Myths*, New York: A Food First Book, Grove Press.

League of Communists of Yugoslavia (LCY) Central Committee member. 1990. Interview, Zagreb, May 28.

Lenardson, G. S. & D. Mircev. 1977. "A Structure for Participatory Democracy in Local Community: The Yugoslav Constitution of 1974," *Comparative Politics*, 11, 2.

Lewicki, A. and J. Friedberg. 1947. *Zarys Historii Polski*, London: S.Z.P.Z. Publishers.

Lida, P. 1989. "Parafie Rzymskokatolickie Na Bialorusi I Ukrainie W 1988 Roku-Obsada Personalna." In *Zeszyty Historyczne*, Paris: Nr. 88.

Lijphart, Arend. 1977. "Conflict Management and Political Institutionalization in Socialist Yugoslavia." In Albert Eldridge, ed., *Legislatures in Plural Societies*, Durham, North Carolina: Duke University Press.

_____. 1977. *Democracy in plural societies: A Comparative Exploration*, New Haven: Yale University Press.

_____. 1984. *Democracies, Patterns of Majoritarian and Consensus Government in Twenty-One Countries*, New Haven: Yale University Press.

_____. 1991. "Majority Rule in Theory and Practice: The Tenacity of a Flawed Paradigm," *International Social Science Journal*, 43, 3.

Lijphart, A., R. Rogowski, and R. K. Weaver. 1993. "Separation of Powers and Cleavage Management." In *Do institutions matter?* R. K. Weaver and B. R.

Rockman. eds., Washington, DC: The Brookings Institute.

Lossowski, P. 1985. *Litwa A Sprawy Polskie 1939-1940*, Warszawa: PWN.

Lithuanian Information Center news release. 1991. Brooklyn: Feb. 10.

Lovric, Jelena. 1989. "Josip Broz's Second Death," *Danas*, June 6; JPRS-EER, 89-086, August 1.

MacKenzie, David. 1985. *Ilija Garasanin: Balkan Bismarck*, New York: Columbia University Press.

Maly Rocznik Statystyczny. 1939. Warszawa: G.U.S.

Maly Slownik Historii Polski. 1967. Warszawa: W.P.

Manteufel, T. ed., *Historia Polski*. 1958-1984, vols. I-IV, Warszawa: P.W.N.

Matley, Ian M. 1970. *Romania: A Profile*, New York: Praeger.

McCrea, Barbara P. 1992. *The Political Dynamics of Federalism in a Marxist-Leninist Setting: The League of Communists of Yugoslavia*. Doctoral dissertation, University of Notre Dame.

Mekina, Igor. 1988. "Hope Expressed for New Political Creations." *Mladina*, Dec. 16. FBIS-EEU, Eastern Europe, 89-001, Jan. 3, 1989.

Miceta, Luka. 1988. "The Errors and Injustices of History," *NIN*, Oct. 13; JPRS-EER 88-096, Nov. 14.

Mihaescu, Barbu. Director, Technology Marketing, Electrical Engineering Institute. 1992. Interview, August 27.

"Milosevic Addresses Plenum." 1988. Belgrade Domestic Service, Oct. 17.

Milosevic, Slobodan. 1989. *Godina raspleta*, Beograd: Beogradski Izdavacko Graficki Zavod.

"Milosevic Speech on Kosovo Anniversary." 1989. Tanjug News Service, June 28; FBIS-EEU 89-124, 62.

Mniejszosci Polskie i Polonia W. ZSSR. 1992. Wroclaw: Ossolineum.

Modelski, George. 1960. *The Communist International System*, Princeton: Princeton University Center for International Studies Monograph.

Modzelewski, Karol. 1994. "What Happened to Solidarity?" *Uncaptive Minds*, 1, 7, Winter/Spring.

Moore, Patrick. 1992. "Croatia." *Radio Free Europe*, RFE/RL Research Report, 1, 39, October 2.

_____. 1992. "Ethnic Cleansing in Bosnia: Outrage but Little Action." *Radio Free Europe*, RFE/RL Research Report, 1, 34, 28 August.

_____. 1992. "Issues in Croatian Politics." *Radio Free Europe*, RFE/RL Research Report, 1, 43, November 6.

Mowery, Mark. 1992. "Czechoslovakia: Good Start on Reform Improves Business Climate," *Business America*, April.

Moynihan, Daniel Patrick. 1993. *Pandemonium: Ethnicity in Inter-national Politics*, New York: Oxford University Press.

"NSF Holds Final Meeting Before Reformation." 1990. *BBC Summary of World Broadcasts*, Bucharest Home Service, Aired on February 3.

Najder, Z. 1990. Interview. *Rzeczpospolita*, May 30.

Narodna Armija. 1991. Belgrade, July 6.

Neher, Jacques. 1992. "Banking: Expanding to Meet New Needs," *Institutional Investor*, March 26.

_____. 1992. "Privatization: A Program of Unprecedented Scope," *Institutional Investor*, March.

Nelson, Daniel L. 1991. *East European Security in the Wake of Revolution,* St. Louis: University of Missouri--St. Louis. Center for International Studies, Occasional Paper No. 9112, December.

_____. 1993. "Balkan Insecurities." In *Post-Communist Eastern Europe: Crisis and Reform,* Andrew A. Michta and Ilya Prizel. eds., New York: St. Martin's Press.

The New York Times. 1989. July 13.

The New York Times. 1991. July 2.

The New York Times. 1992. March 23.

The New York Times. 1992. May 26.

The New York Times. 1993. July 30.

The New York Times. 1993. August 29.

The New York Times. 1993. October 21.

The New York Times. 1993. December 31.

The New York Times. 1994. January 21.

The New York Times. 1994. January 23.

The New York Times. 1994. January 24.

The New York Times. 1994. January 26.

Newman, Barry. 1992. "Vital Signs Point to Poland's Recovery," *Wall Street Journal,* October 22, A-10.

Nordlinger, Eric A. 1977. *Soldiers in Politics: Military Coups and Government,* Englewood Cliffs: Prentice-Hal

"O Zmianach Programowych i Strukturalnych Towarzystwa Polonia." 1989. Krajowa Agencja Informacyjan, 17, 1484; 4, 25-5, 1.

Obrman, Jan. 1992. "The Czechoslovak Elections." *Radio Free Europe,* RFE/RL Research Report, 1, 26, June 26.

O'Donnell, Guillermo and Philippe C. Schmitter. 1986. *Transitions from Authoritarian Rule: Tentative Conclusions about Uncertain Democ-racies,* Baltimore: Johns Hopkins University Press.

Office of the General Commissioner for Elections. 1990. "Sytuacja powyborcza w poszczegolnych regionach kraju," *Bulletin,* May 30.

"The Opinion of the Constitutional Court of Yugoslavia." 1990. *Yugoslav Survey,* 31, 2.

Orchmanski. 1990. *Historia Litwy,* Third ed., Wroclaw: Ossolineum.

Osaghe, R. E. 1990. "A Reassessment of Federalism as a Degree of Decentralization, *Publius,* 20, 1.

Oslobodjenje. 1990. August 11.

Ostojic, Mirko. 1992. "Breaking Up of Yugoslavia," *Review of International Affairs.* XLIII, 1001, February 5.

Palous, Martin. 1992. Cited in "Discussing the Elections: The Czech Point of View: An Interview with Martin Palous and Petr Janyska." *Radio Free Europe,* RFE/Research Report 1, 26, June 26.

Passell, Peter. 1993. "Dr. Jeffrey Sachs, Shock Therapist," *The New York Times Magazine,* June 27.

Pataki, Judith. 1993. "Hungarian Youth Party Comes of Age," *Radio Free Europe*, RFE/RL Research Report, 2, 21, May 21.

Pavlowitz, Stephen. 1988. *The Improbable Survivor*, Columbus: Ohio State University Press.

Petkovic, Gaja. 1988. "Kosovo--Weak Link in Defense." *Borba*, Nov. 4; JPSR-EEU, Dec. 16.

"Petre Roman Presents Government Programme and New Ministers." 1990. *BBC Summary of World Broadcasts*, Bucharest Home Service, Aired on May 25.

Podlaski, K. 1990. *Bialorusini, Litwini, Ukraincy*, Bialystok: Versus.

"Polacy W Kazachstanie." 1989. *Dziennik Zwiazkowy*, Chicago: np.

"Polonia Radziecka-Naturalnym Pomostem Miedzy Polska A ZSSR." 1989. Krajowa Agencja Informacyjna, 8, 1475, Feb. 21.

Polska, Polacy, Mnejszosci Narodowe. 1992. Wroclaw: Ossolineum.

Popovic, Koca. 1989. *Danas*, Jan. 31; JPRS-EER 89-039, Apr. 10.

Privatization Programs in Romania. 1992. Bucharest: National Agency for Privatization.

"Przebudzenie." 1989. *Polityka*, 30, 1682, Warszawa, July 29.

Przeworski, Luiz Carlos Bresser Pereira and Jose Maria Maravall. 1993. *Economic Reforms in New Democracies*, Cambride: Cambridge University Press. Part III.

Przeglad Wiadomosci Agencyjnych, 188. 1989. As quoted in "Po I Zjezdzie Zwiazku Polakow Na Litwie," *Nowy Dziennik*, New York, June 22.

Putnam, Robert. *The Comparative Study of Political Elites*, Englewood Cliffs, New Jersey: Prentice-Hall, Inc.